Contents

For Pearl, Ken, Bernadette, and Roberta

Note from the Author

As I indicated in the first three volumes, the interviews in these books come from *The Directors*, a television series I created, which runs on the Encore Movie Channel in the United States as well as in over fifty countries around the world. Only a small portion of each director's interview was used in the television series. It seemed only natural, then, that we transcribe the entire interview so that we could examine the full scope of each director's talent for making unique motion pictures.

For anyone reading this book who might have a desire to become a film director, know that you have taken on a difficult and sometimes frustrating task. Directing movies is right up there with the most demanding of careers. A film director is part writer, part producer, part technician, part father figure, and certainly the leader of the pack. Everyone looks to him for answers, and those answers can make or break a film.

How can any one person be all of these things? It might surprise you that there is no one answer to that question. The answer lies in the interviews contained in this book as well as in the three books previously published. Each of these directors has his own way of dealing with the demands of making a feature-length motion picture. Most will tell you that it is in their blood, that they cannot wait to get up in the morning and charge full speed ahead into whatever ambushes may await them. Consider what can go wrong on any given day, and you wonder why anyone would put himself through such torture.

Now, consider what happens when things go right. The result is a film that can make an audience cry or laugh, hold people in suspense, and on occasion change someone's life. So, my hat is off to all film directors, because I know from firsthand experience just how difficult—and how rewarding—the work can be. When it works, it is the biggest high in the world.

I sincerely thank all of the wonderfully talented directors who participated and gave of their valuable time, along with the actors, actresses, writers, producers, and cinematographers who appeared in the television series as guests. As always, a very special thanks to the American Film Institute, who helped make all of this possible by partnering with us on the television series.

In transcribing the on-camera interviews into this book, some editing was necessary. However, I have retained as much of the original interviews as possible.

—*Robert J. Emery*

The Directors—
Take Four

The Films of Adrian Lyne

Director Adrian Lyne is the creative force behind some of the most talked-about films of the past decade, including the haunting thriller *Jacob's Ladder,* the spellbinding phenomenon *Fatal Attraction*, the sexually daring *Nine 1/2 Weeks*, the high-energy dance musical *Flashdance*, the international hit *Indecent Proposal,* and the daring *Unfaithful.*

Born in Peterborough, England, and raised in London, Lyne attended the Highgate School, where his father was a teacher. In his twenties, he also played trumpet with a jazz group. An avid moviegoer during his school days, he was inspired to make his own films by the work of French New Wave directors like Godard, Truffaut, and Chabrol. Two of his early short films, *The Table* and *Mr. Smith,* were official entries in the London Film Festival.

Lyne made his feature filmmaking debut in 1980 with *Foxes*, a perceptive look at the friendship between four teenage girls growing up in Los Angeles San Fernando Valley. His next film, *Flashdance,* the innovative blend of rock 'n' roll, new dance styles, and breathtaking imagery, created a sensation in 1983. Lyne's bravura visual style blended perfectly with Giorgio Moroder's powerful score to propel the story of an aspiring ballerina who works in a factory by day and dances in a club at night. The film was nominated for three Academy Awards, with the theme song, "What a Feeling," winning the Oscar for Best Song.

Lyne next took on the controversial *Nine ½ Weeks* and has not stopped challenging film audiences since.

> *What is unique about his directing is his eye. He sees things in a way that I don't think anyone else would or could. He has an unusual mind, but just the way he lights it and shoots makes his scenes really special.*

He can take an average, relatively dull moment and make it into something electrifying.

Woody Harrelson—Actor

The Conversation

I became interested in filmmaking in my early twenties. I used to anxiously await each new Jean-Luc Godard film. I really liked the French new wave more than the English new wave, although there were good English films being made by Tony Richardson and others like that. But I liked French films, and particularly Godard and Truffaut. I don't think it's quite the same now. For example, when you were waiting for a new Ingmar Bergman film, there was such anticipation and excitement. It really was a sort of a reverence for what they were going to do. I don't think it's quite the same feeling anymore.

Early on, I started working as an accountant. I was maybe the least suited for accountancy than anybody you can imagine. I was a disaster. At that time, my one big passion was playing the trumpet. I played the trumpet with a jazz group and when I wasn't doing that I bet on the horses. Then I went into advertising. I heard somebody say that if you don't really quite know what you want to do, go into advertising because there's so many different sides to that. So, I went into advertising and eventually got on the television side and I got to watch people like John Schlesinger make commercials. I eventually got to make them myself.

There was a lady at the agency called Jennie Armstrong, who said to me one day, "I'd like to form a production company with you as director." I'd never directed anything except one little title sequence, so she was taking me on faith. I hadn't the slightest idea of what I was doing for at least three years. When I finally got a commercial to do, I shook with terror, not knowing what was going to happen. It was very much a trial-and-error process. I would do these very ambitious lists of what I wanted to shoot during the day and then I would miss a shot and I would think that the whole thing was screwed because of that. I would literally go into the lavatory while the crew was waiting and I'd be in tears and eventually come out and stagger through it. It was a long while before I really knew what I was doing.

I eventually did a short called *The Table*, which was actually quite good. It was a ten-minute piece about a man who accuses his wife of infidelity. (In fact, it was based on my first wife and myself, to be honest with you.) The man accuses his wife of doing this at a party they attended the previous night. It was interesting the way I shot it in that it never showed all the people clearly. For example, the wife, who is depressed, is stirring a cup of tea. Huge close-up on the teacup and then the stirring would sort of quicken up a little bit because of the guilt involved in what she had done. We'd visually explore cutting up eggs—things like that. Sounds awful, but it's actually quite a good movie that was just shot in huge close-ups.

I've always liked close-ups. I think that close-ups are very important and give you the feel of the scene. For example, I like to shoot with the zoom lens. Not to use the actual zoom, but to move in at the end of a take for a clasp on a mouth or hands, or whatever. I think it's an interesting way to shoot, really.

Foxes (1980)

Jodie Foster; Cherie Currie; Marilyn Kagan; Kandice Stroh;
Scott Baio; Sally Kellerman; Randy Quaid; Lois Smith.

I was in Los Angeles working on a Levi's commercial. I met an English producer by the name of David Puttnam, who had also come to L.A. for the first time and was working for a company called Casablanca Films. He gave me a script to read and said, "You won't do it, it's for an American director, but tell me what you think." It turned out to be the screenplay of *Foxes*, which was about kids growing up in the San Fernando Valley. Gerald Ayres had written it, and I think it was based pretty much on his daughter. I was intrigued with it but didn't think it would get made, and for a long while it didn't.

I remember the meeting David Puttnam and I had at United Artists. Lots of people were there, and there was a general feeling of malaise, and it seemed like nothing was going to happen. Suddenly, Puttnam leapt to his feet and he was virtually incoherent with rage. I remember he was yelling and swearing and hollering, "I'd do anything to get this movie made." Everybody was aghast and the ironic thing is that from that moment on it moved forward. I think they thought that they could blame everything on Puttnam if it didn't go right, but I also think they saw his passion to get the movie made. So, we made it, and I think three people saw it. My mother and a few others, I think. But it's a movie I'm proud of.

When we were getting ready to make the film, I spent three or four months sitting in classrooms in a school in San Fernando Valley watching these kids and learning how they behaved. I think it makes the job wonderful. You have to become an expert in a lot of areas. I don't think you have to be a submarine commander to make a movie like *Das Boot*, but you have to learn about submarines. You have to immerse yourself in whatever it is you are doing, and that's what I learned to do on that first film. That's what a director's job is.

Jodie Foster and Sally Kellerman were both wonderful in the film. They played mother and daughter. I remember there was a scene between them where they were having this extraordinary fight. Sally was playing a single parent. She'd divorced her husband, and Jodie was berating her boyfriend, and Sally screams at her, "What's wrong with Sam? What's wrong with Sam?" and Jodie says, "He wears white shoes."

When Jodie had to cry for the scene, she asked for some Vaseline. But I insisted the tears be real, so we struggled and struggled for a couple of hours and eventually, out of sheer fatigue, I think she started to cry and it was a great feeling for me and for her.

Jodie was just an extraordinarily mature person for her age. Much more so than the other kids in the movie. That's essentially what she was in the film— this strong person. She was the one that kind of united all the characters. To be honest, the film wouldn't have gotten made without her. And, ironically, she was living in a one-parent family in real life, because her mother, Brandy, and her father had gotten divorced.

So, that was my first feature film, for which I wasn't paid a great deal of money. Let's just say the first one is the most difficult one. It got me off the ground, but it didn't do any business, so after that it was almost as difficult as it was before.

I don't think I am ever pleased with my work. I see the mistakes endlessly, and I don't like to watch my own films. That first film was difficult for me because, over the years of directing commercials, I had created a style of my own—I always operated the camera and did the lighting, for example. Then, confronted with *Foxes*, I suddenly realized that none of this was going to work because, rather than doing shots that lasted, say, ten seconds or eight seconds, they suddenly had to last thirty or forty seconds or two minutes long. That was very tough. Evolving a new style and not being enormously frustrated was tough. Also, having to hand over the operating of the camera to somebody else was difficult, although I did continue to operate quite a bit myself whenever possible. So many of my ideas come from looking through the eyepiece. I still spend a lot of time looking through the viewfinder.

I was one of many directors who worked on the film called *Starman*. I worked on developing that with Michael Douglas, who was also producing. I became very friendly with Michael, which I think helped me down the road when we made *Fatal Attraction* together. Anyway, I never got to make *Starman*. Over time, there were many directors involved, including Tony Scott and John Badham. Finally, John Carpenter made the movie.

Flashdance (1983)

Jennifer Beals; Michael Nouri; Lilia Skala; Sunny Johnson; Kyle T. Heffner; Lee Ving; Ron Karabatsos; Belinda Bauer.

He's incredibly passionate about his films. I've never worked with anyone that passionate visually.

Jennifer Beals—Actress

Producer Dawn Steele was passionate about making *Flashdance* and offered it to me. I thought it was kind of dumb. I wasn't crazy about it, and I turned it down a couple of times, which was difficult, because I could tell they were going to spend the eight million dollars on the movie with or without me, so finally I said yes. I suppose it shows that you should always have an open mind.

I thought, well, maybe I can make the dances interesting. I went to Pittsburgh and watched dancers—strippers, really—that this flash dancing was based on. I became intrigued with what I saw, because it was really quite inventive.

I worked on the dance numbers with a man named Jeffrey Hornaday, who really wasn't a choreographer. He was a dancer, and what was great working with him was that he had a totally open mind and was willing to try anything

I asked of him. That's what made it work. There was no ego involved, just a desire to get it right.

I had an idea that I wanted to do a wet dance, and I really didn't know quite how to do it. I had not seen that before and I thought it would be sexy. I remember trying to show the studio heads what I had in mind. We gathered in this rehearsal studio, and the studio guys were sitting at the top of these bleachers, and I was down at the bottom with Jeffrey Hornaday and this poor girl who was about to get wet. I had a hose and I was winding it around this girl trying to show these people what the wet dance was going to be like. All I could see was this desperate skepticism on their faces and that we were doomed and the movie was in the toilet, you know. But, happily, it worked out. The film did over a hundred million dollars domestically. Worldwide, it did about two, two-fifty.

The dancing and who did what became a bit of an issue. For some of the stuff I used a French dancer who was very good. Jennifer Beals had already been cast as the female lead and we knew that her dancing wasn't exceptional. I remember the final audition scene, when she dances for this panel, and we used not only the French girl but an acrobat as well. And we used a male break-dancer from the Bronx who had to put on a wig he wasn't too crazy about. We used four or five different people to make the dance work. I think it's exciting when nobody knows that, you know—until now, that is. But between Jennifer and the other dancers we used, things kind of came together very nicely.

Before we actually began shooting, we were trying out wardrobe. Jennifer had a T-shirt on and I wanted to see what it would look like without her bra on. So, she reached under her T-shirt and, without anybody seeing anything, she managed to take her bra off. I don't understand how she did it, but I was just fascinated by it, so I put it in a scene with her and Michael Nouri. It's quite a funny scene, I think. It's nice when you can use stuff that you've seen in ordinary life and use it as another layer to the scene. It always makes the scene more interesting when it's not just the words, you know—when there's something else going on.

I remember when we were casting the movie and we hadn't decided on Jennifer Beals yet. It came down to three or four girls, of which Jennifer Beals was one. We needed a man to lie in bed with Jennifer and also to run the scene with her. There was a man called Kevin Costner whom I'd worked with on a commercial. He came by and lay in bed with Jennifer Beals and ran lines with her for two hundred bucks. Whatever happened to that guy?

What was fascinating was the way the movie took people over. It was a fairytale story about wanting something bad enough to go after it. If you do want something enough, you sometimes get it, but you have to be passionate about it. People wrote me letters and said the movie changed their lives, and that's very gratifying. I enjoyed the shooting of it.

Nine ½ Weeks (1986)

Mickey Rourke; Kim Basinger; Margaret Whitton; David Margulies; Christine Baranski; Karen Young; William De Acutis; Dwight Weist.

When I decided that I really wanted to do *Nine ½ Weeks,* a sadomasochistic love story, scores of people told me not to do the movie. People said that if I did the movie, it would be like committing professional suicide. But I was intrigued with it. It was a movie that had a stylized quality, which is what I wanted back then. I think if I was doing the movie now, I'd probably do it a little bit differently, but on the other hand it was extraordinary, working with Mickey Rourke and Kim Basinger. Mickey really is one of the most inventive actors I've ever worked with. I remember I had five or six previews at MGM, where I'd sit in the back of the theater with the executives just sweating like pigs. I mean, sometimes half of the audience would walk out, or they'd be screaming and yelling at the screen and you wouldn't be able to hear yourself think. It was really quite frightening. Towards the end of one of those screenings, it was getting so frightening, I thought I'd better get out of there. I went into the projection booth, and I watched the rest of the film from there. It was a film that caused real rage.

I think women were much more inclined to embrace the idea of the movie. I believe they liked the idea of being uncivilized for nine weeks and doing anything that comes to mind and not censoring their feelings. But it was a movie that upset a lot of people, especially men. Their reaction in front of their wife or their girlfriend is very different from their reaction if they're watching the tape by themselves. People aren't too open about admitting to finding something arousing sexually.

Mickey was an extraordinary actor to work with, really, and a very generous actor always. I always think that's a big test for an actor. For example, when he was working with Kim, to keep her fresh, he would change the order of lines of dialogue. He would do this endlessly. Little bits of trickery. Little things to help her. Kim and Mickey pretty much played the movie for real. They never talked to each other except through the movie. I think it worked quite well, really.

I've always thought that sexuality isn't about acres of flesh. I think that sexuality is much more exciting when you glimpse something. Did you see it or didn't you see it? Something suggested is always much more exciting than something spelled out in black and white—for example, when Kim's blindfolded, and he has the ice, and she doesn't know what he is going to do. The same with the scene in front of the refrigerator when he feeds her different things, like the pepper and Jell-O and honey. It's like two kids playing. It started off as fun with champagne, then turned into sexuality when the honey was dripped onto her leg.

I think any film that you make, you have to make it your own. During the course of working on the screenplay, it evolves, and you put your own stuff in. I, for example, have notebooks filled with stuff I've seen during the day. I jot down anything I see that I think is exciting—a visual, a bit of dialogue—I write it all down. Before any film, I always have sixty or seventy pages of ideas that I always try and incorporate in the film that I'm going to do.

I try to mix things up, keep people off guard. I remember the scene where Mickey comes round to Kim's flat and she's showing him some of her artwork. I told her to put her hand on his leg and then put it on his crotch, because I wanted to see his reaction. Mickey didn't know it was going to happen. It's sort of manipulation, if you like, but that sort of thing, when you see it on film, is much more exciting in sexual terms than seeing somebody stark naked.

Kim said something once that was quite interesting. She said that doing the film was a way of being bad, but not really, because it was just a film. So, I think the idea obviously intrigued her. I tested them together, because, in the end, you're not casting Mickey Rourke and you're not casting Kim Basinger. You're casting what happens when the two of them are together. The same with Glenn Close and Michael Douglas or whoever it might be. You're casting the sum of the two. I remember doing a videotape test with Kim and Mickey, and I was fascinated by the fascination that Mickey had for Kim.

I've made a couple of films, and I'd say that *Nine ½ Weeks* and *Jacob's Ladder* are certainly two of them where people sort of latched onto the film later on. *Nine ½ Weeks* grew in its appeal and played in Paris for seven years. I think it's still funny that here in the United States it is quite often on the best-seller's list in terms of videos. In the end, the only important thing for a director is to have a passion for what he or she is doing. I have to have a boiling passion for the project, or I am not interested in doing it. *Nine ½ Weeks* was like that.

He Likes to Work Small and Fast

I think that the important thing is to keep the crew as small as you can. I do a lot of it handheld, so that if the actors move, I move with them. In other words, you don't stop them. I think the kiss of death is when you've got a head of steam going, and then you have to stop them, because it can take forever to get back to that point. And then I think it goes quite quickly. When it comes to love scenes, I think it always helps if they have a couple of drinks. I don't mean get sloshed, but I think it kind of loosens them up a little bit. One of my jobs is to make them feel at home. To make them feel that you're doing it with them. I don't mean this literally, but it's almost like a ménage à trois. I always think there's a danger of this poor pair going at it solemnly in silence, you know. I'm a little bit like a cheerleader and I do cheer them on, giving them little bits of instruction as we go. I think that helps a lot. That's my job really, to make them forget the camera and allow them to just think about each other. Think about the tactile stuff. Think about the way they're doing it.

I think the process of making a film is frightening. It's frightening for me. It's frightening for the actors. It tends to be something that does its utmost to prevent the actors from being natural and relaxed. So, what I try to do is always try and put the clapperboard [camera slate] on the end of the scene rather than the beginning because the physical noise of that so often frightens the actor and creates a feeling of anxiety and suspense. I try and segue into the scene without them really realizing that it's happening. I quite often will shoot things with long lenses so that the camera's not in their face and they can forget about the camera being there. That's very important.

Fatal Attraction (1987)

Michael Douglas; Glenn Close; Anne Archer; Ellen Hamilton Latzen; Stuart Pankin; Ellen Foley; Fred Gwynne; Meg Mundy; Tom Brennan; Lois Smith.

> *I think you get Adrian when you need him. I mean, you get who he is. He's colorful and he's fun. He's eccentric in the best sense of the word. He's risky, you know. He's willing to take a chance and wants you to do the same. I think that is really exciting for an actor.*
>
> Anne Archer—Actress

I was sent this screenplay where I live in the south of France when I'm not shooting. I sat down on the stone steps of the house and started to read. It was such a page-turner that I was still there an hour and a half later, and I finished it. I thought I had to make this because this was going to be a huge movie if I didn't screw it up. I just knew it was, because I felt the audience would identify with Anne Archer, Glenn Close, and Michael Douglas. You knew that they'd put their feet in the shoes of these people. So, it was an absolute *yes* for me straight away.

I'd say that the choice of Glenn Close was sort of unusual. She actually campaigned to be in the movie. At that stage, only Michael Douglas was cast. We actually tested quite a few people with him. But we just kept hearing that Glenn Close was interested in doing it. It's interesting, because up until that point in her career, she'd always played stay-at-home people, always the wife, always the nice person. She'd never had played a part that had a real edge. So we tested her with Michael, and again, it was the chemistry thing. It was just extraordinary, watching them work together. It just shows that you have to have an open mind, that you should never reject anybody out of hand.

There's a moment in the movie when she's seducing Michael in a restaurant in New York and she asks him if he's discreet. When I did the test with her and Michael, we did six takes. Later on, someone cut together these different takes of her doing this scene. It was extraordinary, because I realized that she had said, "Are you discreet?" six distinctly different ways with different emphasis. I hadn't realized at the time that they were so different. It was fascinating to watch and to realize her incredible technique as an actor.

I'd seen Anne Archer a number of times before, in different films, and she was always wonderful. What's interesting about her performance in *Fatal Attraction* is that her best scene was cut out. In one of the original endings, Michael Douglas gets the blame for killing Glenn Close, when in fact she's committed suicide. Anne had an extraordinary scene at the end when she discovers the tape that Glenn Close made saying that she was going to commit suicide if Michael Douglas didn't come through for her. Anne's performance in the scene is most extraordinary, so I always feel very sad that it had to be taken out. I think she's extraordinary at the [actual] end with Michael when Michael owns up to having slept with Glenn. I think she's at the top of her game in the scene.

In the end, I always thought the film was kind of a Hitchcock thriller. But the thing that people remember tends to be the sexuality. There's danger when you're shooting sex scenes. Audiences will laugh because they're embarrassed. So, I think what's very important in a scene like the one with Douglas and Close having sex over that sink is to give the audience something to laugh at so they won't laugh unintentionally. So, I always try to do that with any scene that involves sex. When Michael is carrying Glenn across the floor and he's trying to get out of his pants, I think that's pretty damn funny. It allowed people the chance to laugh and not feel too uptight about it.

Suspense is created by editing and, of course, having the ingredients to make it exciting. Well, I remember when Michael was downstairs in the kitchen and he's putting the kettle on and the kettle starts to boil and we are intercutting this with Anne Archer, who is upstairs, and the Glenn Close character has already entered the bathroom. The audience is desperate to get Michael upstairs to rescue his wife. The fun of a sequence like that is how long can you delay Michael and keep him in the kitchen. How long can you have the water dripping through the ceiling, that the dog is licking up? How long can you play with the audience and manipulate the audience, without them giving up on you? It's really important and fun to create that in the cutting room.

I love it when people will take a phrase or a sentence from your movie and tend to repeat it. Like, when Glenn Close says, "I won't be ignored, Dan." I was also pleased with the rage that Michael brought to the scene—when he threatens to kill her. I remember when Glenn was doing her side of the scene and the camera was on her. Michael was shouting himself hoarse to bring her up and to help her with the scene. By the time we got round to him, he hardly had any voice left.

There's a scene with Stuart Pankin, where they are all a bit drunk at this party. I chose Pankin because, apart from being a good actor, he is a stand-up comic. I knew he'd be doing a lot of one-liners and a lot of improvising that would make the scene natural. Michael is also very good at reciprocating. Half the time, I don't know if they knew whether I was shooting or not. It was like a real party. They were drinking champagne. It was fun.

We previewed the movie and it would go like gangbusters. You could feel the audience was really with you. But with the original ending, it seemed to feel a bit flat at the end. It just didn't seem to deliver. We agonized over what to do. We didn't feel that it worked dramatically, and we searched around and came up with this kind of operatic ending. It wasn't for marketing purposes, as some critics thought; it was to make the movie better.

The film received six or seven Academy Award nominations. I remember Sherry Lansing rang me up at five o'clock in the morning to let me know. We received a Directors Guild nomination as well. I felt pretty good about that.

Jacob's Ladder (1990)

Tim Robbins; Elizabeth Peña; Danny Aiello; Matt Craven;
Pruitt Taylor Vince; Patricia Kalember; Eriq La Salle; Ving Rhames.

You pick up the script to this film and you look at it and read it and you'll say, this is magnificent. But how do you do it? Where do you begin? Where's the middle? It's an exciting project and only a person who is very brilliant, as I feel Adrian is, can do this.

Danny Aiello—Actor

I appreciate movies with hardware, but I don't think I would do something like *The Matrix*, even though I liked that film. I did *Jacob's Ladder*, which involved demonic imagery, and I was very wary about doing blue screen or computer tricks. None of the imagery in that film was done afterwards. It was all done in the camera, because I was mistrustful of doing a film any other way. I wanted it to be something that I produced rather than some guys with a computer produced. Although I can appreciate what the computer guys can do, it's not really for me. But I'm getting ahead of myself.

I had a conversation with a literary agent by the name of Tracy Jacobson, because I was so depressed about the awful scripts that I'd been getting. I asked if anything she might have read took her breath away, and she mentioned [screenwriter Bruce Joel Rubin's] *Jacob's Ladder*. At that time, I was very close to making a film called *Bonfire of the Vanities*. I read *Jacob's Ladder* and I was just blown away by it. I thought it was extraordinary. It had elements of one of my favorite movies, a film called *Incident at Owl Creek*, in that you're not seeing what you think you're seeing.

Bruce's screenplay was full of Judeo-Christian imagery. For example, when Jacob finally goes to heaven at the end, it was very much a staircase to heaven. It was angels. It was pillars. It was clouds. It was everything you had seen before. But I was very anxious to try and do something that one hadn't seen before, because if you had seen it before, it would take the wonder out of it. It would be a cliché. I tried to do something different with the demonic imagery, because a lot of the imagery that was written was the traditional idea of what the devil looks like. I think if I had literally done that, it wouldn't have been frightening, because it would have been familiar.

We struggled with ideas for at least a year before we shot it. We really worked incredibly hard on that screenplay and arrived at a way of doing the demonic imagery. I was fascinated by the idea of it being blurred. I was very interested in Francis Baker's pictures, which are horrifying when you look at them, almost because you can't see them too clearly. They're smeared and blurred, and you think, my God, what's happening underneath that? So, I tried to do the visual equivalent of that by shooting shaking images—running the camera at four frames per second, then running the film at the regular twenty-four frames per second to create a frenetic sort of blur. If you looked at it for a second, it was silly. But if you looked at it for a quarter of a second or less, it was frightening when you put the right sound effect with it. It was fun to think that stuff up and then try to execute it.

I think the film dealt with something that affects us all—life and death. The movie forced you to confront that. I loved the idea that Danny Aiello's character was kind of an angel. He says that if you are hanging onto life, you are seeing demons, and they're pulling your life apart. But if you give yourself over to death, then these demons become angels. I thought it was a very reassuring way of looking at life and death.

It was a complex movie, because what you were looking at and what you thought was happening wasn't, in fact, what was happening. You thought this man was living a life after Vietnam, when, in fact, he wasn't. He was imagining a life after Vietnam. He was dying in Vietnam and, during the course of dying, he was imagining a relationship with this girl called Jessie, played by

Elizabeth Peña. It was a complex idea for people to grasp, and I think some people didn't understand it, because you were dealing with three different time sequences. You were dealing with him dying in Vietnam, which was in the present but looked like it was in the past. You were dealing with an imagined future, and you were dealing with a remembered past before the Vietnam War, with his wife. So, it was a very complicated thing to get hold of.

There was a scene that I particularly liked in *Jacob's Ladder,* where Tim is hanging onto life, and he's essentially in a kind of demonic hospital. He's in hell, and he's strapped down to this bed, and he has pins in his head. He's screaming, "I'm alive, I'm alive," and he's trying to hang on to life. His wife is there with him, and the doctors are telling him that he's dead. I was just bowled over by Tim's performance, so much so that I started to cry. I looked at the cameraman and tried to say something to him and I could see that he was crying as well, and then I looked at the camera operator, who also was crying. After the scene, I remember walking across the parking lot with him in total silence. I finally told him that I thought he was really good in the scene. He took a long beat and then said, "I know."

It was one of the best things that has ever happened to me as a director. It doesn't get any better than that. You know that you've seen and been through something special and that's really why I do it. I do it for the actors. What I really love is working with the actors. That's the fun of it.

Indecent Proposal (1993)

Robert Redford; Demi Moore; Woody Harrelson; Seymour Cassel; Oliver Platt; Rip Taylor; Billy Bob Thornton; Billy Connolly.

Adrian's pictures are always visually stunning. But that's not just what they are. He always has a sense of truth. And so, in all of his movies, the characters come from a point of reality, a point of truth.
Sherry Lansing—Film Producer

Jacob's Ladder was an emotionally tough film to make. The subject matter was kind of depressing, so, when I read *Indecent Proposal,* I thought it was a whimsical, funny sort of fluffy idea that I might like to do. The thought that you would sleep with somebody for a million dollars I felt was just such a great idea. It was not something I thought people were going to take too seriously. But, in the end, the people sort of looked at this much more seriously than I'd expected. The idea seemed to catch people's imagination. Like when Woody and Demi are in bed together and neither is trying to persuade the other to do anything yet. But they're kind of playing "what if." Neither is saying they should do it and neither is saying they shouldn't.

It was fascinating working with Robert Redford, who is a real film star. I'd always known that Robert had come on the set, because even though I hadn't seen him, there would be kind of a hush. There wasn't any hush for me, but there was for him.

I was always impressed with the way Redford walked. He walks perfectly ramrod-straight. I never really called him Bob, you know. Everybody called him Bob. I always call him Robert. He's a very understated man. You'd never see him take a limo. He drove himself everywhere.

Demi Moore was exciting to work with. When I first saw her, she had been pregnant and she had this wonderful sort of womanly quality. She was very rounded and I remember having quite a fight trying to keep her rounded, because she wanted to work out and get in shape. So that was a little bit of a struggle. She's a fine actress and it was great fun to work with her.

Let me tell you about a scene that I like that kind of comes from real life— my life. I remember having an argument with my wife. She was washing dishes and had these rubber gloves on. In the middle of this fight, during the hooting and hollering at each other, I became riveted on those yellow gloves and I thought it was so bizarre. She's got these gloves on, with soapsuds pouring off them, and I'm thinking to myself while we're having this fight, "I've got to use that in the film." I went and wrote it down. So, that's why Demi Moore is wearing yellow gloves in that scene. I always like it when you have another layer going in a scene that isn't strictly the words. It kind of says it's real. I owe my wife thanks for that.

Lolita (1997)

Jeremy Irons; Melanie Griffith; Frank Langella;
Dominique Swain; Susanne Shepherd; Keith Reddin; Erin J. Dean.

Adrian Lyne is a singular person and a singular director. He has a very sharp and very distinct point of view about whatever the material is he's doing, and you can see it in every one of his films.

Frank Langella—Actor

I never wanted to remake *Lolita*; I wanted to make the novel. However much one might like Stanley Kubrick's original movie, it's not one of my favorites. His version doesn't have a lot to do with the novel. It was more about Peter Sellers's performance as Quilty than it was about James Mason's performance as Humbert. I wanted to make a movie about Humbert Humbert, because that's the story. Somebody asked if I was going to make the sexuality erotic. I thought that was kind of a trick question. But I realized that I had to make it erotic, because the movie and the story are being seen through Humbert's eyes. In the novel, it's his eye in the first person. So, I tried to make a movie that reflected this extraordinary but appalling novel. It's monstrous what this man does to the girl, and yet it's hilariously funny. And somehow, when all is said and done, it manages to be a love story. So, I tried to accomplish those three things and, hopefully, succeeded.

It was obviously very, very difficult, because Humbert Humbert isn't a man that you want to sympathize with. It's uneasy, sympathizing with him or liking him or being amused by him. You want to just balls-out hate him for what he's done. In Kubrick's movie, he is a sniveling rat of a man. He's somebody who is very unlikable. He's amusing, but I don't think you sense that in the screwed-up, awful way he loved her.

At the end of the movie, he sees her pregnant and polluted with another man's child. She's only an echo of the nymphet that he'd once known. She's now everything that he despises, but he still loves. She, on the other hand, loathes him. Had she wanted him back I think he would have stayed with her. I may be a romantic, but I think he would have stayed with her.

When I started talking about the movie, the climate was very different than it is now. The Jon Benet [Ramsey] tragedy had happened. Everybody was talking about pedophilia. There was an obsession with it. Less so now, I'm finding out. Now people are talking about violence. Now they've moved on to something else. But at the time, there was a very real fear about releasing this movie. And more and more as it went on, nobody stood up to bat to make this film. I realized that decisions were made not to touch this movie.

I know it's not a question of the quality of the film, because I think it's some of my best work. I think Jeremy's performance was extraordinary. And Dominique Swain was just an extraordinary find because she had done nothing before. She hadn't acted in her life and she turned in a wonderful performance. But, it was just the wrong movie at the wrong time. Even in Europe, people were frightened of it.

It was tough, editing this film, because for six weeks I had to work with an attorney. That was the result of a law, which essentially said that you couldn't have an adult portraying a minor. That was aimed at the Internet, in fact, but it spilled over into films. It meant that the few shots that I had done with a body double were now questionable. There were two scenes that were up for grabs. This lawyer was trying to get me to take them out of the film, and, happily, they stayed in. We were very careful, obviously, because she was a minor. She was fourteen when I first met her, and her mother was always there, and a teacher was always on the set, and we were very careful, as well we should have been.

There was a thing called "the pad" that was kind of a cushion thing that was brought out any time there was any contact between Jeremy and Dominique. I was very concerned about it, and so was her mother. The one that was the least concerned, in fact, was Dominique. Dominique Swain was never concerned or frightened by anything. She was endlessly inventive. Every take would be different, you know.

I must have seen maybe two thousand girls for that role. At first, I was trying to cast people over eighteen, because it would have been much easier. But it just didn't work. There wasn't this feeling that you got with Dominique, whereby she has a foot in both camps. You feel the child on the one hand and you feel the adult on the other. Interestingly enough, by the end of the movie, I couldn't have used Dominique Swain again, because by that time she'd grown up. It was such a fleeting thing, so I was lucky.

The Showtime cable network ran the film, and it was released theatrically afterwards. It was an agonizing process, because I really thought that, week after week, somebody would pick up the movie for theatrical release. They didn't, and I gradually realized that it wasn't going to happen because there was still this fear surrounding the film. Nobody wanted to stand up and be counted as being seen as supporting pedophilia, which is patently nonsense. It's a graphic novel, yes, but taught in universities and colleges all over the world. This movie would have come out easily in the seventies and eighties. It was probably easier in a sense for Kubrick than it was for me.

When I first told my oldest son that I was thinking of doing *Lolita*, he said to me, "We'll need that like a hole in the head." And I realized that, following in Kubrick's footsteps, I would have two strikes against me. But I wanted to do the movie and I do think that it's a film that will linger.

Parting Words

People tend to talk about me in visual terms, and, God knows, that's important. I can't imagine making a film and throwing the visual side out the window. That would be disaster. But what's most important is the actors. You can have an awful-looking movie that's well acted that will go through the roof. And you can have a beautiful-looking film with a bad script and bad acting that will go down the toilet every time.

Adrian Lyne Filmography

Foxes (1980)
Flashdance (1983)
Nine ½ Weeks (1986)
Fatal Attraction (1987)
Jacob's Ladder (1990)
Indecent Proposal (1993)
Lolita (1997)
Unfaithful (2002)

Note: Since completing this interview, Lyne has directed *Unfaithful* (2002), starring Diane Lane and Richard Gere.

Awards and Nominations

Academy Awards, USA

Fatal Attraction, Best Director (nominated), 1988

Golden Globes Awards

Fatal Attraction, Best Director (nominated), 1988

Razzie Awards

Indecent Proposal, Worst Director (nominated), 1994

The Films of Tony Scott

British director Tony Scott has had a consistent string of successes in films and commercials, and he shows no sign of slowing down.

Born in Newcastle, England, Scott attended the Sunderland Art School, where he received a Fine Arts degree in painting. While completing a year-long postgraduate study at Leeds College, he developed an interest in cinematography and made *One of the Missing*, a half-hour film financed by the British Film Institute and based on an Ambrose Bierce short story. He then went on to earn his Master of Fine Arts degree at the Royal College of Arts, completing another film for the British Film Institute, *Love Memory*, from an original script financed by actor Albert Finney.

In 1973, Scott partnered with his brother Ridley, also a hugely successful director, to form a London-based commercial production company, RSA. Tony began his career creating some of the world's most entertaining and memorable commercials, honing his film vocabulary, and picking up every major award in the field.

In 1983, he started his feature-film career with the modern vampire story *The Hunger*, starring Catherine Deneuve, David Bowie, and Susan Sarandon. Three years later, he directed the globally successful *Top Gun*, starring Tom Cruise and Kelly McGillis. His career has been nonstop ever since.

> *You know, on a set time is ticking, which means money is being spent with every second that goes by. And this is a man who brings his attitude of life onto a set. He never loses it. He keeps things buoyant. He knows everyone. He speaks to everyone, and everyone has a voice on the set. It's pretty inspiring. He's a lovely, lovely guy.*
>
> Brad Pitt—Actor

The Conversation

I grew up in the North of England during the postindustrial revolution. It was pretty bleak but had enormous character and was very interesting. It was a depressed mining and shipbuilding area. But within fifteen minutes of where we lived, you had the moors. I am a very outdoor person, so I'd always be on my bicycle or my motorcycle and I'd be up on the moors and climbing. There are rock walls up there about a hundred feet high. All in all, I had a great childhood in what was a very bleak industrial environment.

When I was in school, I was always interested in trying to record what I remembered in terms of people—moments in time, you know. At school, I was always painting, always drawing, and my brother Ridley was a huge influence. Ridley had a photographic memory. He transferred those images and those details through his fingertips with his ability to draw. He was and is a great illustrator, and that had a big influence on me.

I spent eight years in art school, five years as a painter. I kept watching what Ridley was doing. I helped him make his first movie, which was a half-hour movie called *Boy on a Bicycle*. I was the star and my dad was the grip. That was really the beginning of my interest in film. I continued on, and I got my degree in fine art and painting. While I was painting, I persuaded the British Film Institute to give me a thousand pounds to make *One of the Missing,* which was a half-hour American Civil War piece. Based on that, I got into the Royal College of Film School. Went from painting after five years into three years at film school. *One of the Missing* would be my first film, and *Loving Memory* was my second. Actor Albert Finney financed it, and it was something that I wrote, produced, and directed. That was a strange, quirky tale set in the Yorkshire Dales.

When I got out of film school, Ridley said, "You know, I have started up this production company doing commercials. Come and make some money doing commercials and pay Dad back for your eight years as a student." So, I did, and I never looked back, and I loved it. I shot commercials for ten years. Not for the money, though the money was pretty good. But it was for the cute girls. I traveled the world with the most beautiful women. I cornered the market in fashion commercials. It was the best training I could have gotten, you know. I'd shoot a hundred days a year. I turned more film than most feature directors turn in a year, you know. It was fun and very lucrative.

I won lots of awards, but, most of all, I got to understand my craft. I got to understand how to communicate with a crew and how to get non-actors to perform for you. I worked with actors, non-actors, and models. It was great. Every commercial was a different challenge.

Actually, my biography is a little off there. I did my ten years in commercials. I did one film for television, which was an hour-long Henry James story called *L'auteur de Beltraffio,* and that was the thing that actually got me into Hollywood. Michael Eisner at Disney saw it. After ten years of directing commercials, I wanted to try and go into the long-form films. Michael Eisner offered me *Alive,* the story about the air crash in the Andes that led to cannibalism. I spent a year working on that, and, for a number of reasons, it didn't happen. But, somehow, I got *The Hunger* after *Alive* fell apart. So, I went from *Alive* and its theme of cannibalism into a vampire movie with Catherine Deneuve, David Bowie, and Susan Sarandon.

The Hunger (1983)

Catherine Deneuve; David Bowie; Susan Sarandon;
Cliff De Young; Beth Ehlers; Dan Hedaya; Rufus Collins;
Suzanne Bertish; James Aubrey.

The original script for *The Hunger* was really sort of a B-horror-movie script, you know. I tried to do something more artsy, esoteric, and strange, and I accomplished that. But, you know, I was criticized by the industry and especially Hollywood. They all hated it. They hated it because they said it was indulgent, it was esoteric, and it was slow. Well, it was all those things. But I think it showed that I had the ability and an understanding of my craft and I was able to get the performance out of actors. And I demonstrated how I could make things look good, you know. It's a mood-and-mysticism piece with a very slight story. But Hollywood hated it. And it took me four more years to get another movie.

I was devastated because the critics slammed me, especially [the] U.K., which is my home. They just devastated me, and they took cheap shots. They said the film was a classic product of something that comes out of advertising—far too glossy. But I was actually trying to disguise what I felt was a weak story. When I look back at it, I think it's an interesting movie, you know. It was my first movie and it really did show that I was able to actually deal with performances and the story. Now it's a huge cult movie.

There's a funny story attached to *The Hunger*. My mother, who lived in a retirement community on the southeast coast of England, told all her friends that her son just finished his first film, and they'll all get in to see it free. I said, "Mum, I don't think this is the sort of movie that your friends want to see." She brought forty of her friends to see *The Hunger*. When she came out of the theater, she denounced me. She said, "No son of mine would make this movie. It must be a different Tony Scott." In the film, Susan Sarandon and Catherine Deneuve get it on, not in a lesbian scene but transference of blood, but it was very sexual. My mum had this heart attack sitting in front of forty of her best friends. And she denounced me.

> Top Gun *has become a picture that is beloved by the public. It's still selling in videocassettes and DVD. But look at* Enemy of the State *and* Crimson Tide. *These pictures really stand out. Tony hasn't made a bad picture for us, ever.*
>
> Jerry Bruckheimer—Producer

Top Gun (1986)

Tom Cruise; Kelly McGillis; Val Kilmer;
Anthony Edwards; Tom Skerritt; Michael Ironside;
John Stockwell; Barry Tubb; Rick Rossovich;
Tim Robbins; Clarence Gilyard Jr.

Producer Don Simpson was a strange character, as we all know. Don would sit and look at the movies like *The Hunger* at three in the morning with a bit of chemical help, if you know what I mean. It was in, back then, for Hollywood film types to smoke grass and watch *The Hunger*. They all thought it was a great movie. It was about that time that Don's partner, Jerry Bruckheimer, saw my commercial reel. So, based on my commercial work, they offered me *Top Gun.*

Here's a true story. I went on a river rapids trip to the Grand Canyon with Simpson and Bruckheimer. Mr. Simpson said, "If you swim these rapids we'll let you direct this movie." So I did, and they gave me the movie, and that's a true story.

To be honest, I wasn't sure that I wanted to do *Top Gun* in the beginning. I was a painter and an artist, and *The Hunger* was much closer to my sensibilities, you know. *Top Gun* was this out-and-out popcorn movie. I hemmed and hawed, even though I had chased it for a while because I was desperate to do another movie. Then it sort of clicked. I said, I'm going to take it for what it is, which is rock 'n' roll and blue skies. It's silver jets against blue-black skies with Tom Cruise and Val Kilmer. And that's what it was. With rock . . . with real rock 'n' roll music to accompany and push it along.

To get ready for *Top Gun,* I looked at all the old aerial movies. I was obviously concerned, because all the aerial sequences I saw were boring. I hadn't seen any aerial sequences that I thought had any excitement in them. So, I brought my skills that I learned in advertising to the aerial sequences. In terms of the true strength and the energy and the pacing, the excitement comes from the editing. So, I figured out what I would need to get to actually make the editing work.

In aerial sequences they normally shoot plane-to-plane. I'd shoot closer to the faces with more reactions. We got permission to mount cameras on the wing tips for a one-second shot of a barrel roll. Then we'd put another camera on a mount on top, and they're coming at you at six hundred miles an hour. But in the end, it was all those elements that strung together.

I storyboarded all the aerial sequences. I had a vision in mind based on my previous advertising work. I'd give these Navy pilots a storyboard, like a comic strip. We'd do briefings with these guys with little jet plane models, telling them that I wanted this or that. I'd give them their storyboard, and they'd paste them up in their cockpit. Then I had a flight leader who would be the director in the air, and he would call it. But no matter how much I tried to plan and control it, it all really finally came together in the cutting room. I had all the ingredients for the canvas—all the paint was on the pallet, and it was ready to be massaged in the cutting room.

Everyone thought Kelly was an unusual choice to play opposite Tom, because she looked a bit older than he did. But I thought Kelly was a great choice, as did Tom. She wasn't as glamorous as a lot of people expected the woman to be. But I think she had more of a reality base, you know. The chemistry between the two of them was actually created between them on camera and by me in terms of how I staged stuff.

When I first came to the film industry, I kept saying I was an artist and I wanted to do serious work. I wanted to do movies like *Blade Runner*, which was Ridley's film. But in the end, I loved doing *Top Gun*, once I'd gotten my head around what the movie was all about. I got a vision of what I wanted to say in the film. That was my challenge. That's what kept me going for eighteen months of my life.

Beverly Hills Cop II (1987)

Eddie Murphy; Judge Reinhold; Jurgen Prochnow;
Ronny Cox; John Ashton; Brigitte Nielsen; Allen Garfield;
Dean Stockwell; Paul Reiser; Gilbert R. Hill; Paul Guilfoyle.

After we finished *Top Gun*, Don Simpson and Jerry Bruckheimer asked me if I wanted to do *Beverly Hills Cop*. I said, "I'm terrified of comedy. I don't know how I can contribute." Eddie Murphy was a god in my eyes, you know. I have great difficulty in communicating with stars. I am in awe of these people, and I get nervous, you know. But then I woke up one morning and said, "I know what it is. I can actually bring contemporary action to an Eddie Murphy comedy, which nobody has done before." It would be a glossy look at a comedy. And nobody had done that up until then. So, that was my hook, and I had a blast. It was fun.

The most difficult scene that I found was at the very end of the movie, when Eddie is in the building looking for the bad guy. I was trying to think how could I give this something a little different from what we've seen in Hollywood action pieces. So, I made everything go very quiet. Then this wall explodes, and this car comes through, which the bad guy is driving. It was the least expected, and it worked, but that was the most difficult scene I had to stage.

He is a great, great talent. He's giving; he's supportive. He's encouraging, and he's very, very funny. Just the way he wears his ball cap will make you laugh. That pink ball cap and the fact that he hardly ever wears trousers—always shorts.

                              Anthony Quinn—Actor (1915–2001)

Revenge (1990)

Kevin Costner; Anthony Quinn; Madeleine Stowe; Tomas Milan; Joaquin Martinez; James Gammon; Jesse Corti; Sally Kirkland.

After *Top Gun*, it was a whole different world there, because of the success of that picture. The world became my oyster. But I got pigeonholed into doing action movies. I loved doing them, but I really wanted to get back to the darker side of my character. So I chose to do *Revenge* with Kevin Costner, Anthony Quinn, and Madeleine Stowe. It was actually brought to my attention by a girlfriend of mine. She thought I should do it. She was with another guy at the time, so it was our story, kind of. It's about forbidden love, and it was a very dark piece. It was very close to my own life at the time. That's why I had a passion for it and wanted to do it.

John Huston had wanted to make *Revenge* for ten years and kept pushing producer Ray Stark every year to make the film. But Stark didn't think it was John Huston material. He didn't like the darkness and the violence, so he didn't make it during Huston's life, but after Huston died, Stark decided to make it his homage to John Huston.

I think it became kind of a cult film because it was a forbidden-love story. It took people down a different road than what the genre had done in the past. It was a shame, because I thought my cut was much better, and it was twenty-four minutes shorter. You can't say everything with words. You have to rely on the moment and capitalize on what you feel is the connection between the two lovers. And Madeleine and Kevin were great. But they made me go back and reshoot another twenty-four minutes of talking heads to articulate and tell everybody what was going on. And so, it lost the mystery. I think my version was much more mysterious and more dangerous and much more powerful and certainly very dark, very violent, and very passionate.

I loved working [with] Anthony Quinn, who was a brilliant storyteller. He has got such a wide spectrum of adventures and experiences in his life, and you'd die laughing when he told a story. Up until his death, I stayed in touch with Anthony on his birthday and Christmas. He was a larger-than-life individual who was charming, funny, articulate, and very smart. I thought he was perfect for the character of Tibby in *Revenge*. It was great fun working with this legend, and I looked up to him. For me, he will forever be Zorba the Greek, and certainly no one will ever forget his magnificent performance in *Lawrence of Arabia*. It was a privilege to know and work with him.

It was great fun working with Kevin Costner and Madeleine Stowe in that film. There's darkness inside of Madeleine that worked so well in the movie. We shot it down in Mexico in some strange and unusual and dark places. It's a beautiful film—strange, dark, and esoteric—and it doesn't pull its punches, and I wish they would have left my cut intact.

Days of Thunder (1990)

Tom Cruise; Robert Duvall; Nicole Kidman;
Randy Quaid; Cary Elwes; Michael Rooker; Fred
Dalton Thompson; John C. Reilly; J. C. Quinn.

We didn't have a script when we started that movie. We were actually writing the script as we were shooting. I always wanted to do a motor racing movie, because I was a street racer in my youth. I went to motor racing school in England and I've ridden motorcycles and always driven fast cars when I had the money. My whole life has been sort of dedicated to speed. Even though I didn't know much about NASCAR, we wanted to do a Formula One racing movie. So, when this project came along, I started doing my homework. But we had to commit to a release date before we really had the script. That was one of the toughest movies I've done, because we were shooting during the day and writing at night. On the other hand, I think it was really the lack of time that enabled us to bring something fresh to that genre.

Tom Cruise is a speed freak like me. I got him into motorcycles and cigars back when we were shooting *Top Gun*. And that's my claim to fame. Tom is actually a great car racer. He kept saying to me, "I'm good." I would say to him, "Bullshit," but he actually is very, very good.

Listen, I thought I had a lot of energy, but Tom Cruise is tireless. He is so prepared when he comes to work it's scary, you know. And he's tough. He's tough and very opinionated, with lots of ideas. But he listens, too. It's a push and pull, you know, but it works, and he's a team player.

Robert Duvall is also tough, and he is brilliant. There is just something about Gene Hackman, Anthony Hopkins, and Robert Duvall. There's a lot of anger and there's this boiling inside these guys. That's what makes them so great, I think. But Robert's tough to deal with. He gives directors a hard time, and on this picture, I was at the brunt of it. I've offered him three other movies since *Days of Thunder,* because I kept thinking his picking on me was personal. I worked with Gene Hackman twice, and Gene has all this stuff built up inside. But that's what's so great, because he gives an internal performance. The same with Duvall, and it's the same with Hopkins, who I did a commercial with and my brother did *Hannibal* with. Those three guys have their own little box. There's this power and energy that comes from what's going on inside them. But if you cross Robert, you're in trouble. [*He laughs.*] We couldn't make it work, but he's one brilliant actor.

The Last Boy Scout (1991)

Bruce Willis; Damon Wayans; Chelsea Field;
Noble Willingham; Taylor Negron; Danielle Harris;
Halle Berry; Bruce McGill; Badja Djola;
Kim Coates; Chelcie Ross.

The Last Boy Scout was written by Shane Black, who also wrote *Lethal Weapon.* I'm trying to think how I would actually pigeonhole Shane. He's smart, articulate, funny, and very twisted. The twisted part is what came out of the opening sequence of *The Last Boy Scout.* It was dark and twisted, and it was so outrageous it was funny. This football player was actually carrying a gun inside of his uniform during a game. I thought it was a very interesting opening to a mainstream movie. If you haven't seen it, please do, so I don't have to give the opening away.

It didn't do that great. Having said that, it did about a hundred million, which by today's standards is not great. Going in, the expectations were higher. I'm not quite sure why it didn't do better, because Bruce Willis was great in it. He had a solid handle on who his character was—this real anti-hero. And the little girl who played Bruce's daughter was brilliant. I was surprised it didn't do better than it did.

I have one story about that film, and I don't know whether I dare to tell it. Okay, here goes. The first day we worked with Bruce, we were out in a remote area, and it poured rain that night. The cleaning service left the trailer door open when they were finished cleaning Bruce's trailer. Bruce had a hairpiece hanging next to this hat. A cat got into the trailer, took the hairpiece underneath the trailer in the pouring rain and tried to fuck it. So, we couldn't figure out why Bruce was so late the next day. And then one hour went by, and then two, and I said, "Where the fuck is Bruce?" Eventually he turned up and told us what this cat had done to his hairpiece.

> *We had a scene where Chris Walken shoots me in the head, and the gun is actually put to my head, and I didn't want to do that. So, Tony said it was safe, and puts the gun to his head and pulls the trigger, and blood was oozing out of his forehead. The thing was not put to my head, obviously, but that's the kind of director Tony is. If he asked you to do something he's prepared to do it.*
>
> *Dennis Hopper—Actor*

True Romance (1993)

Christian Slater; Patricia Arquette; Dennis Hopper;
Val Kilmer; Gary Oldman; Brad Pitt; Christopher Walken;
Bronson Pinchot; Samuel L. Jackson; Michael Rapaport;
Saul Rubinek; Conchata Ferrell; James Gandolfini.

It was Quentin Tarantino's first script before he wrote *Reservoir Dogs*. I had just finished *The Last Boy Scout* and I was flying off on holiday to Italy. My ex-secretary gave me this script to read and said, "This kid is quite talented." He'd come down while we were shooting *Last Boy Scout* to see how things were done. And I kept saying, "Fuck, who is this guy?" because he always had this boundless energy. I thought he was some sort of film groupie. But there's something really interesting and odd about him that attracted me to him. So he came down to the set and I had dinner with him and we talked a bit. Then my secretary said, "You got to read his script," so I read two scripts in one sitting.

When I got off the plane in Italy, I said, "I'll take both of them." I called up my then- secretary and told her I wanted them both, but she said we could get *True Romance* but not *Reservoir Dogs*. *True Romance* was a brilliant piece of writing, brilliant in terms of character development. Quentin does so much homework in terms of who his characters are. So, whether a character has one line or is the lead in the piece, he has a clear understanding of who those characters are.

Unfortunately, the film wasn't successful. It bombed, really. I think maybe it's too violent. But if you ask me to make a choice and state which of my films is my favorite, I think I would say *True Romance,* because it invaded my life so easily, because it was so well written. The characters were so well drawn. Every day, I went to the set and had an amazing smorgasbord of the best actors around.

Everyone loved that script so much nobody wanted to change anything. The only thing I'd change is the very, very end of the movie, the very end. In Quentin's draft, Christian Slater's character dies and Patricia Arquette puts a gun in her mouth, threatening to kill herself, but instead says, "Ah, he's a piece of shit anyhow." Then she gets out of the car with the money, hitches a ride, and goes to another life. I shot the film in continuity, so by the time I got to the end of the movie, I was like, romantic at heart. I really wanted to see these kids win, you know. I honestly felt in my heart of hearts that's how I wanted to see this movie end. It was a sad, strange adventure between two people who were desperately in love.

The critics were mixed, and the film got about 50 percent good reviews and then the other 50 percent slammed me good. It's tough to read the bad ones, but I love what I do, and I get very well paid for what I do, so I should care.

Let me say something about the scene between Dennis Hopper and Chris Walken that takes place in Dennis's mobile home. Those two really brought their full talent to that scene. On the written page it didn't come off that funny, but those two brought humor to the scene with their impeccable timing, and they had never worked together before. They were springboarding off of each other. That was one of the best scenes I've ever had to shoot. We rehearsed it for a day and then it took a day and a half to shoot it.

One more story about *True Romance*. Again, the scene between Dennis and Chris Walken. At the end of the scene, Chris puts the gun to Dennis's head. When we were rehearsing it, I decided that Chris would put the gun right on Dennis's forehead and pull it. Dennis says, "I'm not doing that." I said, "Dennis, it is perfectly safe. There's nothing to it." Dennis said, "I don't like that. The gun against my head freaks me out, man." So, I said, "Dennis, watch me. I'll do it. I'll rehearse it for you." So, I got the prop guy to put this gun against my head and he pulled the trigger. But I didn't realize it's one of those guns— a Beretta—where the barrel comes out and then recoils when fired. So, the prop guy put it right against my forehead and fired, and it left this perfect hole in my forehead. So, Dennis is standing there and says "Oh, my God." And then there's this blood. There was this ring in my forehead the size of a wedding band, with blood pouring down between my eyes. And Dennis said, "I told you so. Look at that. Look at that." I'll never hear the end of that as long as I live.

But, going back to Quentin's script, it was just so masterfully put together, and so well crafted, and purely driven by characters who had a sense of humor. The piece had humor, darkness, violence, and then whatever else I brought to it in terms of camera shots, sound, and music, you know.

Crimson Tide (1995)

Denzel Washington; Gene Hackman; Matt Craven;
George Dzundza; Viggo Mortensen; James Gandolfini;
Rocky Carroll; Jaime Gomez; Michael Milhoan; Danny Nucci;
Lillo Brancato; Eric Bruskotter; Rick Schroder; Steve Zahn.

Denzel Washington and Gene Hackman were the first two ideas out of my mouth in terms of actors. It wasn't a black-white thing. Gene Hackman was the commander of the ship and Denzel Washington was the second in command. It just felt right with those two in those roles.

Producer Jerry Bruckheimer and I bounce ideas off of each other, and we are good in terms of picking leads for films. All Hollywood studios, Disney included, want to go the route of examining other actors, even though we had made our overtures to Gene and Denzel before the script was fully there.

We did end up trying other people, but they were the guys that I wanted. To get the script where the actors felt it needed to be, Quentin Tarantino came in and did a total rewrite in terms of the dialogue, and he totally reexamined the characters.

In terms of preparation, Gene goes off and sits in his trailer. He likes to have everything buttoned up before we get to do the scene. So, with Gene, you read the script, do rehearsals, make whatever changes, and that's it. That's what we're going to shoot. Denzel comes in a different way. He sometimes likes to improvise and likes to pull and push and move things around. That tension between the two actors actually helped me in terms of the two characters in the movie.

My favorite submarine movie of all time is *Das Boot,* which was directed brilliantly by Wolfgang Petersen. He did this as an ensemble piece, but each and every character in that film was memorable. He made a wonderful film in a WWII submarine, which is essentially a long tube. That film gave me inspiration.

The Fan (1996)

Robert De Niro; Wesley Snipes; Ellen Barkin;
John Leguizamo; Benicio Del Toro; Patti D'Arbanville;
Chris Mulkey; Andre J. Ferchland; Brandon Hammond.

That came to me with the idea of Robert De Niro being attached, and he's my god, you know. He's just such a great, strange, gentle sweetie. Such a contradiction of everything you hear about him. He'll call you up at four o'clock in the morning and say, "You know that line? What if we did this with it and not that with it?" And, in the end, it is always brilliant. He uses a director, too, because he likes input. But whether he accepts advice or not, I guess it's sort of a comfort to him. I'd love to work with him again.

I've had very few critical acclaims as far as my films go. I've always been slammed. What happened with *The Fan* was devastating when I read the press. Generally, I don't read the press, because it just kills me. So I'll just keep going. I love my life. So, I don't read the reviews, good or bad, anymore. With *The Fan,* it was a shame, because I had such a great experience making that film. I think part of the problem was I made some bad character choices. For instance, I thought De Niro's character was such a gentle human being. But by the time we finished the first two acts, it became a stalker movie. It's about a guy stalking a baseball star. And by the time you came to the third act, De Niro's character is a lost soul. I made him into that vindictive stalker. So, the fault was mine in terms of the choices and the way I was trying to push it.

> *Tony was the first director I ever saw with millions of tear sheets of things. Colors of things that he liked and furniture that he liked. He was just so into everything. I think that is a crucial part of looking at his work. There is also that wonderful spirit of his.*
>
> *Patricia Arquette—Actress*

Enemy of the State (1998)

Will Smith; Gene Hackman; Jon Voight; Lisa Bonet;
Regina King; Stuart Wilson; Laura Cayouette;
Loren Dean; Barry Pepper.

Jerry Bruckheimer and I were looking for another movie to do. Jerry brought the screenplay to me. Luckily, I always wanted to make a movie about the invasion of privacy, especially in today's world. Now, I always do my homework before I commit to a script. In this case, I spent time in Washington and got access to NASA and to the CIA; so, I get a look at this world and say, "Does this world really interest me?" For *Crimson Tide,* I went and hung out on a Trident submarine. It helps when you are trying to develop who your characters are. For *Crimson Tide,* we found a real submarine commander who'd been in service twenty-one years. That was Gene's role model for his character and the same for *Enemy of the State.* We found a role model in D.C. for Gene's character. That kind of background research is what makes me commit to a film. You have to spend time in the real environment.

Enemy of the State was all factual. I was fascinated by the invasion that can occur from a satellite. One of my all-time favorite movies was *The Conversation,* which was a Francis Coppola movie that starred Gene Hackman, and it was about the invasion of privacy but in a different time frame. Modern technology has made it even easier to get into people's lives and into the privacy of their homes. That's what fascinated me. So, everything you saw in *Enemy of the State* was absolutely true. Sometime in the very near future, you will be able to call a service and say, "I want surveillance of my house between 8:00 A.M. and 11:00 A.M." And they'll say, "What do you want? A one-block radius—a hundred-yard radius—a hundred-feet radius?" You'll be able to pay for it like you pay for a telephone call, by the minute. If your house is broken into, you'll see the bad guys go into your house, unload your furniture, put it in the back of a truck, and drive off. And then you're able to get a slight down-angle, so you can read the numbers on their license plates. You'll be able to pay for it, like a regular service. If it's raining, like today, they'll give you an infrared rendering.

Enemy of the State was high energy and was a good film for me to make, because I think I have a short attention span, so three-hour movies put me away. There are very few movies over two hours that I want to sit through, you know. I like momentum, and I like energy, whether it's in my daily life at home or whether it's in the work that I create. Sometimes you want to drive material forward, because you don't want to give the audience too long to examine it, because it's a sleight of hand and you don't want to be caught, you know. I'm trying to give energy to what I put on the screen. I want the audience to go to it, respond to it, and enjoy the fun I had with *Enemy of the State*.

> *He's very good about letting you speak first and letting you exercise whatever things you need to get out. And then he comes in as a kind of referee to keep the overall story in line.*
>
> Brad Pitt—Actor

Spy Game (2001)

Robert Redford; Brad Pitt; Catherine McCormack;
Stephen Dillane; Marianne Jean-Baptiste; Larry Bryggman

I thought *Spy Game* was a very interesting premise. It was attached to another director, and I kept watching it and watching it, and then things started going a little bit south. And so, I saw an opening and dove in. But it was different for me. It was a purely character-driven piece. It's about a father-son-type relationship. It's Robert Redford and his last day at the CIA, and the day that he retires, this kid he's known for twenty-five years has been thrown into jail in China. It's an old-fashioned spy movie, but it's very contemporary in terms of the way it's actually presented.

Two-thirds of the movie is in flashbacks. You never see Redford and Pitt onscreen in present day. You only see them in the flashbacks. Robert Redford's in this conference room with all these heavies and the story flashes back to Vietnam, Beirut, and China. It's a wild ride, and Redford and Pitt are brilliant in it. Catherine McCormack is the love interest who had a relationship with Redford years before, and now the true love in her life is Brad Pitt's character. She gets herself into trouble and Brad goes off to rescue her.

I don't think that it's me that attracts these wonderful actors. I think it's the material that attracts them, you know. In the beginning, both Redford and Pitt had certain misgivings about the script. Early on, there was a little bit of a push and pull, and then through rewrites we managed to seduce them and get them aboard, because in the end they liked the material. But, obviously, I have a track record working with performance and working with big actors, so that does have a little bit to do with it.

I always wanted to work with Redford, ever since I was a young man in art school. *Butch Cassidy and the Sundance Kid* and *Three Days of the Condor* are certainly two of my all-time favorite movies. What a great job. I get to work with guys who were my gods, my idols—De Niro, Hackman, Redford, and Brad Pitt. I'm still intimidated by these stars, and I'm always nervous.

On Producer Jerry Bruckheimer

I've known Jerry for a bit over twenty years now. We've been in business together on five movies, which is like ten years of my life on a day-to-day basis. That's longer than any of my marriages have lasted. I was married three times, you know. I've been married to the latest one for ten years. Jerry and I have a great relationship. He gets the best out of me, and I get the best out of him. It's always been a pull-and-push relationship, but somehow we seem to have met in the middle with films like *Enemy of the State* and *Crimson Tide*, which had integrity and good characters and a certain quality to them. They were a bit different from the popcorn movies like *Days of Thunder* or *Beverly*

Hills Cop II. We broke ground together on *Enemy* and *Crimson* because they were intelligent and mainstream.

But Jerry never changes. Jerry has always been the same Jerry. He's so hardworking, and he loves the business so much, you know. He has always been the kind of guy that shows up on the set at seven-thirty in the morning. And he and Don Simpson [deceased] had a great relationship because it was like left hand, right hand. Jerry was the details guy, and Don dealt with the broader structure. But that combination was great, you know. Jerry split up from Don before Don died, you know. I'm sure Jerry must have thought, "Hmm. Whether I think I need Don or not, it was a good karma and good luck we shared." But since that breakup, Jerry has gone from strength to strength. He's very smart, very articulate, and he has a brilliant handle on story and character.

The Next Project (Maybe)

I've got Tom Mix and Pancho Villa together in the same picture. Something I've always wanted to do, which is like *Lawrence of Arabia* and *The Wild Bunch* rolled into one, so it's a big epic. And since I am a rock climber, I want to do a film about that. Climbing is not about man against nature or man against the mountain. It's about man against himself, you know. The world of climbing that I'm involved in is really like a rock gymnast's, but on the big walls. It's a surfing mentality in the vertical world. Before I get much older, I'll make that climbing movie.

How Will He Know He's Finally Made It?

I will know I've made it when I'm sitting in my office at Paramount on my toilet with a telephone in my hand. Sitting in a major studio with a telephone in the loo, wow! Coming from where I come from, that would be the ultimate. But answering your question in a more serious way, you never know when you've really made it. Making it is something inside each individual's mind. Making it is actually satisfying your own desires for that particular movie or time frame or moment in time, and feeling good about yourself, you know. But I'm so paranoid and so insecure and that's what keeps me struggling and working harder. I am constantly trying to do something different and not necessarily better. The true challenge every day is trying to produce something different, so you are not repeating yourself. I love what I do. I love where I live and whom I live with. It's a great environment I work in, and it's a great business.

Tony Scott Filmography

Loving Memory (1969)
One of The Missing (1971)
Nouvelles de Henry James, TV series, segment "The Author of Beltraffio" (1976)
The Hunger (1983)
Top Gun (1986)
Beverly Hills Cop II (1987)
Revenge (1990)
Days of Thunder (1990)
The Last Boy Scout (1991)
True Romance (1993)
Crimson Tide (1995)
The Fan (1996)
The Hunger, TV series, episode "The Swords" (1997)
Enemy of the State (1998)
Spy Game (2001)
The Hire: Beat the Devil (2002)
Man on Fire (2003)

Editor's note: Since completing this interview Scott has directed *The Hire: Beat the Devil* (2002) and *Man on Fire* (2003).

Awards and Nominations

British Academy Awards

Michael Balcon Award for Outstanding Contribution to British Cinema, 1995

Catalonian International Film Festival

One of The Missing, Best Short Film, Medalla Sitges en Plata de Ley, 1971

Fantasporto

True Romance, Best Film, International Fantasy Film Award (nominated), 1995

San Sebastian International Film Festival

The Fan, Golden Shell Award (nominated), 1996

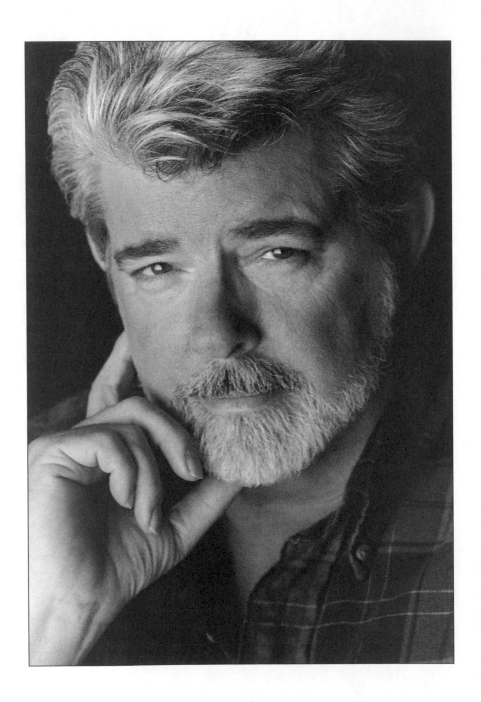

The Films of George Lucas

George Lucas was raised on a walnut ranch in Modesto, California. As a young man, he had hoped to become a racecar driver, but after high school graduation, a serious auto accident sidelined that career goal forever. Looking for direction in his life, he attended Modesto Junior College before enrolling in the University of Southern California film school. It was there that he made several short films, including *THX 1138*, which he would later turn into his first feature film.

In 1967, he was given the opportunity to apprentice at Warner Bros. Studios, where he met Francis Ford Coppola for the first time. Eventually, the two formed Zoetrope Studios in 1969 and moved their operation to San Francisco. Coppola went on to direct *The Godfather,* and Lucas formed Lucasfilm Ltd. In 1973, he wrote and directed, with Coppola's encouragement, the box-office hit *American Graffiti*. Between 1973 and 1974, he wrote the screenplay for *Star Wars*. That film would eventually redefine the term "blockbuster." Lucas continued on with the other *Star Wars* films, as well as producing the *Indiana Jones* series, which his friend Steven Spielberg directed. It seemed that when it came to movies, Lucas had the magic touch.

Most of Lucas's time between 1980 and 1985 was spent building Skywalker Ranch, south of San Francisco. It is truly a place of beauty and tranquility, where Lucas and his staff could apply their craft. The interesting thing about George Lucas is that he has continually fought for his independence as a filmmaker, and he has won. To this day, he does just about whatever he wants to do, when he wants to do it. All of his *Star Wars* films have proven to be huge box-office successes, and he and Spielberg have yet another episode of the *Indiana Jones* series in store for eager audiences.

He has the most amazing imagination of anybody that I've worked with. It just goes on and on and on.

Carrie Fisher—Actress

The Conversation

I grew up in Modesto, California, which is a little farming community. It's very rural in nature and very small. Growing up in the 1940s and 1950s was a very post-war Norman Rockwell–type existence. Very much like the Midwest, except we were only about sixty miles from San Francisco. I had a lot of influence from being around San Francisco but at the same time lived in a very small-town environment.

In my early years, I was very interested in cars, and some of my first obsessions really were with cars and working on cars and fixing cars and racing cars. When I was about thirteen or fourteen years old, I was either on a motorcycle or in a car getting myself in trouble, because we lived on a ranch where there were a lot of private roads that I could race around on without any real problem. Right before I was going to graduate from high school, my obsession with cars led me into a rather disastrous automobile accident, where I was all but killed. I sat in the hospital thinking how I might have been killed and how I survived the accident. I was wearing seatbelts and had roll bars and all these things but, fortunately, was thrown free of the car before it completely wrapped itself around a tree. Had I stayed in the car—had the roll bar worked, had the seatbelts worked—then I wouldn't have survived it.

It was one of those odd things where through a quirk or something or other I managed to get out of it alive. It made me think a lot, and I decided to give myself a little bit more direction in my life, so I started college. I started taking a lot of humanities, sociology, psychology, and a lot of anthropology courses—and became very interested and fascinated by it. I spent a lot more time on school than I had in previous years, when I was mostly a little foreign-car service working on my car.

My interest in making things had always been there. When I was young, I loved being a carpenter, and I used to build things. I used to build dollhouses and chessboards. We used to build these houses in the back, you know, forts and tree houses and that sort of thing. I was building carnivals and roller coasters. That transferred itself into working on and building cars and putting them together.

I'd always been interested in art and it was one of my better subjects in school, especially in high school. I had a fantasy at that point of going to art school and becoming an illustrator. I'd also picked up in high school an interest in photography. I got an 8-mm movie camera and began making movies for my friends that were racing cars. But that was as far as my interest in film went. It was really sort of an adjunct to me going to the Art Center and becoming an artist.

My father was very much against me becoming an artist. He said it was not a really worthwhile profession and I would have a very hard time of it. He said, "You can go to art school if you'd like, but you're going to pay for it." The Art Center was actually one of the more expensive schools around. So I said, "Well, that doesn't sound like a good idea," so I was just going to go on to San Francisco State and be anthropology major, and I didn't quite know what I was going to do with that. I didn't really envision myself being a professor.

Just by circumstances, a friend I grew up with and knew my entire life was going to go to USC to study business, and he talked me into going and taking the test with him in Stockton. So I applied and passed the test and got into school, and I said, "Well what am I going to do there?" And he said, "Well there's a cinematography school there. You know you like photography. It's not quite fine arts, but it is something you're interested in." And I said, "Well, yeah, okay, I'll try that." And that was really my first experience with film. I didn't really know anything about it until I got to film school, which was in my junior year in college.

He has a mellowness on the set, which I do admire in directors. I feel
very at ease with him and he seems very at ease with what he's doing.
Liam Neeson—Actor

Film School

In film school, you first take history classes and some very early production classes. But I took an animation class my first semester there. They gave us one minute of film to practice with on the camera. I took that one minute of film and I made a one-minute movie out of it. I put a soundtrack to it and then ended up winning a lot of awards all over the world. From that moment on, I realized I knew how to do this really well. It came naturally to me, and I really loved doing it. Then, after that, I made a series of student films. I think I made five or six of them, and about half of them won awards in all the film festivals. Eventually, I won a scholarship—a sort of work-study scholarship—at Warner Bros. to observe production over there. At that point, I really had no interest in theatrical filmmaking at all. That was not what I got into film for. My only experience with film was from going to the movies and chasing girls.

There were a bunch of underground filmmakers in San Francisco. I'd go up there on the weekends and watch these little 16-mm movies, and that's what I thought I was going to do. That was my desire. When I got into film school, I learned about cinema verité documentaries, which were just starting to come in. So, I thought I would become a cinema verité cameraman, edit my own films, and then I'd do these little avant-garde art films on the side. That was really what I wanted out of the world of cinema at that point.

The Coppola Connection

I went off to do this Warner Bros. scholarship just on a lark because I ended up winning it and I thought I'd go and see what feature filmmaking and this Hollywood thing was about. When I got there, Warner Bros. had been shut down because they had just been bought out by another corporation. Jack Warner was actually leaving the lot the day I arrived. They were making one film *Finian's Rainbow,* which was being directed by Francis Coppola. And they said, "Well, we'll stick you on this film because all the other departments are closed down." So, I got stuck watching this movie being made, which I wasn't that interested in. I think Francis was kind of offended that I didn't have a lot of interest in what he was doing, and I told him that I wasn't really interested in this kind of filmmaking. I was just trying to get over in the animation department because it was empty. I figured if I got some short ends of film, I could go over there while nobody was around, and I could start making animated films in their animation department. But Francis said he would give me a job to do. I could come around and be his assistant and give him one good idea every day, and I should go around picking out camera angles. That actually worked out very well. I was very prone to the cinematic side of things. I was more into film editing and into the photography, whereas Francis is very much into the writing and working with actors. So, he kind of took me under his wing and taught me all the parts I didn't like, which was the writing of scripts and the working with actors, and I helped him and became an assistant in the cinematic side of films.

When my scholarship at Warner Bros. was over, Francis decided that he didn't really like the experience of making *Finian's Rainbow.* He wanted to get back to doing street films and avant-garde kinds of movies. He decided we could do the *Rain People,* which was going to be shot all across the country with a small crew. I had the choice of going back to graduate school or going off on this little adventure, and I decided to go off on the adventure with Francis. He couldn't pay me, so he said he'd get me a deal to write a screenplay of *THX,* a short I'd made that had just won the National Student Film Festival Award. I was trying to see if I could get it off the ground as a movie. He said, "You can write the screenplay, and you can be the assistant everything on this movie, and we'll travel across the country." I thought that would be a great idea. So, we went to make this movie of his, and we started in New York and came back across the country.

We were shooting in Nebraska, and I came back to a conference in San Francisco and met John Korty, who had a little film studio there. I went back to Francis and said, "Why don't we continue on to San Francisco," and he thought that was a fantastic idea. He didn't like the idea of going back and working in Hollywood, and he really wanted to start a whole new idea up there in San Francisco. *Easy Rider* had just come out, you know. There seemed to be a possibility that avant-garde, youth-oriented films could make it in the world. So, we decided to make that kind of alternative studio in San Francisco, and called it American Zoetrope. That's how that whole thing started.

THX 1138 (1971)

Robert Duvall; Donald Pleasence; Don Pedro Colley; Maggie McOmie; Ian Wolfe; Marshall Efron; Sid Haig; John Pearce.

THX was the very first film that Zoetrope did, because I'd already written a script. Francis went down to Hollywood, and, again, Warner Bros. studio was being sold to another corporation. Francis went in and said, "You know, we already had this deal to make movies, and you have to give us the go-ahead." He really did a lot of fast talking, and he told them we had seven projects ready to go, and we wanted funding, and they said yes. They had no idea what they were saying yes to. Later on, the whole thing went sour when they finally saw *THX,* and they saw the seven scripts we'd written, and they basically closed the place down and forced Francis to pay all the money back.

That put Francis in about $350,000 worth of debt. We were going to have to shut down at that point. I was sort of thrown off on my own to do my own thing and Francis had to go off and do a gangster picture that had been offered to him. He had a lot of concern about whether to give up his freedom and do this work for hire or whether he would try to continue on doing his own thing. As it turned out, I went on and did my own thing with *American Graffiti,* and he went off and did *The Godfather.*

I've never actually described my relationship with Francis as being volatile. I think the media has, though. Francis and I were very good friends right from the moment we met. We're very different. Francis is very flamboyant and very Italian and very sort of "let's go out there and do things." I'm very sort of "Well, let's think about this first. Let's not just sort of jump into it." He's called me the eighty-five-year-old man, but together we were great, because I would kind of be the weight around his neck that slowed him down a little bit to keep him from getting his head chopped off. I think that allowed us to have a very active working relationship, and we actually had a great time working together. We've worked together on a lot of films over the years. But, you know, he helped me. He basically taught me everything about writing and directing. And then, at the same time, he got my first film off the ground. And then he helped me get my second film off the ground. Later on, I went and produced a film for him, and I worked on second-unit things like *The Godfather.* I developed, along with John Milius, the script for *Apocalypse Now.* So there was a lot of collaboration between us on all the movies we were doing at that time, and we still do collaborate. We still show each other our movies and communicate with each other about what we're doing. I read his scripts, and there's a lot of communication that goes on between us.

He exudes his wisdom and his creativity, and you want to match it. So, whatever he wants from you, you want to give it to him because you want to be part of that incredible magical creation that is him.
                                                    Cindy Williams—Actress

Writing in Longhand

I write scripts in longhand. I started out that way, and it's just a habit. I think we all have different ways of being inspired and do our thinking best under certain conditions. I just like to do cursive, and it makes me feel better.

> *I went into this meeting and I didn't know anything about the script. I looked, and there's this little guy sitting behind a desk, and I thought, this is the director? My image of a director was like John Huston, you know.*
>
> Paul Le Mat—Actor

> *George said, it's a musical. And I said that I didn't sing. He said, it doesn't matter that you can't sing. And that was the end of the interview. It was a very cryptic sort of conclusion.*
>
> Ron Howard—Actor-Director

American Graffiti (1973)

*Richard Dreyfuss; Ron Howard; Paul Le Mat;
Charles Martin Smith; Cindy Williams; Candy Clark; Mackenzie
Phillips; Wolfman Jack; Bo Hopkins; Manuel Padilla Jr.; Beau Gentry;
Harrison Ford; Jim Bohan; Jana Bellan; Debby Celiz.*

The anthropologist side of me never went away, and I was very interested in the mating rituals of the fifties. A uniquely American mating ritual of meeting the opposite sex in a car was very fascinating to me. I really liked this kind of lost ritual that had gone on in the United States between 1940 and the beginning of the 1960s. I saw the beginning of the sixties as a real transition in the culture because of the Vietnam War and all the things we were going through, and I wanted to make a movie about it. I had always liked the idea of Fellini's film *I Vitelloni,* which was kind of the same issue about growing up and about taking responsibility and moving out of the house and that whole trauma. It was one of the things in *THX,* and I wanted to expand on it. Francis kept saying that I should do a regular movie, because *THX* was way out there. He suggested I do a comedy, something that would be really acceptable to people. And so, *American Graffiti* was the closest thing I could think of to an acceptable movie. The problem was that the studio didn't see it that way. They said it was not about anything. There was no story. They didn't think I could tell four different stories and intercut them when they weren't related to each other. They said that was impossible. They said I couldn't put that much music in a movie. They didn't think I could have a music track going through the whole thing.

There were a lot of issues that were very controversial at the time that kept it from being made. For over two years, I struggled, trying to get it off the ground and get it made. Finally, I got a studio to approve the project. They liked the script and wanted me to do it. But they needed a name to go with it. Francis came back after doing *The Godfather* and said he'd be producer on it. Then I panicked and realized that I needed a better script and hired some friends of mine to rewrite it and make it work.

I spent a great deal of time casting. I worked for about six months, seeing thousands of kids. I had them come through one after the other. I would talk to them for about two minutes to get a sense of who they were. I would narrow that down to a smaller group that I would bring back and talk to in more depth. Then I would do readings and eventually screen tests. I would do screen tests with different groups of people working with different people. I was really looking for an ensemble cast.

I think the hardest thing about making the film was that it was all shot at night, and it was a very short schedule. It was twenty-eight nights, and it was short nights in that the sun went down at nine o'clock and came up at five o'clock in the morning. That made for a very short day. It was shot very, very fast on location with cars that broke down and all the other drama that would go on in that kind of situation. It was just physically a very difficult thing to get through.

The studio wasn't that happy with it when they saw it. But we began to show it to people. Every time somebody from studio marketing wanted to see it, we'd always pack the house with the secretaries and all the assistants and everybody in the studio we could. We never let anybody see the film by themselves. Eventually, the word got out that it was a good film, and we managed to have it released as a feature and not as a TV movie, which is what the studio had wanted to do.

I got all this feedback from people about how important it was to their life and what a difference it made in their lives. There were kids that had forgotten that you could be stupid around girls, and it was okay for girls to be stupid around boys, and for girls to be obsessed with boys was okay, too.

That generation in the sixties, of free love and drugs and dropping out, was very different from when I grew up. I grew up in the fifties, and just as I got out of high school in 1962, it switched to this other world, and all through college, I didn't have anything to do with that. Everything was very topsy-turvy, but ten years later, people were saying it was all right not to be so cool. Going back to the way it was I think helped a lot of people get their bearings again and to figure out how the world really worked. That kind of influenced me in terms of making a movie that transferred a lot of the information from the past generation on to the next generation. I could take the values from the westerns, which were the last American mythology, and move them into a new genre, a new idea that was very contemporary that young people would be able to relate to.

> *My agent said that George was kind of interested in my picture and that he wanted to see me right away. I went in and he said he was making this film called* American Graffiti *and asked me if I could drive, and I said yes, and he said, thank you very much, and I got the part.*
>
> Suzanne Somers—Actress

The Birth of Lucasfilm

When Zoetrope ran into problems, and the studio pulled all the money out from under us, we stayed in San Francisco. It was then that I started Lucasfilm. The difficult part was there weren't many infrastructures in San Francisco at that time. We had a few people that worked in the film business, but we didn't have things like a sound-and-mixing studio. We didn't have a lot of the technical things you needed to run a full-fledged production company.

> *I think one of the great, often ignored, facts of the success of* Star Wars *is that it is reintroduced in each generation of young filmgoers. People who may not know who I am until they are introduced to me*

at age five, six, eight years of age, because they have seen Star Wars *for the first time. That's had an enormous and positive effect on my career.*

Harrison Ford—Actor

Star Wars (1977)

Mark Hamill; Harrison Ford; Carrie Fisher;
Peter Cushing; Alec Guinness; Anthony Daniels;
Kenny Baker; Peter Mayhew; David Prowse;
Phil Brown; James Earl Jones.

When I finished *American Graffiti*, I was broke, because I didn't get paid very much to do the film. It took me two and a half years to do, and when I finished, I was desperate to get another job. United Artists is where I developed *American Graffiti*, but it was Universal who ended up backing it. But while I was developing it at United, they asked if I had anything else I wanted to do, and I told them about this space film idea. They said they were interested in doing that. Initially, Universal was not going to release *American Graffiti*. I was dead broke, and so I had to get a job just to live on. I went back to United Artists with my space film idea, but they now turned it down. Then I went to Universal and they turned it down. Finally, Alan Ladd Jr., the head of Twentieth Century–Fox, saw *American Graffiti* and loved it. He asked me what I wanted to do, and I told him I was trying to get this space thing off the ground. He agreed to fund the development of the screenplay. I got $20,000 for writing the screenplay, and it was, like, more money than I'd seen in two years. So I was very relieved that I could now sit back, write a screenplay, and eat a decent meal for a change. When *American Graffiti* came out and was this giant hit, I used that opportunity to secure my position with the film that I had been working on, which was *Star Wars*.

I had made the deal with the studio. With the success of *Graffiti*, they expected me to come back and ask for more money, because I was now the hottest director in Hollywood. But I didn't do that. By this time, I had written a very long script, which would run about six hours, and I knew they weren't going to do that. I came to the reality that I was going to have cut it into three pieces. I'd do the first two hours and then hope, somehow, some-way, that I'd get the other four hours made. I managed to get the sequel rights and licensing rights. I wanted to make enough money promoting the film with the licensing to where I'd get the next one made, which is all I was wor-ried about at that point. In truth, I really expected the first film not to do that well, and so you're constantly on the defensive. You're constantly worried that if the first one doesn't do well, how do you get the second one done? It turned out the film was successful, and I realized that I had a chance to be-come really independent from the studio system. I didn't have to go to them for the money. I didn't have to go to them for permission. I was able to set myself up using the profits from *Star Wars* to build a company, completely in-dependent, up here in San Francisco. That's what I did, and that's why I stopped directing at that point.

The deal on the first *Star Wars* was that I got a salary and then I got 40 percent of the film profits. In those days, profits didn't mean anything. It still doesn't mean anything. The only thing that means anything is a percentage of the gross. If you get a piece of net profits, you never see anything out of it. All I had was a little deal memo that had these points on it, and I went back and did what nobody had done before, which was to negotiate all the other points. You see, usually they hand you a boilerplate contract, which you sign, and then they plug those little deal points in. I told them I wanted to go back and look through the entire draft of the agreement and change everything to be in my favor. The studio didn't care, because they didn't think the film would be profitable, and they didn't care about sequel or li-censing rights. To them it wasn't worth anything. And up until that time, li-censing was not a big thing to begin with. There's no money there. I was only doing that, really, to get T-shirts and posters to promote the movie, be-cause I was afraid they weren't going to do it. So they were giving away things that didn't mean anything to them, and, in exchange, I could have asked for a million dollars for the film, but I didn't do it. They thought they were getting a good deal. I thought I was getting a chance to make sure that I had a better shot at getting my second film made, and so we were both happy at the time.

When I was ready to do *Star Wars,* I went through a whole long process of casting. I saw hundreds of people who didn't have established names.

We were looking for new, young, and fresh people, and that's a very hard and arduous process. But, again, as I did on *Graffiti*, I interviewed people very fast. I brought back the people that made an impression on me, and eventually had them do a reading. Then, we put different people together in screen tests. Then I would take these three Princess Leias, and I would move them around and test them with three different Lukes and see who played well with each other. I really was looking for a group of people that would work well together. It takes six to seven months to do something like that.

I would push the technology occasionally. I'd develop a way of panning in outer space. I would develop a way of creating a two-and-a-half-foot-high character that could act. But I had real challenges, especially with the first film, where I had very limited resources. That budget was $9,999,000, and for a film of that scope, it was an almost impossible exercise. The other movies I'd made had all been under a million dollars, so I could sort of deal with tight budgets. But at the same time, I was frustrated. I got the film finished somehow, but not at the level that I'd wanted it to be.

There's a saying among directors that a film is never finished; it's just abandoned. At some point, it's taken away from you. But no matter how the story goes, the director is usually left frustrated and not feeling that he's been able to complete his vision, or it's been altered one way or another. When we were thinking about reissuing the films for the twentieth anniversary of *Star Wars,* I had the opportunity of fixing them up. I thought this was a great chance to experiment with the new technology and see if I could fix a lot of things that I was really frustrated with the first time around. Now, the DVD version of the original film will have all of the nuances that I had been looking for when I first did the film.

> *I have a lot of respect for the fact that George has pursued his own truly singular goals, some in and some out of the film business. I'm very envious of the fact that he's made enough money so that he can indulge that. But he's done some remarkable things for that reason. He's really taken advantage of the opportunity that he was given, and it's wonderful in a whole bunch of areas.*
>
> *Richard Dreyfuss—Actor*

Making Indiana Jones a Film Reality

About the time I was finishing *THX,* I was looking for something else to do. I had a number of ideas. *American Graffiti* and *Apocalypse Now* were two of them. I also had an idea for a 1930s serial-type film as well as this space adventure. *Star Wars* was the space adventure, and the 1930s serial thing was the adventure of an archaeologist looking for supernatural artifacts. I landed on the space thing because I thought that had more potential, and I thought it would be more fun to do. So I put the archaeologist idea on the shelf and then started doing *Star Wars.* As I was doing *Star Wars,* I was sort of talking to friends to see if I could get somebody to do the archaeologist film. But nothing really happened until I'd finished *Star Wars.*

After [*Star Wars*] was released, I was sitting on a beach in Hawaii with Steven Spielberg, and he was telling me how he really wanted to do a James Bond film. I said, "I've got a great idea, and this is much better than a James Bond," and I told him the story of Indiana Jones. Well, he immediately wanted to do it. That was really where it started, and we agreed to go back and hire a writer and get going on the project.

My day-to-day involvement on *Raiders* was just to enjoy myself. That was the perfect producing opportunity for me, because I had a brilliant script, I had a brilliant director, and everything came together in a great way, which doesn't really happen that often. It was one of those things where, as we developed the script, it just kept getting better and better, and Steven made the picture better and better. I would go to the location or the studio every two weeks or so, because I was developing *Empire Strikes Back* at the same time.

On Technology

All art is technology, and all artists eventually end up pushing against that technology, whether it's developing a new red or a new blue or whatever. You're always faced with some kind of constraint that holds you back. The cinema is an extremely technological medium. So you're defined by two barriers: One is resources; one is technology. And *Star Wars,* especially, bumped up against those. So I was never able to tell the story that I wanted to tell. I had to self-censor the story down to something that I knew that could be done given the technology I had available.

On Life Changes

When I finished the first trilogy, I figured that was the end of *Star Wars*. That's what I'd set out to do, and I'd finished it. I had also become a new father, got divorced, and was determined that what I was going to do was stop everything and raise my daughter. So, I changed my life goals at that point. I produced a few films and ran the companies that I created and produced a TV series, which I enjoyed. I just did things that were less stressful than actually directing a movie.

I was in the process of working at my hobby, which is building my ranch, the facility that I now work out of. I was raising my daughter and I was producing some films. I really wanted to be in a position where I didn't have to come to work at five o'clock in the morning. I wanted to be able to come in at ten o'clock and leave at four or five in the afternoon if I needed to do something with my daughter. I didn't want to work on weekends, and I wanted to be able to take a day off now and then. I didn't want to be in a locked in, rigid schedule that you find yourself in when you're a director.

During this time, I had adopted two more kids. When my son was about five years old, I thought I could go back and direct again. I was then faced with the decision about what I was going to do. Was I going to go back and finish the kind of movies that I'd started out doing? Or would I go back and pick up where I'd left off with *Star Wars* and do this back story, which I'd never really intended to do, and which couldn't have been done when I finished *Return of the Jedi*. But now, fifteen years later, I had the technology. ILM had developed digital technology to a point, after *Jurassic Park,* that I could actually consider doing some of the things that I was thinking about for the back story.

So I said, well, do I finish *Star Wars* or do I go off and do these other things? I knew if I went off and did these other things, I'd probably never go back to *Star Wars,* and that would be the end of it. But I really thought it would be an interesting challenge to take the medium in new directions, pushing it in a way that I'd been wanting to do in the first *Star Wars*. I wanted the medium to meet my imagination, because when you're doing science fiction, you're always bumping up against the technology.

The Birth of Skywalker Ranch and Other Enterprises

As I said, we didn't [originally] have a lot of production support facilities in San Francisco. When Francis and I first opened Zoetrope, it was basically an editing-and-mixing facility. I realized I was going to have to start my own, and that was really where the idea for Skywalker Ranch came from. Originally, it was a little house in San Anselmo, and then, after *Star Wars*, we outgrew that, and I built this place.

When I did *Star Wars,* I had an idea of doing this crazy 1930s action adventure film, and it would be very, very fast-paced and very exciting. The problem was there really were no special effects facilities at that time. Doug Trumbull had the closest thing to a special effects facility, but he was trying to be a director and had retired from the special effects at that point. So I went to a few of the people that had worked for him doing industrial films.

I was forced to start my own company in order to make the movie. That's really how Industrial Light + Magic got started in the first place. I knew that I wanted something that was going to push the limits of the technology of the film medium in order to make this movie work. I couldn't just have space ships slowly moving through the frame. I wanted to be able to pan and move with them. To get that vocabulary added to my lexicon, I needed to invent some new technology, which was what we did at ILM. We were able to create motion-control cameras that locked the foregrounds and backgrounds together, so I could have much more freedom of movement. I was able to then have shorter shots and have a much more kinetic visual style to the film. Since I was making three of these films, I kept ILM going, and, eventually, we took on outside projects to pay for the people that worked there in between the times I was making my movies, and it turned eventually into a big company.

[While] I was trying to get my company and ILM built up and independent, I started a video-game company. I'd started a computer division, which was designed to develop high-end computer graphics technology, and we developed a nonlinear film-editing system. I wanted to develop a system that was based on pure editing. It was the kind of thing that I wished we had when I was in school. So we spent a great deal of time and effort building the Editroid. We eventually sold the system to Avid Technologies, which ultimately became the editing system most people now use.

At the same time I was building the ranch, we built a sound-mixing facility. I wanted to get the best sound possible in this mixing facility, so we developed a whole new way of putting together a sound room in a theater. Tom Holdman, who was in charge of the project, developed a whole different way of looking at the sound environment in a theater. When we finished, we had people from Los Angeles come up, and as soon as they saw what we had done, they wanted it, too. So, then we started building sound theater systems for everybody in Los Angeles. Then we came to the conclusion that wouldn't it be great if we could get movie theaters to sound this good. Then what we hear here at this facility would be the same they would hear there. That really started the whole THX sound program.

We then expanded into quality control, which was always a very big issue in terms of the exhibition of films. We have this system where we review film prints to make sure they are as good as the original answer print. We go into theaters to make sure that the film is run correctly, that there's no scratches, that it's not chewed up, and that the last reel is actually on the picture and that it's being shown at the proper foot candles [projection light source]. It's the ultimate quality-control process for the exhibition of films.

> *It always amused me when the film came out and certain aspects of the media would hold George Lucas up as a Hollywood Studio. This is probably the most expensive independent film ever made* Attack of the Clones. *It has nothing to do with the studio system or Hollywood. I always get a chuckle out of that, as did George.*
>
> Liam Neeson—Actor

Star Wars: Episode I—The Phantom Menace (1999)

Liam Neeson; Ewan McGregor; Natalie Portman; Jake Lloyd; Ian McDiarmid; Pernilla August; Oliver Ford Davies; Hugh Quarshie; Ahmed Best; Anthony Daniels; Kenny Baker; Ray Park; Frank Oz; Terence Stamp; Brian Blessed.

Star Wars: Episode II—Attack of the Clones (2002)

Ewan McGregor; Natalie Portman; Hayden Christensen; Ian McDiarmid;
Pernilla August; Ahmed Best; Anthony Daniels; Samuel L. Jackson;
Frank Oz; Andrew Secombe; Kenny Baker; Silas Carson;
Christopher Lee; Jimmy Smits.

I decided I would go back and finish the back story of *Star Wars*. I realized that I was going to be working in the medium that was considerably different from the one I left when I did *Star Wars* fifteen, twenty years before. I'd shot a TV series where we used a lot of these new techniques. I did produce a film, *Radioland Murders*, which was a way of experimenting with these new ideas of digital filmmaking. I ended up creating little 3-D computer versions of the scenes that I'm going to shoot. I can actually pre-visualize a scene.

On *Phantom Menace,* we had very crude representation. On *Attack of the Clones,* we got something very, very sophisticated and started adding in the color palettes that I wanted and the look that I wanted.

I had a group of kids upstairs, and we'd do storyboards. I would say, "This is the storyboard I want, but I want it in action. I want it to be like this or to be like that," and they would go up and work on it. They'd bring it down, and we'd work together until we got it just the way I wanted it. So now, when I'm working with ILM, I turn over a reasonably finished shot for them. I mean, it's sort of 60 percent finished, and I tell them that is what I want. A lot of the initial work is already finished. They show me a preliminary of what their version is going to be, which usually is very close to what we've already developed. They show me the shot on the big screen. I either approve it because it works, or I'll suggest changes, and then they bring it back. But it's much more sophisticated than it was when I first started. The final shot more often than not is fine when I finally see it on the big screen.

The Digital Camera Revolution

About 1980, I started the computer division, and one of the mandates they'd had was to develop special-purpose computers for computer graphics. We worked on that over the years, and then we finally got to *Jurassic Park*. Then I realized that it would be much better to actually capture the material in a digital medium, because it all had to be put into a digital medium in order to work in these computers. I mean, with the *Star Wars* films I knew the whole film was going to be in a computer at some point. I also knew that if I captured it that way and put it in that way, it would be much less cumbersome, because it's very hard to transfer from one medium to another medium. That's what really got me interested in trying to shoot a film digitally.

We started working with Sony to develop these cameras—to develop them so they recorded at twenty-four frames per second, like a film camera. Then we had to find somebody who would build a lens that would go on the camera, and that took a while, because nobody wanted to build lenses for this thing. By the time we got it finished and we got all the deals together, it was two weeks before I was going to shoot *Phantom Menace*. It was impossible to really shoot *Phantom Menace* using this digital technology. Later on, we were able to get a prototype camera with a prototype lens and shoot a couple of scenes digitally. I wanted to do that so we could see how well it matched into the film that we'd shot. It matched in so well nobody ever noticed it. That meant that I knew we had the cameras and lenses, and I could shoot the next film completely digitally. I wouldn't have to move back and forth between mediums. I felt at that point that the quality was close enough to film that I wasn't going to end up with any less of an image. The process itself is so much more malleable, so much easier to use, so much less restricted that it would give me a huge advantage in terms of the actual day-to-day process of making the movie. And it would save me a lot of money. I'm still an independent filmmaker. I still pay all my own bills, and I really have to be careful. I don't have the unlimited resources of the giant megastudios. I still have to worry about where I'm going to get the money for my next film. We're always trying to do it the least expensive way possible, and digital really made a huge difference there.

We wanted to begin showing digitally with *Phantom Menace*. We got it into four theaters, and then I was hoping to be in a few hundred theaters. Three years later, when we did *Attack of the Clones,* we ended up in about eighty theaters. I'm hoping that number will continue to grow. It's the best way to project it to get the best quality. It goes hand in hand with what THX is doing to keep quality in the theaters. The great thing about digital is that what you see on the first day in a theater is the same thing you will see on the first day of the tenth week. Whereas with film, what you see on the first day is not at all what you're going to see in the tenth week. In the tenth week it's going to be scratched and jittery and torn up, and the quality is going to be disintegrated to a rather alarming degree. I do think digital films will have a profound influence on the audience's enjoyment of the movie.

A Bit of Philosophy

I'm not really into breaking box-office records. I'm only concerned that the film make its money back so I can go ahead and make another movie. Whenever you work for yourself, the important thing is to be sure you can afford the next project. I focus really on the quality of the theaters and the quality of the presentation rather than trying to break records.

Star Wars Forever?

There's only one more installment, and it's a darker version of *Star Wars*. It's not as dark as a Quentin Tarantino movie, but, at the same time, for *Star Wars,* it'll be pretty dark. I'm not sure how popular it's going to be. It may be popular with the fans, but I'm not sure it will be popular with the general public. So, I expect that one to be less financially successful than the other ones. But, you know, I've got to tell a story. I see *Star Wars* as a six-part movie done in twelve hours. I don't see them as individual pieces or individual episodes. I see them as one six-episode movie.

On Work

I'm not too great at multitasking, so I mostly do one thing at a time. I get one thing in order, and then I get people in charge of that, and I move away and do something else. I have a lot of friends, Francis Coppola and Steven Spielberg, especially, who can produce and direct and write and do all these things all simultaneously, and it just drives me crazy. I get one thing under control, and then I go off and do something else, and then I come back and see what's happened while I was gone. It's especially true of directing. When I'm directing, I'm pretty single-minded, and that's all I can say.

On Blockbuster Films

Well, it's funny. Everybody says that somehow I had something to do with the invention of the blockbuster. People forget that there were a lot of block-busters around. *Gone With the Wind* was a blockbuster in every sense of the word—even bigger than anything I have ever done, and it's still number one. Closer to when I was making my films, there were the James Bond films, which were big blockbusters. There were Irwin Allen's disaster films like *The Towering Inferno* and *Poseidon Adventure*. Those films were big blockbusters. And then Francis's *The Godfather* and Stephen Spielberg's *Jaws,* which were both big blockbusters. I came along after that group. Every year, there's been a couple of blockbusters. *The Sound of Music* is still the blockbuster of all time if you take inflation into consideration. You know, I really don't know what blockbuster means.

I hope my work is going to be remembered in a better light than it is today. In time, once the kind of superficial aspects of the film have been for-gotten and people actually look at the movies for what they are, I think they will find them rather fascinating. I'm hoping that they will have delved into them further than some contemporary analysis and see that they are more social in nature. Right now, that's all been kind of mixed up in a funny kind of way and gotten very controversial, and people have very strong opinions one way or the other. [My films] are very simple and very complex at the same time.

George Lucas Filmography

THX 1138 (1971)

American Graffiti (1973)

Star Wars (1977), revised as *Star Wars: Episode IV—A New Hope* (1997)

Star Wars: Episode I—The Phantom Menace (1999)

Star Wars: Episode II—Attack of the Clones (2002)

Star Wars: Episode III (2005)

Awards and Nominations

Academy Awards, USA
Irving Thalberg Memorial Award, 1992
Star Wars, Best Director (nominated), 1978
Star Wars, Best Writing, Screenplay Written Directly for the Screen (nominated), 1978
American Graffiti, Best Director, 1974
American Graffiti, Best Writing, Story, and Screenplay Based on Factual Material or Material Not Previously Published or Produced (nomination shared with Gloria Katz, Willard Huyck), 1974

Academy of Science Fiction, Horror and Fantasy Films, USA
Star Wars: Episode I—The Phantom Menace, Best Director, Saturn Award (nominated), 2000
Star Wars, Best Director, Saturn Award (tied with Steven Spielberg for *Close Encounters of the Third Kind*), 1978
Star Wars, Best Writing, Saturn Award, 1978

British Academy Award of Film and Television Arts, Los Angeles
Stanley Kubrick Britannia Award for Excellence in Film, 2002

Csapnivalo Awards
Star Wars: Episode I—The Phantom Menace, Golden Slate Award (nominated), 2000

David di Donatello Awards
Kagemusha, Best Producer—Foreign Film, David Award (shared with Francis Ford Coppola, tied with Hungaro Film for *Angi Vera*), 1981

Emmy Awards
Ewoks: Battle for Endor (TV), Outstanding Children's Program (nomination shared with Thomas G. Smith), 1986

Golden Globe Awards
Star Wars, Best Director—Motion Picture (nominated), 1978
American Graffiti, Best Director—Motion Picture (nominated), 1974

Locarno International Film Festival
American Graffiti, Bronze Leopard, 1973

National Board of Review Awards
Special Award for Visionary Cinematic Achievement, 2002

National Society of Film Critics Awards
American Graffiti, Best Screenplay (shared with Gloria Katz and Willard Huyck), 1974

New York Film Critics Circle Awards
American Graffiti, Best Screenplay (shared with Gloria Katz and Willard Huyck), 1973

Razzie Awards
Star Wars: Episode I—The Phantom Menace, Worst Director (nominated), 2000
Star Wars: Episode I—The Phantom Menace, Worst Screenplay (nominated), 2000

Sci-Fi Universe Awards
Lifetime Achievement Award (Readers' Choice), 1995

ShoWest Convention
Director of the Year, 1978

Video Premiere Awards
Star Wars: Episode I—The Phantom Menace, Best Audio Commentary (nomination shared with Rick McCallum, Ben Burtt, Rob Coleman, John Knoll, Dennis Muren, Scott Squires), 2001

Writers Guild of America
Raiders of the Lost Ark, Best Comedy Written Directly for the Screen (nomination shared with Lawrence Kasdan, Philip Kaufman), 1982

Star Wars, Best Comedy Written Directly for the Screen, 1978

American Graffiti, Best Comedy Written Directly for the Screen (nomination shared with Gloria Katz and Willard Huyck), 1974

Young Artists Awards

Jackie Coogan Award, 2000

The Films of Phillip Noyce

The films of director Phillip Noyce include the political thrillers *Patriot Games* and *Clear and Present Danger*, along with the films *Dead Calm, The Saint,* and *The Bone Collector.*

Born in Griffith, New South Wales, Australia, Noyce moved to Sydney at the age of twelve. As a teenager, he was introduced to underground films produced on shoestring budgets, as well as mainstream American movies. He was seventeen when he made his first film, the fifteen-minute *Better to Reign in Hell*, utilizing a unique financing scheme selling roles in the movie to his friends.

In 1973, he was selected to attend the Australian National Film School in its inaugural year. During his first year in film school, he made *Castor and Pollux*, a fifty-minute documentary, which won the award for best Australian short film of the year.

Noyce's first professional film was *God Knows Why, But It Works,* in 1975. This film helped pave the way for Noyce's first feature film in 1977, titled *Backroads*. In 1978, he directed and cowrote *Newsfront,* which won Best Film, Best Director, and Best Original Screenplay awards in Australia. In addition to opening the London Film Festival, *Newsfront* was the first Australian film to open the New York Film Festival.

In 1982, *Heatwave*, cowritten and directed by Noyce and starring Judy Davis, was chosen to screen at the prestigious Director's Fortnight at the Cannes Film Festival.

> He's a unique human being. You can get a sense of who he is if you look at the range of interests that he has shown in his films. He's a very good guy to be with on the set.
>
> Harrison Ford—Actor

The Conversation

I was born in 1950 in Griffith, New South Wales, a small farming town about four hundred miles to the west of Sydney. I grew up seeing only American or English movies every Saturday, when I would go to the Lyceum Theater in Griffith. I went because I was drawn by those fantastic adventure stories that took me to faraway places. But I also went because it gave me the opportunity at intermission to swap my comics for someone else's comics. All the kids in the town would go along with their comic book collections and refurbish them each week.

I grew up seeing only two films that were set in Australia for the first eighteen years of my life. I became interested in making films when, as a teenager and now living in Sydney, I left my suburban home on the outskirts of the city and went into town. I was walking along, and I saw a poster on a phone pole that was advertising American underground movies. It was rather an elaborate sort of LSD-type image, which is the first thing that attracted me, being eighteen in 1968. But the word "underground" sort of conjured up everything that would appeal to an eighteen-year-old at that time. Risqué, alternative, maybe even drug-induced.

You have to remember that 1968 was the year when all of those baby boomers, like myself, were attempting to redefine themselves as everything that their parents weren't. So, I went along to the screening and saw the movies and walked out of that cinema wanting to be a film director. I walked into the cinema having no idea, no dream, no intention, because the idea of being a film director in Australia was out of madness. There was no such animal. We didn't have a film industry. No one was making films. But what I saw on that screen that day was a new kind of cinema. Not movies that were made to feed the sausage factory of Hollywood, as I had been brought up on. But movies that were made as personal expression by artists.

They were mainly movies of the American Underground Movement. I saw films that were made for little cost, using nonprofessional actors, with portable equipment, with unconventional techniques of storytelling and cutting. And I thought, "Hey, I can do that." So, after the last year of high school, when I was almost nineteen, I set to work digging sewerage ditches. I realized that I was gonna have to dig them for a long time to raise the money to make a film. And so I decided that with the script that I had written during my lunch hours, I would appeal to my friends for money.

The film was called *Better to Rain in Hell*. It was about the sex fantasies of a teenager. So, I said to my friends, "If you give me money you can be in the movie. You can have one of these sexual fantasies." I got a lot of offers. Unfortunately, and fortunately, one of them was from a doctor's son who, for $400 of his father's money, became the star of the movie. Fortunate, because I got to make the film. Unfortunate, because he was an absolutely lousy actor. So that was the first lesson in moviemaking. It's better to pay for the actor, because then you can choose and tell them what to do.

My interest in cinema grew out of being fascinated with the vaudeville shows that would come to my small country town. The greatest day of the year was the agricultural show, when the farmers and their wives would show their wares. There were tent shows that came to town during those times. It was like the Roaring Twenties.

There was Jimmy Sharman's boxing troop. My parents used to give me the equivalent of $2 to spend on these sideshows. The money would go pretty quickly. So, then there were two ways to get into the show. Either under the tent flap at the back, which was sometimes full of perils. Or you could offer yourself as a stooge. Being a stooge for the show was even better than the show inside. That is, the real show that took place outside to attract the audience. I remember being involved with one show where the guy took a little piece of paper a couple of inches long. He said, "Stick your tongue out, son." I stuck my tongue out, and he put the paper on the end of my tongue. And then his wife, who was about five feet two, took a four-foot-eight-inch sword, raised it in the air, and brought it down and cut the paper in half. I was so impressed with the sighs from the audience, I thought, "Hey, I did that." They're responding to me.

It was just the lure of this sort of relationship between performer and audience that started me thinking about not a career in show biz, but just wanting to engage people—to entertain them. So, between each year of that agricultural show, I would invent my own shows. I had my own version of The Roaring Twenties. I had a ghost train, and the kids would come around to our farm, and I'd try and get them to give me a penny to go through my show. Sometimes they would, sometimes they wouldn't. But, for me it was watching them respond to something that I created for their amusement or entertainment. That's what got me going.

But then there was one other thing. When I was a young teenager, a movie came to Australia called *Psycho*, directed by Alfred Hitchcock. Even before I went into the cinema, I was petrified and electrified. I was electrified by the relationship between the anticipation of the experience and the audience. We were all talking about it. I think the ad said, "No one will be admitted to the cinema after the first fifteen minutes of this film." So, that made you want to go even more and get there early. I watched that movie, and for a thirteen- or fourteen-year-old it was quite sensual at times. But that wasn't the thing that impressed me the most. I can remember sitting at the back of the cinema, as I would do many times in future years, and seeing the audience move, duck, weave. Seeing them sort of grip themselves in terror. And I thought, well, you know, that's extraordinary, because that's just the same thrill that I saw in the audience when I was performing in that tent show. But I didn't really think that I'd ever get to do that.

It was all but impossible to become a film director in Australia. Australia had no film industry. We imported our movies from mainly England and America. All the cinemas were owned by foreign interests. So, to say you wanted to be a film director was probably certifiable, you know. It was at the age of nineteen, while I was studying law at Sydney University, I announced to my parents that I wanted to be a film director. Their first thought was that maybe I should see a doctor. There I was, about to follow in my father's footsteps. I was going to be a good suburban lawyer, and now I told them I wanted to be a film director. It soon became clear to them, as it was to me, that the thing I enjoyed most was making these little short films on weekends. And even more than making them, I enjoyed showing them.

The late sixties and early seventies were a time of great change within the Australian culture. There was a cultural rebirth. The baby boomers were being given a chance to express themselves, thanks to the labors of their parents. We had the time, thanks to their money, to goof off. There was a real nationalism in the air. Australians wanted to create stories on the stage that reflected the Australian lifestyle and images using Australian language for the first time. And the filmmakers followed.

In 1971, along with a group of friends, I started a little cinema above a socialist bookshop in Sydney. We would screen our short films one night a week. It became popular, because so great was the audience's passion to see themselves in that mirror up on the silver screen, that one-night-a-week screenings quickly became a seven-night-a-week venue. Within six months, we had three cinemas, all operating illegally all around Sydney. Into those cinemas came many of the names and the faces of the so-called new wave of Australian film. Peter Weir screened his films one week. Next week, it would be

Bruce Beresford, and then it would Gillian Armstrong or George Miller. We were all making short films, not imagining that this hobby could ever be a job. Still not expecting that anyone would ever give us money to make films. And still not expecting that we would ever actually receive a salary for doing it.

The audience was so hungry to see themselves in their own culture that the first fledgling attempts to make feature films were met with instantaneous success. We could make movies in the early seventies in Australia for a couple of hundred thousand dollars. We could make a profit within eight weeks, because the audiences were lining up to see their own experience on that screen that previously had been the exclusive domain of England and Hollywood.

Dead Calm (1989)

Nicole Kidman; Sam Neill; Billy Zane; Rod Mullinar;
Joshua Tilden; George Shevtsov; Michael Long.

When my first Australian feature was released in America, one of its biggest fans was an American producer and director by the name of Tony Bill, who had directed *My Bodyguard* and produced films such as *The Sting*. Tony and I formed a long relationship, always talking about maybe the possibility of making a film together. I was visiting him in 1994, and, as I was leaving, he said, "Wait a minute." He threw a manuscript across the room and said, "You've got a lot of water down in Australia. Why don't you read that?" It was a copy of Charles Williams's novel *Dead Calm*. I put it in my bag and there it remained for several months.

I was trying to give up smoking at the time, and I'd run out of chewing gum. So, finally, I dig back in my bag to find something to stave off the feeling of panic of not having that nicotine hit. I pulled out the manuscript and started to read it. And, of course, I realized immediately what a fantastic movie this would make. I got to the airport in Los Angeles three and a half months later, eight o'clock in the morning, and rang Tony Bill. I woke him up and said, "I've got to make that movie." He explained that the problem was that Orson Welles had attempted to make *Dead Calm* back in the early sixties, and about halfway through production, he had lost his leading actor, Laurence Harvey, who died. The film remained unfinished.

The rights to the material were owned by his de facto widow, Oja Kodar, who had starred in the movie in the part that would be played in my film by Nicole Kidman, the part of Rae Ingram. She was quite reluctant to sell the project to the Hollywood establishment that, I guess, in the back of her mind, she felt had persecuted Orson during his career. I know that Tony felt that she identified him as part of the Hollywood establishment. So, I carried the story with me again for a couple of months.

I was back in Australia, talking with Australian director George Miller, who had made the *Mad Max* films, among others. He was about to go off to America to direct *The Witches of Eastwick*. I told him the story of this couple on this boat and the struggle between three people in the middle of the Pacific. He immediately warmed to it, as I did. So, I sent a telegram to Tony Bill and said, "Would you give me permission, together with George Miller, to try and obtain the rights?" George was, before he was a film director, a doctor, so he has a marvelous bedside manner. He went and saw Ms. Kodar and convinced her that we were not part of the Hollywood establishment, although, ironically, once we finished the film, we sold it to Warner Bros. for worldwide distribution.

The first person we cast for *Dead Calm* was Sam Neill in the part of Captain John Ingram. And then we were looking for Rae Ingram, his wife. Nicole Kidman had starred in a miniseries for George Miller's company. Nicole was eighteen years old at that time. Clearly, too young to be the wife of the forty-year-old Sam Neill. But I was so impressed with the emotional purity of her performance. I looked at one of the episodes she had done for George Miller. It was the scene where she was playing an antiwar protester. And suddenly, her brother, who had gone to fight in Vietnam as a soldier, came on the air. I was reduced to tears just watching that scene even though I had no knowledge of the previous several hours of the story. So, I asked Nicole to do a screen test playing several scenes from the film, and I was just knocked out by her. Even though she was so young—still a baby, really—a teenager, I just thought that here was such a talent that I had to bend over backwards and do anything we could to get her in the movie.

There followed several months of training for Nicole. Voice training to deepen her voice. Movement training to try and change her from that sort of freewheeling, free-spirited teenager that she was, into a woman, say, of the mid- to late twenties. And finally, training so that she herself could sail that sailboat. To turn the sailboat and be the commander and rescue a husband as we see her do in the movie.

In the restaurant business, they have a rule about running a successful restaurant. Well, there're three rules, actually: location, location, location. The same rule applies to shooting on water. It could not just be location, location, location, but sea, sea, sea. You have to find workable water. We searched all over the world. You've got to study the prevailing wind patterns. You got to work out the tides, the undertow, the wave formations, and so on. Particularly for a film that's called *Dead Calm,* because so much of that film takes place with the water just absolutely placid.

We finally realized that inside the Great Barrier Reef—the reef that's just under the surface and stretches for several thousand miles up the southeastern coast of Australia—inside that reef was an area of water that was relatively placid. And we then chose an island inside the reef that had a rather large mountain on it that would protect us from the prevailing winds. And then we chose another island nearby that would protect us from any winds that came up in the other direction. And then we chose another island, about three-quarters of an hour's sailing away, which was a resort island that had accommodation on it. That's where we lived and that's where we built our studio.

We built a tank, which is just a large swimming pool, and filled it with water. That's where we would later film our underwater sequences. Around that tank, we built a studio. What this meant was that every day of filming, we could go out to sea if we wanted to. If the water was right, if it was workable, we could film. The trick when you're filming on water is not only location, location, location, but also you've got to be able to take advantage of that greatest of all talented art directors, the master art director, the one that wins the special Academy Award every year—God. Because God will make things that no man can make. And you've got to just be there at the moment that the storm comes up. You've got to be there for the sunset, because He may not turn it on again. So, the longer you can give yourself access to water, the more varied your shots are going be.

The film was shot over a four-month period. Initially, we would venture out each day. Eventually, we just all moved out to sea and lived on a flotilla of boats parked in one of those bays that I spoke about. We would just transfer to our master boats each day. Eventually, we cut the crew down because just transferring from boat to boat takes so long. Eventually, we had a very tiny crew and we all lived onboard each of the boats and would go to sleep, then get up and start filming. It was quite a wonderful experience. Wonderful, because you're out there with nature. But it was also wonderful because it was whale-mating season. The whale-mating season is a thing to behold, because the male dances for the female. He dives up out of the water, turns and twists like a peacock before finally mating for life. They're never un-faithful, like humans.

As much as the actors were the stars of *Dead Calm,* so were the boats stars in their own right. For the Sam and Nicole's boat, we chose a racing yacht that was built in South Africa in 1961. For the *Orpheus,* the abandoned ship, we found an old Merchant Marine sailing ship from Tasmania that was built in the early part of the twentieth century. In order to film the sequence where the *Orpheus* goes up in flames after Sam Neill sets fire to it, we actually built a replica of the *Orpheus.* Because we were not able to always use the real ship (it was out taking tours around the Great Barrier Reef), most of the shooting that you see was done on that replica. Then, of course, one night in June in 1988, with seven cameras filming, Sam Neill threw the torch into the water and the whole thing went up in flames. It was spectacular but just another part of the make-believe world of moviemaking. That replica ship had to be towed everywhere it went, because it was just a balsa wood replica.

Dead Calm was quite a departure for me. That departure came about as a result of directing a miniseries in Australia about three years prior to *Dead Calm.* In the miniseries, an Australian soldier and a Japanese soldier find themselves facing each other in the middle of a clearing in New Guinea. In directing that story, I was suddenly exposed to the whole question of how to create tension for the audience when you've got very few elements to play with. Two men, facing each other, one with a bayonet, one with a machine gun. What will happen? That's when I just discovered that I had a little talent for creating tension. Without that experience, I don't think I would have responded to *Dead Calm* in the way that I did. I would have felt that it was too remote from the sort of interests I had in terms of subject matter at the time.

Viewing Orson's Work

After I finished making *Dead Calm,* I was lucky enough to see some of Orson Welles's footage. Actually, it was a trailer that he had made to try and raise more money. It was quite funny to watch the same story with different actors—although, oddly enough, a lot of the shots he had chosen originally were very similar to my angles. I guess you're restricted on a boat to how many angles you've got. Both Orson and I chose, as one of the more dramatic shots, a shot where the camera is up on the mast and looks down on the deck. It's almost geo-metrical in its properties, and it's distancing. I use it in *Dead Calm* just before a shock moment to sort of take the audience away from the character. Orson used it in his version during the sequence where Rae Ingram is kidnapped.

Blind Fury (1989)

Rutger Hauer; Terry O'Quinn; Brandon Call; Noble Willingham; Lisa Blount; Nick Cassavetes; Rick Overton; Randall "Tex" Cobb; Charles Cooper; Meg Foster.

I began thinking that maybe I should go to America, do a movie there, because maybe I won't be able to raise any more money to make movies in Australia. So I came to Hollywood and made the $6 million *Blind Fury*. I cast Dutch actor Rutger Hauer as the blind samurai. We shot that in Texas and Reno, Nevada, in 1990, while we were still editing *Dead Calm*.

Making a film about someone that's blind but is also a master swordsman had its difficulties. What I usually do is go through a long process of not so much rehearsal but preparation. In doing that, you're exposing yourself and the actors to information and experience. You hope that it's going to rub off on each of you, so you've got a shared experience that you can draw on. But also, you hope that at the end of that preparation period, the actors will become the character they're playing without trying. You hope it just seeps into their skin. So I took Rutger Hauer to the Braille Institute in Los Angeles, and we spent a lot of time talking to and being with blind people. But then, for the real test, and for several days, all of the cast and myself and the key crew prepared for the film blindfolded. It produced a great camaraderie, and you learn to depend on someone when you're impaired in that way. Then, for the agile sword work Rutger trained with a swordsman for eight weeks, starting fully sighted during all of those moves and then doing them actually blindfolded.

I'd Rather Be Directing

A lot of young filmmakers ask me, "How do I get to be a director?" I always ask them, "Well, you've got to ask yourself the question first, 'Why do you want to be a film director?'" And if they say, "Well, because I like such and such a person or because it seems like a better job than the one that I otherwise have," I usually tell them, "Well, maybe you're not really cut out to be a film director." You've got to have a passion to tell stories. I want to tell stories and connect with people. I want to move them. I want to involve them. That's really what makes a film director. That passion to connect with the people and to tell them stories. You know, a film director is just part of the ancient tradition of storytelling, and storytellers have always been prized for their abilities to engage the audience. That's what we do.

Patriot Games (1992)

Harrison Ford; Anne Archer; Patrick Bergin; Sean Bean; Thora Birch; James Fox; Samuel L. Jackson; Polly Walker; J. E. Freeman; Richard Harris.

After *Dead Calm,* I was sent truckloads of thriller scripts from Hollywood. At one point, I decided to actually leave Australia and come and live in America. Not just because I wanted to become a Hollywood movie director, but I guess, in part, because I looked around and saw all my forty-year-old friends sort of closing their lives down. And I thought, I'm not ready to settle down now. I want to reinvent myself. I'm ready for my second life, and after that, I'll have my third.

When I did come to Los Angeles, I was offered a script called *Patriot Games,* adapted from Tom Clancy's novel of the same name. There had been one film made already in the series, called *The Hunt for Red October,* that featured Jack Ryan, the CIA analyst, who was played by Alec Baldwin. When I read the script, I hated it. My initial reaction was that it was politically insensitive to the Irish Republican Movement. And secondly, that it was more concerned with gratuitous action, rather than with the character or the story. But I was attracted to it for one reason, and that was because of my father.

Like the OSS in America, Australia had its own military intelligence unit. In 1944, my father became a part of Zed Force, the Australian equivalent of the OSS. The OSS in America was the forerunner of the CIA. For fifty years, I heard stories of my father's exploits as a military spy training to go behind enemy lines and so on. These stories always fascinated and intrigued me and I was excited by that cloak-and-dagger stuff. So I decided to do the film for that reason. Soon after I came onboard, Alec Baldwin pulled out, and we were left with no one to play Jack Ryan. As it happened, Harrison Ford had been preparing to do a movie at Paramount that had fallen through because of projected cost overruns, and Harrison was suddenly available. So, together with a couple of Paramount executives and producer Mace Neufeld, we flew up to Jackson Hole, Wyoming, to see Harrison at his home there.

Interestingly enough, Harrison had a lot of the same comments about the screenplay as I had; that it was not concerned with the character of Jack Ryan as much as it should be. It didn't deal with the process of being a spy or being an analyst. The one-hour discussion turned into a whole day of talking about what the film could be as opposed to what the script was or even what the novel had been.

That was the beginning of probably the most fruitful relationship that I've ever had with an actor. Harrison is blessed with two things: experience, because he's worked with some of the best film directors in the world, and an innate understanding of the relationship that the characters he plays have with the audience. He just knows how to connect with them, and that's always his focus.

I've always been the kind of director who treats the screenplay not as Shakespeare, where you have to honor the sanctity of every single word and its meaning, but rather as a map to another destination. You can deviate from it if you want to have a more interesting journey. The question is, will you arrive at your destination on time? In other words, it's the finished product, not the process. The process should be one of investigation of all of the possibilities. Harrison likes to work like that as well.

I've always encouraged my actors to become the character, to take upon themselves the responsibility of being storytellers as much as the director or the writer is. Harrison is just that sort of person. Off-screen, he's as much like Jack Ryan as he is on-screen, a man who relies on an intellectual process to work out an emotional problem. He's analytical. At the same time, he's humane in the best sense. And so, the qualities that he brings to Jack Ryan, as he does to any of the roles that we love him in, are those qualities. There are the same qualities I admired in my father. A sense of what's right and what's wrong. Wanting to listen to all of the evidence before you make a decision. Always taking the attitude that the underdog might be right, not wrong. Looking at the other man's point of view. Harrison has all those qualities, and he brings all of those to the screen.

Here is a typical day working with Harrison Ford. We arrive on set at about six-thirty in the morning, knowing that we've got, say, two scenes to shoot before six-thirty that night. We read through the first scene. By lunchtime, we still haven't shot the first shot. But during that time, the scene has gone all the way to the left, all the way to the right, all the way up, all the way down, in terms of being twisted and turned into something else. Try this. Try that. Let me start here. Let me say this instead of that. What do you think about this? Is this good? Is this bad? So, the first half of the day usually becomes a workshop investigating not what's written, but what could be filmed. Investigating what we can do between all of us, with all this equipment, with all this talent, with all this money, on that particular day. And then in the afternoon, having played around and explored the possibilities, we would quickly film the scenes that were scheduled and usually finish before six-thirty came around.

   The big difference I found shooting films in Hollywood as compared to in Australia was that, on the day you started filming in Los Angeles, they were already telling you the day that the movie was going to hit the screens. Not one screen, as I'd been used to in Australia, but several thousand screens. That date was always indelibly etched in your memory. Even while you were filming, buses would be traveling around with the *Patriot Games* opening date notices on the sides of them. So, what I found was that I was going into a system.

   I discovered that I had entered a system that was churning out product. Within that system, you could express yourself, but you always had that opening date in the back of your mind. The advantages of that are that you know that the film is going to find an audience. Even if they don't want it, they're going to be exposed to the movie by the Hollywood marketing machine all around the world. The disadvantage is that there is the pressure of that judgment day awaiting you, and all that money that's been invested not just in making the film, but sometimes an equal amount in marketing the movie. That tends to make filmmakers more conservative than they otherwise might be, and you're going to play for the tried-and-true. You're going to tend not to be as inventive as you would like to be, simply because you want to make sure that you connect. Of course, some of the best films in cinema history have been within that system as well as some of the worst.

   When I finished the first cuts of my movies, I always showed them first to my daughter Lucia, who is now eighteen. She cuts through the BS and usually gives me a straight opinion about everything. I think she was about eleven when I showed her *Sliver*. It was a screening just for her, me, and the editor. She came out of the cinema and she said, "Well, can I ask you just one question before I say anything?" I said, "What's that?" She said, "Have you signed the deal? Have you set up your next movie yet?" I said, "No. Why?" She said, "All right. Well, I don't think you should show this film to anyone in the world until you've done that." And, at the same time, Paramount offered me *Clear and Present Danger*. So, before I showed them *Sliver,* I made sure that I signed everything to direct *Clear and Present Danger*. After finishing *A Clear and Present Danger,* as was the custom, I showed the now-fourteen-year-old Lucia the movie. With a wry smile on her face, she came out and she said, "Just one question." I said, "Oh, oh. My God, what's she gonna say now?" She said, "Have you done the deal on your next movie?" And I said, "No." She said, "Well, don't until you show this movie to the whole world."

> *I must say that we all felt having done* Patriot Games *that we would be obliged to the audience to present them with an entertainment that was at least as good as the first and hopefully better. That's the obligation we took on for ourselves, to make it better.*
>
> Harrison Ford—Actor

A Clear and Present Danger (1993)

Harrison Ford; Willem Dafoe; Anne Archer; Joaquin de Almeida; Henry Czerny; Harris Yulin; Donald Moffat; Miquel Sandoval; Benjamin Bratt; Raymond Cruz; James Earl Jones; Hope Lange; Anne Magnuson; Dean Jones; Ellen Geer.

I never really was passionate about the subject matter of *Patriot Games*. I was passionate about what we turned it into. I was passionate about the character that Harrison and I were able to create. I was passionate about particular sequences in the film. But the story itself, a story of revenge, a story of a man protecting his family from a terrorist, didn't excite me that much. But when it came to *Clear and Present Danger,* I was really excited. This was a story that was inspired by the Iran controversy during the Reagan administration. It was a story that dealt with very real issues about executive power and its use and abuse within the American political system. It was a film that dealt with America's new position as Sheriff to the world and the responsibilities that came with that. And, it was a film in which I felt that Jack Ryan's character would be really tested. And I really wanted to make it. There was a whole different feeling going into the film.

Sliver (1993)

Sharon Stone; William Baldwin; Tom Berenger; Polly Walker;
Colleen Camp; Amanda Foreman; Martin Landau; CCH Pounder;
Nina Foch; Keene Curtis; Nicholas Pryor; Anne Betancourt.

Sliver was a film that was released in 1993; it starred Sharon Stone and Billy Baldwin. It was adapted from Ira Levin's novel of the same name by Joe Eszterhas, who just previously had written *Basic Instinct*, which also starred Sharon Stone. When I read the screenplay, it unearthed latent voyeuristic tendencies in me as I hope it did in most of the audience. As a kid growing up in that small country town in Outback, New South Wales, I would amuse myself in the afternoons after school by choosing a person to follow secretly, like a spy. I'd shadow them as they journeyed through the town.

I think the catch line for the film was "You like to watch, don't you?" And I did. Not in the way that Billy Baldwin does in the movie, of course, planting cameras in all of the rooms of an apartment building in New York. But I was just attracted to the film for that reason. There's something about every movie that I make that attracts me. It's not usually what's in the story; it's more something underneath. It's something about the relationships and the characters that connect with me. In this film, it was the intensity of the relationship between the two central characters played by Sharon Stone and Billy Baldwin.

The success of any film depends on the right casting, and it depends on the off-screen relationship between the performers as much as it does on the pretend on-screen relationship. In *Sliver,* we had a story of passion, a story of animal attraction that unbalances the characters. Unfortunately, I cast two people who were not only not attracted to each other, but just didn't get along. So it was a real stretch doing those love scenes in the movie. For whatever reason, Billy Baldwin and Sharon Stone never hit it off from the first day. I always blamed myself for that. The director's job is to unruffle all the ruffled feathers, to calm everyone. I should have perhaps listened when Sharon expressed her reservations when we were initially going to cast Billy. Not that I don't think Billy is a great actor. But together they didn't work off the screen, and that made it even more difficult on-screen.

When the film was cut, as is the custom in Hollywood, it was test-screened for an invited audience, and the response was quite ambivalent. They were not positive, or as positive as we would have liked them to have been. In particular, they seemed perplexed by the ending of the film. In the original ending, as written by Joe Eszterhas, the couple played by Baldwin and Stone were married. On their honeymoon, they fly into a volcano and then disappear into the lava. It was an enigmatic ending, and that's probably a kind way to describe it, that left audiences both perplexed and cold and seemed to reverberate back on their appreciation of the whole movie that had come before.

When I first finished the cut, I sent it to Joe Eszterhas. I usually involve everyone in trying to get his or her responses to the material. I don't hide it from people. What's the use of hiding it, because, eventually, it's gonna be seen by hundreds of millions of people? Well, Joe was really happy. He thought it was a great translation of his adaptation of Ira Levin's novel. But after a few negative screenings, Joe realized that the film wasn't working. I can remember sitting in the office of Sherry Lansing, who was head of Paramount at the time, and we were brainstorming and trying to work out what to do. Joe said, "Well, why don't we make Tom Berenger character the killer? Won't that turn the whole ending on its tail?" It was such an outrageous idea that I said, "Yes. Let's try that." I just didn't know what else to do. It wouldn't have been an idea that I thought of myself. Maybe, if I had been in a more rational place and not with all the pressures of trying to get the film finished for an already-set release date, maybe I would have said, "No. Let's just persevere with the ending we have now and try and find a way to make it work." But we didn't.

So the cast was brought back a mere three weeks before the film was to hit screens around America, and we filmed a new ending with a new perpetrator, a new killer. And that's the version that went into the cinemas. It's a version of the film that meant the movie could go on to be profitable for the studio. But it's not the film that we all signed on for. I think that the original ending would have been better as cinema, maybe not as entertainment, maybe not as a product, but certainly better as art.

The Saint (1997)

Val Kilmer; Elisabeth Shue; Rade Serbedzija; Valeri Nikolayev;
Henry Goodman; Alun Armstrong; Michael Byrne; Evgeny Lazarev.

As a teenager in Sydney, I would watch *The Saint* TV series that was made in England and starred Roger Moore as that dapper solver of other people's problems. But my interest in *The Saint* goes back to Leslie Charteris's stories, which I read when I was about seven. I used to always imagine when reading the stories that I was The Saint. And so, when I was offered *The Saint* movie, it was with those recollections of the series and the stories that attracted me.

However, I didn't want to make a remake of the TV series. I wanted to make something new. And so I decided to make the story of how Simon Templar became known as The Saint. The story that we came up with is a story that Leslie Charteris never told. It starts in Hong Kong, when The Saint is in an orphanage.

In the style of the original TV series, the screenplay that we wrote had a certain tongue-in-cheek quality to it. It was real but it wasn't real. You were meant to take it seriously, but not quite. In the original version, we killed off Elisabeth Shue's character about two-thirds of the way through. When we screened this for audiences, they seemed to like it. But, as you often do when you're editing, I decided to play around with some of the technical aspects, the story and the music. I also decided to see what would happen if, through the sleight of hand that you can do with editing, Elisabeth Shue's character was kept alive. What I found was that during the last part of the movie it seemed as though the audience was on the same sort of almost funny roller-coaster ride that they'd been during the previous two-thirds in the other version. It seemed in the original version that we had two movies: one, a tongue-in-cheek, action-adventure story that you were meant to take half seriously; and then another, following the violent murder of one of the central characters, which was a completely different story. It became a story of revenge and a story of a man who is determined to bring to justice the killers of his lover. That was a very, very different movie. So we decided in the end to go with the version where Elisabeth Shue's character lives.

What Makes a Successful Performance?

Successful performances are, as so many directors will say, 80 percent due to the right casting as well as the right chemistry between the characters. So the first thing that you look for when you're casting is not what that actor brings to the movie, but rather you feel confident that the actor will be able to inhabit that character. What I always look for are not actors who just want to turn up in the morning and go home in the afternoon, but people who are seized by the personality that they play.

Ever since Henry Hathaway and Dennis Hopper had that famous encounter on an MGM stage during the early years of the so-called method acting style, directors all over the world have feared the inevitable moment when their actor or actress says, "But my character wouldn't do it like that." Feared, because it means that maybe the actor is afraid. Feared, because it means that maybe the actor is trying to assert him- or herself. But I've always viewed that statement with mixed feelings. And one of them is maybe that it's the eureka moment. It's the moment to be cheered, because maybe it's the moment when finally the actor is possessed. Finally, they've become that person. Finally, they're not acting; it's just seeping out of them. They don't need to think about it anymore. And so, in some ways I expect that the actor will always say to me, "But my character wouldn't do it like that." Because that's also the beginning of the process between actor and director, where you are really discussing the nature of the personality that they're portraying. There is no story without that flesh-and-blood person that joins the director, the writer, and the audience together. The audience is going to invest in that actor and the person that they're portraying. You want the actor not to just say their lines the way they are told to, but to be a part of that process, to engage in a dialogue, not just with the audience, but with the director. If that means that you get into arguments, so be it, because out of the argument might come something better. And after all, a good idea is maybe the most precious thing in the whole world. It certainly is on a film set.

> *Phillip is intense. He is very funny. He is a hard, hard worker. He works too hard. I had no idea he was only a year or two older than me, because he's wearing himself out.*
>
> Denzel Washington—Actor

The Bone Collector (1999)

Denzel Washington; Angelina Jolie; Queen Latifah; Michael Rooker; Mike McGlone; Luis Guzmán; Leland Orser; John Benjamin Hickey; Bobby Cannavale; Richard Zeman.

When I first read the screenplay for *The Bone Collector,* I thought it was a wonderful opportunity for any director. Most of the film is set in one room. Your central character is bedridden and mostly paralyzed. He spends almost the entire movie in a bed. I thought if I could overcome that disability that's going to limit the scope of the film, then that's potentially going to really engage an audience. But the question was how to do that?

I knew from the outset that we needed the very best actor we could find. Not the biggest star, but the best actor for this part. Because on a Friday afternoon, when the audience is thinking of going to the multiplex, they're gonna say, "Do you want to go and see the one about the bank robbers who are chased across America? Or do you want to go and see the one about the guy who's paralyzed and lies in bed the whole movie?" Probably, they'll want to see the one about the bank robbers. I thought the only way we can overcome a natural and understandable prejudice against this character is to make the performance so compelling that the audience just has to see it.

The only way you can make the performance compelling is to find an actor of extraordinary ability. In Denzel Washington, I found that actor. He's a man who has great intelligence and great humanity. And because of his theater background, he really prepares for each and every role. For *The Bone Collector* he met with a lot of quadriplegics on both the East Coast and the West Coast. During the shoot, we employed a caregiver that had worked all her life caring for quadriplegics. She was always there beside Denzel to answer all of his questions and he had a lot of them because, most of all, Denzel wants to get it right. He realized that the film would also fail if the audience felt that we were taking advantage of the character's disability. That it was only there as an impediment to make things harder, but was not doing justice to the agony of someone who's in that position.

For the part of Amelia Donaghy in *The Bone Collector,* I needed to find an actress who could convince the audience that she's about to bloom or destroy herself. I was lucky enough to see a tape of *Gia,* an HBO movie starring Angelina Jolie. I was knocked out by her performance. She came in to see me and spoke about a character that she might play in *The Bone Collector,* and I sort of felt that I was sitting there talking to the character of Amelia Donaghy, not to Angelina Jolie. She just seemed to have so much talent bursting out of her, that like years before, when I screen tested Nicole Kidman for *Dead Calm,* I felt compelled to put her in the movie. It wasn't a case of thinking about anyone else. I felt that I was lucky just to get her. I was afraid that someone else was going to reach the same conclusions before I had a chance to sign her up and get her on the screen. Each day working with her was a joy.

What's Up Next?

The next two movies that I'm planning to make are on a completely different level from the films that I have been doing for the last ten years here in Hollywood. The first of them is called *Rabbit-Proof Fence*. It's a film set in Australia in 1931. It tells the story of three Australian Aboriginal children who, as was the custom and government policy at the time, were taken from their parents to be retrained as domestic servants for white families. This is based on a true story. Eventually, the children escaped and, despite a huge manhunt over several months, traveled the two thousand miles back to their homeland. They followed the fence that was built from the top to the bottom of Australia in the early part of the twentieth century to keep the rabbits on one side and the rabbit-free pastureland on the other. The kids knew that the fence went through their territory, and if they could find the rabbit-proof fence, then it would guide them home, and it did.

The other film I want to do is *The Quiet American*. It's adapted from Graham Greene's novel of the same name. It's a love story, a political thriller, and a murder mystery, set in Saigon, now Ho Chin Min City, in 1952, when the French were fighting the Vietnamese Independence Movement before the Americans became involved. This is a story that's on quite a different level to the kind of films I've been making.

Parting Words

I grew up in a country that had no cinema. I only saw two films that were even set in Australia in the first eighteen years of my life. So when I started making movies, everything that happened to me was a gift. It was a gift to be able to spend my own money making short films. Then it was a gift that other people would give me money and also pay me a salary to make movies. So the whole thing has been a joy that's not about a job, but about being given an opportunity. And so the first thing that I want to achieve is just to keep on making movies, because that is a privilege, particularly given the cost of making some of the films that I tend to make. I'd like people to look back on the movies and see in the ones that I made in Australia, a filmmaker who was seizing the Australian experience and putting it up on the screen for an indigenous audience, for his family.

In the American movies that I've made I think I'd like people to feel that these were movies that could not have been made by Americans—that somehow, American life, that American experience, was viewed maybe through a particular set of South Pacific glasses that were able to reveal something different about the American experience and the American personality. That can only come from not being a part of it, admiring the nation and all that it stands for, and the personalities that have emerged from that great melting pot of cultures. Admiring the principles upon which the nation was founded. But also looking at it sideways and seeing other things. Not worshiping America, not condemning her, but maybe just being able to view perhaps, as an outsider, more realistically some parts... some aspects of living in this country.

Phillip Noyce Filmography

That's Showbiz (1973)
Castor and Pollux (1973)
Backroads (1977)
Newsfront (1978)
Heatwave (1982)
The Hitchhiker, TV series (1983)
The Dismissal, TV mini-series (1983)
Cowra Breakout, TV mini-series (1984)
Echoes of Paradise (1987)
Dead Calm (1989)
Blind Fury (1989)

Editors note: Since completing this interview, Noyce has directed *Rabbit-Proof Fence* and *The Quiet American,* both released in 2002.

Nightmare Café, TV series (1992)
Patriot Games (1992)
Sliver (1993)
Clear and Present Danger (1994)
The Saint (1997)
The Repair Shop (1998)
The Bone Collector (1999)
Rabbit-Proof Fence (2002)
The Quiet American (2002)

Awards and Nominations

Australian Film Institute Awards
Dead Calm, Best Direction (nominated), 1989
Newsfront, Best Direction, 1978
Newsfront, Best Original Screenplay (shared with Anne Brooksbank and
  Bob Ellis), 1978

Mystfest
Heatwave, Special Mention, 1983
Heatwave, Best Film, nominated, 1983

Razzie Award
Sliver, Worst Director (nominated), 1994

The Films of Cameron Crowe

Cameron Crowe was born in Palm Springs, California, and raised in San Diego. He began his career in journalism at the age of fifteen, writing for such publications as *Creem, Rolling Stone, Playboy,* and the *Los Angeles Times.* When he was only sixteen years old, he joined the staff of *Rolling Stone,* where he was a contributing editor and later an associate editor. During his tenure with the magazine, he profiled many of music's most influential artists, including Bob Dylan, Eric Clapton, David Bowie, and Neil Young.

In 1979, Crowe, then twenty-two, returned to high school to research a book, which resulted in the best-selling novel *Fast Times at Ridgemont High,* published in 1981 by Simon and Schuster. But even before the book came out, Crowe was tapped to write the screenplay adaptation, marking his screenwriting debut.

In 1989, Crowe made his feature film directorial debut with another of his original screenplays, *Say Anything.* He subsequently wrote and directed the widely praised romantic comedy *Singles.* But it was the 1996 release of *Jerry Maguire* that brought him the recognition as one of Hollywood's brightest young writer-directors to come along that year. He quickly followed that film with his semi-autobiographical *Almost Famous* in 2000, and the complicated and visually challenging *Vanilla Sky* in 2001.

> *I think he's a specialist on transmitting the magic of the small moments, the little things in life that are the most huge moments. He's someone who has the subtlety and can transmit those moments. It looks like something done with little effort, but it's the most difficult thing to do.*
>
> Penelope Cruz—Actress

The Conversation

I grew up in the desert. I was born in Palm Springs, California. I'm the only person that you'll meet who was actually born in Palm Springs. It's incredibly hot, and the funny thing was, there were fields everywhere in between the houses. So, you'd go play in these fields, and you'd find desert tortoises, and people kept these tortoises instead of dogs. So, it was a completely different kind of childhood. It was a little like the childhood in *To Kill a Mockingbird*, which is a movie that I've referenced a couple times in stuff that I've done. But it was a nice, hot community, and I remember the radio station used to have these contests every summer. What's the day you think the temperature will reach a 114? Not "Will it?," but "What's the day that it will?" I just remember this not oppressive but kind of beautiful heat. My dad was a real estate man, and my mom was a teacher, and later we moved to India [California], which is kind of a smaller, more countrified Palm Springs.

My mom was a great student of comedy and still is and, in her classes about English or sociology, would always reference comedy because she felt joy was the most infallible sign of beauty in life. So, she very methodically turned us all on to the great comedians—Woody Allen, Robert Klein, Mike Nichols and Elaine May—and from that came a real joy of words and a joy in art, really.

I fell in love with journalism and music, and so I became a rock journalist at a young age, because my mom had skipped me all these grades. The whole other thing that was going on was, she felt—and this is in *Almost Famous*—she felt American schools just underestimate the brainpower of children. You don't need fifth grade, for example. What happens in fifth grade? Fractions, maybe? You should go straight to sixth grade. Anyway, I had this accelerated life in school and went to summer school, and I skipped one grade by accident, two grades on purpose, so I graduated high school at fifteen and kind of took off on this road of interviewing musicians for a local underground paper. I was a little bit of a mascot for all the bands and the people that worked at this underground paper. We had moved to San Diego at that point.

I think it was an amazing time in the world, and it was an amazing time for music. This is back in the early seventies, and my sister had gone to work for a local underground paper called the *Door* in San Diego. It was this big ramshackle house near downtown, and in that house was brewing all these ideas, you know. Guys would be passing out with huge joints in their hands. Other people would be having these committed conversations about how we've got to stop the Republican Convention from coming to San Diego. I remember my sister took me to this house, and I started to meet these people, and, slowly but surely, I got them to give me assignments. One day, I remember John Lennon sent a song to this newspaper because the Republican National Convention was in fact going to come to San Diego. So, he and Allen Ginsberg wrote this song called "Going to San Diego," and they sent it to this house and to this newspaper. I felt like I was just at the epicenter of everything that was culturally happening.

I got them to give me some album assignments. The pay was that you got to keep the album if they publish your review. So I wrote, like, fifty reviews of anything I could get my hands on. They would have promotional copies of records sitting around in this commune, and I'd review everything. They published a few, and I took those tear sheets, the copies of the things that they published, and sent them out to other magazines to get other assignments, and one of the magazines was *Rolling Stone*. The cool thing about the *San Diego Door* was they had also published Lester Banks, who was a San Diego resident and one of the very first rock critics. There's a character in *Almost Famous* who is literally Lester Banks, based on my memories of him. Lester would write streams and streams of record reviews, sometimes never even mentioning the record that he was reviewing. These reviews would go on forever, and then they were just kept in files at this underground paper. So, I'd sit and read these files of Lester Banks's writings. Stuff that should have been published, but I don't know what happened to it. I fell in love with the idea of writing about music and writing about culture, and, ultimately, editors at *Rolling Stone* noticed my work, and I got published in *Rolling Stone*.

I loved movies, but I never felt that was my destiny to write or direct them. What I loved was journalism, and I had a love of detail, and I loved capturing a moment and writing about how real life happens. Slowly but surely, I started to realize that my favorite movies did the same thing. A movie like *Carnal Knowledge* felt like a series of stolen moments. Here's what people really act like in tough relationships when they don't think anyone else is around. That's journalism to me. So, I began to discover more of what I loved in movies as well as in the written word. Movies come from the written word, so I started to study scripts. But, again, from a distance. I never thought that I would ever be involved.

Then, I wrote the book *Fast Times at Ridgemont High*. I was writing these profiles of rock stars for *Rolling Stone*. More and more, I started to interview the fans in the audience, because I loved the juxtaposition of the rock star in the plush hotel room and the fan that saved up for months to buy these tickets for himself and a date. The guy that worked on cars, for example, to get that concert ticket money. The guy who bought the clothes so that he could go to the concert. It started to shift for me, and, all of a sudden, it was like the kid was more interesting than Rod Stewart ordering champagne in the hotel room. So, *Fast Times* was a book about the kid that goes to those concerts. The whole book is about real life. It's about a year in the life of this high school in San Diego where I posed as a student. So, I guess I had my senior year that never happened the first time around. I think *Fast Times at Ridgemont High* is still my favorite writing that I've ever done. There's a real kind of bliss in between the sentences of that book, because I was swimming in great research, and I just loved capturing real life in that way.

The movie of *Fast Times* happened because of Tom Mount, who was then a big executive at Universal and knew my writing at *Rolling Stone* and had a hunch that the book could be kind of a modern *Catcher in the Rye*. He put me in touch with Art Linsen, who was a rock manager who had transitioned into producing movies. Art and Tom Mount decided that I would be the cheapest guy to adapt my own book. They gave me the job of writing the screenplay, figuring it probably would never get made or some other writer would come in. But, as time went on, they protected me, and I went through several drafts of that script, and I began to fall in love with screenwriting.

Then, we found a director, Amy Heckerling, who had done this wonderful short for AFI [American Film Institute]. She came onboard, and I found that she had the same sensibilities. "Let's not talk down about kids," she said. "Let's talk up about kids. Let's honor their lives rather than look down our nose and laugh at the funny teenagers. Let's say these are great characters, and they're as important as adults are. Let's see what their life is like." That's how she made the movie, and I think to this day that people appreciate that it didn't exploit anybody. It honored those characters in their pain and in their joy. Also, Amy was great because Amy shot the sex scenes in this beautifully documentary-style way. She caught the anguish of adolescent love.

That was like a buzzer to the people that came to see that movie when it first came out. Somebody was speaking a language that they hadn't heard in movies in a while.

The studio didn't believe in *Fast Times*. They put it out in a few theaters, and, at the last minute, they cut our release in half. I remember driving across country to a wedding with a friend of mine. I was really depressed because they sort of dumped the movie out. There were a few bad reviews that came out from the establishment press, and I just wanted to get out of town. I just wanted to drive across the country. We stopped in Arizona, and it was a Saturday after the Friday the movie had come out and it was like, yeah, let's just go by this theater that's running it and see what it's like. Let's see what that empty theater will be like. Well, we drove by the theater, and it was packed. We went inside, and there were kids that had already seen the movie two or three times. They had checkerboard vans like Sean Penn's. They were talking like Sean Penn. People were laughing their ass off at stuff that I didn't even know was funny. It was a great experience, and on that day, I knew I had to do this for as long as I could because there is nothing like making people laugh by showing them real life. *Fast Times* started everything.

What about Mom?

My mother lives and dies with everything that I do. We're very close. She felt real anguish over the possibility that the movie might just be dumped off by the studio and off into a bin of poor releasing. She comes to test screenings with me because we don't believe it until we see it. One laugh will hit and then another laugh, and we won't trust it. This happened when we first screened *Jerry Maguire* for an audience. The people laughed a lot, and they seemed to really enjoy it. So, the movie was over, and we thought it played okay. It wasn't a disaster. Could have been better, but they're not going to throw spears at us. This is real. I remember walking out into the lobby with my mom, and we were both just kind of furtive, and this enormous woman recognized my mom from a brief cameo in the movie and said, "You're in that movie. I love that movie. I love you." And, she just smothered my mom in this huge loving hug, and my mom's face basically said, "We made it through. This movie is reaching people." It's nice to have that partner in crime. I treasure my relationship with my mom and with my wife. The two of them are twin pillars for me because it's tough being a writer, and writers are not easy to live with. It's great to have people that live and die with your stuff right along with you.

Say Anything (1989)

John Cusack; Ione Skye; John Mahoney; Lili Taylor;
Amy Brooks; Pamela Segall; Jason Gould;
Loren Dean; Glenn Walker Harris Jr.

After *Fast Times,* we made a movie called *The Wild Life,* which was a misfire. In an attempt not to do a sequel to *Fast Times,* we did a movie that was aggressively not a sequel. The movie should be what it is and not be something else. *The Wild Life* was another movie about young people that did not have the same loving touch that Amy Heckerling brought to it.

I met James L. Brooks, who, from *Mary Tyler Moore* onwards, has created some of my favorite characters ever. To meet him was a huge privilege. We had a mutual friend, and I went in and talked to him. It turned out he liked *The Wild Life.* He thought it had some great character touches. We began a five-year conversation about art, love, movies, writing, everything, and out of that experience came the script for *Say Anything.* Jim taught me something truly, truly important, which was: Nothing beats writing about that embarrassing thing that happened to you that you don't think anybody else will appreciate, but it turns out that it's so vivid to you that you've got to write it. That's the stuff people love the most. That's the stuff they remember.

I would have these conversations with Jim, and I'd pitch ideas for things I was thinking about. He'd kind of listen, and then he'd say, "How's your wife doing, man?" My wife's a musician, and I'd say, "Well, there's this roadie who's in love with her, and the way he looks at me, I know what he's thinking." Jim's like, "That's what you should write about. That's your life. That, you know. Write that." And so *Say Anything* was the result of years of this great kind of life-enriching conversations with Jim.

We had this story about a golden girl that falls in love with the one guy nobody appreciated quite the way she did. As it turns out, she ultimately picked great. She picked the one guy who really honored her and was there to save her when she needed help in her life. A story of how well that guy loved and how smart she was to pick him out as her great love. This story just kind of builds and builds and builds.

When it was finished, we had a list of directors that we wanted to approach. One of them had done a movie that I really loved. He read the script but didn't want to meet me. He talked to me on the phone while a Lakers game was on. He was rooting for the game and calling out coaching tips to the guys on his TV screen while discussing my script with me, so I moved on. The next one was unavailable altogether. The third one was Lawrence Kasdan, and he loved the script and asked to meet me. I went to his office, and we sat for a long time talking about the script. He said, "I would do this movie if I did a movie a year. But there's this other movie that I've been working on for a while, and it's important to me. It's called *The Accidental Tourist*. But you remind me of the kickboxer in your script. You know this guy. I think you should direct your script." Now, that's something that Jim Brooks had mentioned to me, too. Basically, he said, if you can't find someone who'd be better than you to direct your own script, you should give yourself a job. Kasdan sort of echoed that. He called the studio and said, "I think Cameron Crowe should direct this script." So, they give me the job as director of *Say Anything*.

Well, I was scared to death. You know, I didn't know about scene blocking. I didn't know much more than instincts, which, oddly enough, was a lot of what this movie was about. I sort of learned as I went, and I got a lot of help from Jim. Watched his dailies while he was making *Broadcast News*. I studied the way he directed. I studied the films of Billy Wilder and read anything I could get my hands on. I read an AFI transcript of a seminar that Billy Wilder gave, and that helped a lot. But nothing helps like being there.

On the first day, I shot a master shot of John Cusack addressing old folks in an old-folks' home. It seemed to go really well, and I did a few takes. I said, "Cut and print the last two and let's move on." Polly Platt, who was one of the producers on the movie, came up to me and said, "You know, you have to go in closer now and shoot close-up shots of the same scene." I said, "Right, close-up shots, masters, and then you put it together, that's directing. Okay, great! Hey, let's do this scene again." But I was dying inside. I went into

my trailer at lunch and my buddy Clay Griffith, who was an assistant director at the time and has gone on to be a great production designer, said,
"You've got to beat this right now. You've got to leave the trailer. You've got
to show the crew that you're confident, and you've got to go have lunch with
them. It would mean a lot to them." I'm like, "It would mean a lot to them if
I went and sat with them?" And he's like, "You're damn right. Get out of here.
Get out of this trailer. Go and have lunch with your crew." It was one of the
greatest pieces of advice I ever got in directing. Hang with your crew. They
are your people. That's your gang, and they can help you. They can also hurt
you. They can do it all for you.

I found that crews are like sweet little brothers, in a way. Show them some
love, and they'll never forget you. They'll work their ass off for you if you just
recognize them as people. It's shocking to me how few directors really ac-
knowledge and bond with their crew. It's like one of the great relationships
you can have in your life, knowing everybody and them knowing you, and
it seeps into the movie.

I learned pretty early on that casting is just behind writing in terms of
the important elements of a movie. You can have what you feel is a great
scene, but if the person doesn't inhabit it or give you the total kind of physical being of that character, you're going to be working hard to get there the
whole movie. I flew to Chicago to try and get John Cusack to do the film.
He kept turning us down. I walked in this restaurant, and I saw John Cusack sitting there, and for me he was the character of Lloyd. But I did leave
Chicago without signing him, because he kept turning it down. Then, finally, he sort of backed into doing it. And, as soon as he started doing the
part, I knew that that's the standard that I had to hit as a director every
time out, because it was the beautiful marriage. It did sound like he was
making up the words. Like they were just coming to him, and that's great
acting.

I've always loved actors. I've always loved the commitment that actors
have to the material. I've always appreciated seeing them with their scripts
and all these notes in the margins. They've got all these impressions of their
characters and beats they want to hit.

The first day of *Say Anything* seemed great to me. I had to become more
critical of my own stuff, because I was just so grateful that these scenes were
coming to life. Now, I look back, and I realize I had really great actors who
did a lot of the work for me. There was John Cusack and John Mahoney, two

great Chicago actors. Ione Skye had a real natural kind of quality, and they all worked their ass off for me. They would say things like, "Let's do a laughing take now, so you'll have a version in the editing room of us laughing as we do the scene," or, "Let's do an angry take now, because later you'll really appreciate having all these options." Because of that, we found our way on *Say Anything* together. I'm just so proud of that movie.

On Universal Storylines

I read somewhere that most directors tell the same story, and they hone that story over a period of time, and I think that's true in a sense. Probably more true is that, whether the director wrote the script or not, the movie is a diary, in a way, of the director's life. If you watch all the movies in a body of work of the director, you can see his life in a lot of ways. *Say Anything* for me was about optimism as a revolutionary act. It celebrates the idealist, not in a golly-gee way but in a noble, fierce way—optimist fighting against the opposition that occurs in life. That's what *Say Anything* was about. I think, to some degree, that's what everything I've written has been about. I think it's my life, and it's also what interests me. That's a hero to me. Somebody that can just take the knocks and take what life throws at them and remains positive. It's much easier to buy a gun and shoot someone or become a drug addict or do all those things that many movies glorify. Many of them I really like. But I have, like, the greatest love for a story about somebody that takes everything that comes at them, somehow learns from the experience, and grows that much while remaining an idealist. I've always had a soft spot for the story of the battered idealist. I love the tale that's told about the person that takes the knocks that life gives you and they make it through. They don't buy a gun and murder people. They don't commit suicide. They don't embrace the dark side of life for eternity. They suck it up and continue living life as an optimist. I got that from my upbringing. I love real-life heroes and I love to write about them.

> *I think he's a guy who is mostly comfortable in his own skin, you know. I think he knows who he is as a person, and there's something kind of relaxing about that.*
>
> Bill Pullman—Actor

Singles (1992)

Bridget Fonda; Campbell Scott; Kyra Sedgwick;
Sheila Kelly; Jim True; Matt Dillon; Bill Pullman; James LeGros;
Eric Stoltz; Jeremy Piven; Tom Skerritt; Peter Horton.

The critical success of *Say Anything* allowed me to get *Singles* made. It wasn't an expensive movie, but the success of *Say Anything,* critically, and the success of Nora Ephron's movies, gave Warner Bros. the feeling that people might embrace a love story within a romantic comedy. But I don't think they ever understood the backdrop. The idea that a love story could be told with the budding grunge generation was a surprising mix to the studio. I remember somebody said at one point, "Why do you have to make Matt Dillon look like Charles Manson? Can't he just look like Matt Dillon?"

Singles was going to be a love letter to Seattle, a romance set in that city. It had a really simple theme—single people coming together to create their own family. A family made up of separate single people, all living in this apartment. That was the spine of *Singles.*

Casting *Singles* was all about surrounding Bridget Fonda with wonderful actors. I loved Bridget Fonda. I saw her in a movie called *Scandal,* and there was something about her that just talks. She was like a blond Audrey Hepburn. She reminded me of girls that I knew in Seattle who worked at coffeehouses. It was a young generation as opposed to a beatnik generation. Bridget Fonda reminded me of one of those girls who juggles her relationships and her friends. So, I knew I wanted to focus the movie on Bridget Fonda, and it was about building it from there. Matt Dillon came in, and then we sort of built from there.

You should always get the feeling that you can easily follow any one of these actors and their character off into their own little movie, and *Singles* was like that for me. That was the standard we wanted to set. I thought, even though there were about six main characters, each one could have been its own other movie.

When the film was finished, I don't think the studio felt, once again, that it fit into an easily identifiable box. Now, I've come to realize that's sort of a badge of honor. But I always end up in the room with a marketing person who says, "What is this movie? What is the genre? It's not this; it's not that; it's not this. It's just kind of like real life or something." I'm like, *yes*, thank you. But how do you market real life, was the problem with *Singles*. I wanted to sell it as a love letter to a city and a love letter to these characters, and that was the poster in my mind. The studio decided to take a shot. But, ultimately, what made them believe in the movie enough to release it was the explosion of the band Nirvana. This thing that we'd captured a year earlier was part of what was going on for real in Seattle. A year later, Nirvana had become huge, and it was a pop-culture explosion.

I've never watched the film since we finished it. I do hear about it a lot. People kind of rediscover it and that's great. To me the problem with *Singles* is the structure. I loved every *Singles* vignette, but I don't think they hang together as they should have. I went to a movie not long after *Singles* came out, and I saw a film that did it. I realized, sitting in the theater watching this other movie, that they had cracked the code on the idea of vignettes that could come together as a movie. The movie was Quentin Tarantino's *Pulp Fiction*. I realized that you've got to make the vignettes hang together to tell a bigger story, and then you're not going to have a stop-and-start feeling. *Singles*, to me, has a little bit of that stop-and-start feel. Each individual part stands alone, but together they stand on rickety legs. So, the big lesson in making *Singles* was, always honor structure in the best way you can—even if an audience is unaware of how you're doing it. Structure is best when it's invisible.

When *Singles* came out, it was released in the heyday of the grunge explosion, and some of my very good friends who were part of that scene looked at me a little differently. They felt like that movie exploited Seattle a bit, which it was never meant to do, nor was it a big enough hit to truly exploit Seattle. But there was a perception brought on by the year that movie spent in the can and the fact that it was released after Seattle had become this huge cultural hotspot. There was a perception that the movie was a part of Hollywood coming in and trying to capture this very private, beautiful thing that was going on up north. It was the oddest thing to be in a room with people that months earlier were your dear friends, and now they're just a little distanced. They're putting on the act that they're still your friends, but something's changed. I felt so kind of disconnected and sad. It reminded me of this interview that Elvis Presley gave. He said, "I feel lonely, man. Sometimes I feel loneliest in a crowded room." The bones of *Jerry Maguire* came from that feeling.

You get this vibe on the set that everybody's there to support him. And so, he would play music so that the crew and everyone was in an environment where everyone was relaxed, yet focused on the same thing.

Tom Cruise—Actor

Jerry Maguire (1996)

Tom Cruise; Cuba Gooding Jr.; Renée Zellweger; Kelly Preston; Jerry O'Connell; Jay Mohr; Bonnie Hunt; Regina King; Jonathan Lipnicki.

I wanted to write a story about a guy who had been tossed out of his kingdom but still had to work in that kingdom. And I wanted to write about [the question of] who's really there for you. Who's truly your friend? Usually, you find in a stressful situation that the people you least expected were your friends. The ones you depended on the most weren't. That was the beginning of *Jerry Maguire*.

Once again, I was working with Jim Brooks. I had Nancy Wilson—my wife—and Jim Brooks, two of the greatest listeners in the world. It took four years to write the story, cast it, and make the movie. It is the closest of anything I've done that has come to really nailing the way it sounded and felt when I wrote it. It was a dream to shoot it. Everybody couldn't wait to get to work every day. Nobody wanted to leave. I had the greatest relationship with Renée Zellweger. The two of us would sit and watch the film trucks leave at the end of the night and go, "Can you believe we're making a fifty-million-dollar movie with Tom Cruise? How did we get here? You know, this happens to other people, not us."

I remember very early on in the writing asking my wife, Nancy, and Jim Brooks, how do I make a movie that has a story like *The Apartment,* where it draws you in? It's like the kind of movie you see late at night, and it's black and white, and you go, "Damn, they don't make movies like this anymore." I wanted that to be *Jerry Maguire*. I studied *The Apartment* until the videos broke. And I love Fran Kubelik, Shirley MacLaine's character in *The Apartment*. She's the battered optimist, and I loved her spunk and the way she cried and how she laughed when she was supposed to be crying, and she cried when anyone else would have been laughing. Who do you find today that can be like that? The character of Dorothy Boyd was my own little private Fran Kubelik.

In trying to cast that part we met everybody. One day, casting director Gail Levin said she wanted me to meet someone who probably was not right for the role, but she wanted me to meet this girl anyway. Gail told me the girl was from Texas, and her name was Renée Zellweger, and that she wouldn't consider changing her name. Renée came in with her dog and read for the part, and I couldn't get her out of my mind. She wasn't quite Fran, and she wasn't quite Shirley. But she was Dorothy. Gail and I looked at each other, and we knew something had just happened again. A couple days later, Renée came back when Jim Brooks was there. She was distraught. Her dog was sick. She was having a bad day. She wanted so much to deliver. It didn't work. But even Jim saw that there was something there, but it just wasn't the right day. So, we continued looking.

Cameron Diaz was one of the people that came in, and she was great, but it wasn't that Shirley thing that I was going for. Then, Tom Cruise came to town, and Tom started reading with some actors. Gail and I looked at each other and said, let's bring Renée in. I actually have video of Tom and Renée meeting for the first time, and it's amazing. She walks in the door, and she's sparkling. She twirls around the room. I'm recording it on video, and she kind of twirls and presents herself. And she read with Tom, and it was magic. Very shortly after that, we gave her the job, and she was probably the most unknown of any of our potential Dorothy Boyds.

Renée gave me some of my great joys as a director. In fact, there's a moment in the kitchen in *Jerry Maguire* where she watches her kid kissing Tom. Her kid kisses a man for the first time that is not his father. We move the camera in on Renée just a little bit, and I could hear this Bruce Springsteen song that I wanted to use as I was seeing the shot happen. It made me cry while directing it. That was the moment that I knew I wanted to be a director for always. It was such a joyful moment.

At one of our first screenings, Jim Brooks invited Shirley MacLaine. We had a little get-together afterwards, and Shirley MacLaine was standing there, and I went up to her, and I said, "What did you think?" And she said, "That girl Renée, that's me, you found her."

Jerry Maguire was written for Tom Hanks, who read the script and found himself with a dilemma. He wanted to direct his own movie, *That Thing You*

Do. It was one of those passes where you hang up and you go, "Wow, that was a great phone call," and somebody says, "Is he going to do it?" And you go, "No, he passed." Tom Hanks could hold a seminar on how to say no to a project with class. I felt great and yet had no movie.

So it was then time for plan B, and immediately I thought, Tom Cruise. I could definitely see Tom Cruise in this part. He's actually a little more realistic to the sports agents that I've met. I could see how he would be a little bit of a missile as this character.

We sent the script to Tom. It took him two days to read it and call with great, detailed notes about what he liked and what he was fascinated with. He said, "Look, I really like your script. I may not be right for it. Let me just come to town and we'll sit down and we'll talk." He came to L.A., walked into a room with James Brooks and me, and had the script with him. It was well thumbed, and he said, "Look, who knows if I'm right? Let me just read for you, and see if it makes any sense." He opened the script and he started reading it.

Now, everybody said, beware of big star, beware. Watch out, watch out, watch out! Now, back to that meeting. Tom Cruise walks in the room. He's got my script. It's already well thumbed and folded and he's clearly been reading it like crazy. He opens the script and starts reading. I looked at Jim Brooks and went whew, oh man: (a) it's great, and (b) he's auditioning for us. This is really cool. So began the process of fitting it to him like a glove, and it didn't take long. He signed on, and the first thing I did was play him the song "Magic Bus" by The Who. This is, like, five minutes after he said he'd do the movie. He stood in my office, and he did the lines, and the song is playing on the boom box, and the next thing I knew, I was in the theater watching the movie, and it was exactly like that. He was born to play *Jerry Maguire*.

Tom gave me great gifts as a director because he was the first guy that said, "Whatever you want, even if I'm in the middle of a take, tell me. Shout a line out at me. Do whatever you want. I want to make your dreams of this script come true." And so began a different mode of directing, where I play music while he was doing the scenes. I would shout out lines like, he says, "I don't like black people." Half a second later, it's coming out of Tom's mouth, and it's in the movie. He'll spoil you in that way, because soon after that, you'll find yourself with another actor going blah, blah, blah, and they go, "What are you talking to me for, I'm performing now, you're speaking in the middle of my take." Then I go, "Oh, just a little something I picked up on *Jerry Maguire*. Sorry." My relationship with Tom that began on that movie was a really inspiring one.

For the part of Rod Tidwell, there was only one actor that was right for that part, and it was Cuba Gooding. Oddly enough, he was the first guy that I saw do it. He had a read-through at a table reading. There was another actor that was going to play the part during the read-through. On the day of the reading, he cancelled. We put out these agonized calls all over the place to find somebody who could come in to read the part of Rod Tidwell. The studio was coming to hear the script read out loud. We couldn't find anybody, and then an agent Tracy Jacobs said, "I have a client by the name of Cuba Gooding. He's going to be coming from a press conference for an HBO movie. I can get him the script. He can come from the press conference and just sit at the table and read it if you want."

Robin Williams was reading the part of Jerry Maguire. Tom was pretty much in at that point, but he wasn't in town, so Robin Williams read the part of Jerry as a favor to Jim Brooks. Anyway, Cuba Gooding comes in, opens the script, starts reading it, and, as he's reading it, he finds the character, and he just keeps revving it from there. He's going, "Show me the money." Robin Williams is going, "Show me the money." They just exploded. They reached across the table and they're hugging each other. But, foolishly, we thought, if this could happen with the first actor that reads the part, we have to try, like, other actors and see what happens. But a hundred people later, nobody had the exuberance of Cuba, and Cuba knew it.

He was sitting at his house waiting for the phone call to come. When I called him, he was in the shower, and his wife picked up the phone, and I said, "It's Cameron Crowe. I'm calling for Cuba about the part of Rod Tidwell." She goes, "Honey, it's Cameron Crowe calling about . . ." and he started to scream in the background. You hear Cuba going, "Aaaaaah, aaaaah." He gets on the phone and says, "Where do I have to be, what do I have to do? I'm going to pee all over this part, man. Get me in there." And I said, "Well, Tom's coming in. Would you do the part one more time with Tom?"

It was even more explosive than the read-through with Robin. He had his pants down. He was doing stuff in these locker-room scenes. They were doing "help me help you." I just didn't believe it. It was great. He never stopped being perfect for the part. He's still perfect in the part. He showed me something that had never happened before. Crew members on their day off would show up to see his scenes with Tom. It was like magic, and I'll never forget it.

Lots of people were intimidated with Tom, but Tom puts them at ease really skillfully. But never Cuba. You'd have scenes with Tom and Cuba, and Cuba would literally be throwing Tom around like a marionette. He would just shove him out of a frame, you know. And Tom would come back, and these scenes began to have this amazing quality. I can't imagine the movie without Cuba.

The line "show me the money" came from an interview that I did with a player for the Arizona Cardinals. I was interviewing him at an owner's meeting. He had stopped by to show off his new physique because his contract was coming up for renewal. He was waiting to walk through the lobby to show himself off, which I later put in *Jerry Maguire*. He was sitting with his friends in his hotel room, and CNN *Moneyline* was on in the background, and he was saying, "I don't have that much more time left to play in the NFL. I had a really good season. My contract is up. I have kids. I have a wife that needs me to bring more to the table, and you know what, where is the money? Where is the money? Where is the money?" I couldn't get that guy out of my mind as I was writing the script. The clock running on how much more he could play and be an earning force, and those kids were crying at home, and he wanted to get paid. And it became "Show me the money."

I was knocked out about the success of *Jerry Maguire*. As soon as we started showing the movie, something about *Jerry Maguire* got under people's skins. At one of our first screenings, the lights came on. A couple that was sitting there stood up, and the guy proposed to his girl. Another woman who worked in our editorial office came in one day and said, "You know, I've been thinking about this movie that we're working on, and I'm going to divorce my husband. It's a good thing though. It's a good thing." It was the break-up scene in *Jerry Maguire* that affected so many people. The way Renée says, "I don't want ten years just being polite. Let's just say what we have to right now and let's face the facts." It just gave people the feeling that they could seize their life.

The level of success was unexpected and much appreciated, because before the movie came out, I was in a room with marketing, who were people saying, "It's a sports movie and it's a romance. You're going to alienate both audiences that see this movie. Guys don't want to see a weepy romance, and women definitely don't want to see a sports movie. So, this may be an in-between movie for Tom Cruise." I remember that phrase "in-between movie." But they were wrong. That was one time when the movie came out and people instantly responded to it in a very positive way.

I've had a hard time getting stars to do my scripts, particularly male leads. It's a little more in vogue now to be emotionally upfront and to say "I love you" and to play a male romantic starring role. There was a while there where it was really hard. Tom was a breakthrough for me because Tom showed up and said, "I love this part. I love the love story. I love the line 'you complete me.'" That was a big breakthrough, because he threw himself completely into this love story. He trained for those scenes emotionally.

Jerry Maguire has spawned a cottage industry of guys who say they are "the real Jerry Maguire." But *Jerry Maguire* is a creation of the script and of Tom Cruise's. We both did a lot of research. A lot of people in the NFL—agents, players, and all kinds of people—had opened their door to me to do research. I sort of knocked around the NFL for a long time. I was like the longhaired guy that nobody was quite sure belonged. A lot of people told me a lot of stuff, and the movie is what I consider the best of all my research. There is no real Jerry Maguire. One of the biggest sports agents around, a guy who later went around claiming he was Jerry Maguire, read the script, and he said the problem was, there's no sports agent like Jerry. Tom really did a great job in making that character the kind of person that you can look around and say, that's a Jerry Maguire. He doesn't have to be a sports agent. He is somebody who has a revelation that their job can mean more and fights the opposition around them and follows their positive instincts.

Both *Say Anything* and *Jerry Maguire* were the results of long periods of research and writing. I think that the scripts both benefited from that. They cooked a long time on the stove, those two scripts, and I advise anybody to research and really live with your script before you go out and make the movie. Both those movies took a long time, and it was worth every minute. We just wanted everything to be right, and a lot of that is the influence of James Brooks, because he is a brilliant perfectionist, and he breathes perfection in everybody around him. Every line matters.

On the set, he is gentle and a real fan of actors. He's got a big kid qual-
ity to him. But the movie is about this band and he still has that fan en-
ergy, which is really wonderful for somebody as successful as he is.

Philip Seymour Hoffman—Actor

Almost Famous (2000)

Billy Crudup; Frances McDormand; Kate Hudson;
Jason Lee; Patrick Fugit; Zooey Deschanel; Michael Angarano;
Noah Taylor; Anna Paquin; Jimmy Fallon; Philip Seymour Hoffman.

I will say the film is about 93 percent fact in that it happened to me. The other 7 percent is on the DVD. The film is a tribute to my mom, and it's a tribute to the music that I love. And I wanted to help bring my sister and my mother back together, and they did come together as a result of the movie. It gave my mom and my sister a communication point. My sister felt that there were things that she'd always wanted to communicate that were in that movie for my mother and other people to see. The two of them are as close, closer than I ever thought they would be, as a result of that movie. Some of those lines my mom had forgotten she said, but my sister remembered. When I showed my sister the film, she kept grabbing my hands, going, "Oh my God, I thought you were too young to remember that." We did an international press tour for *Vanilla Sky*, and everywhere we went people talked to us about *Almost Famous*. They had discovered it on video.

Almost Famous is totally from the heart. I tried to do a glib version of those years, because I'd always wanted to write about what it felt like to be in the front row of the rock scene of the early 1970s. Whenever I tried to be glib about it, it sucked. There would be great scenes here and there, scenes that I felt really good about. But, it was sort of like a personal version of *Spinal Tap*. Eventually, you make that tough decision as a writer to throw out the glib stuff and to go solely with the real stuff—to throw out the smooth, snappy stuff and go with the stuff that is hard to write because it's true. There is that agonizing period of getting it on the page, and then a great gift is delivered to you later, because you've done something totally from the heart. That was *Almost Famous*.

Friends of mine told me not to make the movie because I am too sensitive. I would take things that people say about me to heart, which was much more true a couple years ago than it is now. If people didn't like it, they're criticizing more than just the movie. They would be criticizing me. That was the high-wire act of *Almost Famous*: to do it in a way so that you are not saying, "Look at my life and my adolescence." That was the challenge.

I wanted to work with Brad Pitt because I had the idea the Russell Hammond part would be great for him. So we had Brad Pitt do a couple scenes from *Almost Famous,* and he was great. He was funny, spontaneous, soulful, and ultimately couldn't quite get there. It was kind of an emotional process for both of us, because we both wanted it to work. But he said one day, "Guys, there's something about it that doesn't feel right." I thank him for that because as great as he would have been in the part, him not doing the part opened the door for the truly right way to make the movie, which is spying on real life with actors that you forgot were acting. Billy Crudup ended up in that part. We got the feel that I always wanted, which was like Truffaut's film *Stolen Kisses.* I crave to work with Billy Crudup again. I love his stuff. It's invisible acting, and that's some of my favorite stuff because it lets your writing shine through. We also had incredible actors like Frances McDormand and Philip Seymour Hoffman.

Almost Famous could have easily been the first movie that I did, but because I did it after *Jerry Maguire,* I was able to do it correctly, having had a little bit more experience. But *Almost Famous* was tough to make. A lot of times, my mom was on the set, and it was very strange directing Frances McDormand, who's acting the part of my mother, with my real mother who's right over my shoulder. It was a strain. Sometimes I had to go for a walk and just get out of the psychedelic emotions of making this movie. Sometimes I would do a zillion takes of the little detailed stuff, you know. I could feel some of the crew saying, like, okay, therapy might have been a little cheaper and slightly more private.

Some people asked me, where were the drugs and the brutal rock sex. Well, I didn't see that when I was fifteen. I've read books later about some of the bands I wrote about, but I didn't see it. There was, in fact, a whole other world happening but I didn't see it. I saw what's in *Almost Famous.* The one thing that I'm proudest of is that it's a movie about rock that captures the moment when you fall in love with music, which is why people become musicians, and not just because they're going to have drugs and sex. They fall in love because they hear a song on the radio that changes them. The movie captures that, and I'm really proud of that.

It was a rough ride getting *Almost Famous* released, but when we did, people really responded. It was nice, and my fear didn't happen, that people thought we were glorifying my life. They saw that it was my Truffaut movie. Truffaut wrote about things that were very personal to him, and he never felt that he was beating his chest. It was just a slice of life. So, I'm very proud of the fact that people understood it and critics understood it.

> *It's such a layered movie in that it's so skillfully written and directed that if people have a chance to see the picture a second time, it's going to be a different experience the second time around.*
>
> Tom Cruise—Actor

Vanilla Sky (2001)

Tom Cruise; Penélope Cruz; Kurt Russell;
Cameron Diaz; Jason Lee; Johnny Galecki; Jennifer Aspen

If you're lucky, as a director, you get to make all kinds of movies, and that was the motivation to do *Vanilla Sky,* an adaptation of the original Spanish film *Abre Los Ojos,* which was a deeply emotional science-fiction-romance-thriller-love story. It was an unwieldy combination. You can't trust where it's going to go. You can't predict how it's going to end up. The love story at the beginning of the movie just sucked me in, and then they took it away, and I didn't know where we were headed. I thought that was great. But I wanted to make the characters as much of the star as the story. So we made the characters more real, and I wanted that jump at the end, the guy who's ending a life to begin a life. I wanted that to be celestial and not just a look at how the movie was going to end. I found, even as we were filming, the more you believe in those characters, the more you agonize for the choices they make. The more you're hurt for Tom. You hurt for Cameron Diaz's character. The movie became more real, and it polarized audiences.

Some people loved the film, and some people hated it. Some people felt that we had taken away that love story and replaced it with a coldly scientific third act. And some people were grateful for that ride, and other people, as I quickly found out, were pissed off. But the pissed people couldn't stop talking about it, and the pissed people sometimes went back to see it again and began to like it. For a long time those people drove the success of that movie. I kept hearing that people at parties would be like, have you seen this movie, *Vanilla Sky?* You want to go with me tomorrow? And their early reactions would change, but as Mr. Wilder once told me, his goal was to make movies that you'd want to talk about for fifteen minutes afterwards. Or, you're standing around the water cooler the next day, and you talk about it. That's a successful movie. Beware of the movie where you go, that was cute where are we going for dinner? Say what you will about *Vanilla Sky,* but nobody ever said that it was cute. People stayed in the lobby and argued about it.

We did a two-month promotional tour. We went around the world and argued about it. The reaction was the same everywhere we went. People got their heads spun around. Some people wanted to know how I could have made a movie like this, and the answer in many different languages was always the same. It's a cover album. You know how a band makes an album quickly after the one before, and it's, like, a whole bunch of other people's songs. Well, that was this movie. So, I think when we make the next movie, more people will say, "I get it, *Vanilla Sky* was a cover." One of the great things is that the original director, Alejandro Amenábar, really dug it. He said, "I so feared Hollywood was going to simplify my story. You made it more complicated. Thank you." He also said the two movies were like two very special brothers having a conversation. One likes opera and one likes rock 'n' roll, and I thought of that through the promotional tour. I sat in those rooms with people jousting with us for a long time, and I would think about what Alejandro said; the movies are brothers, and they have a conversation between two movies. Both directors are happy with the conversation. I can't think of a situation like it. We did something different, and his faded to black, and mine faded to white, and I dig it.

I came home from mixing the sound of *Vanilla Sky* one night, and I sat down with my wife, and I said, "You know, as much as I would like to just go and write the new script, this is a movie we're going to have to talk about. I'm going to have to talk to a lot of people about this movie, and I think it's a good thing." And Tom felt the same way. It's a movie that demands conversation among audience members and from us. I think people needed to know that it's a movie from the heart. Nobody was profiteering. Nobody was preening. Nobody was just providing grist for those Hollywood filmmaking mills. It's a movie we felt passionate about. I remember walking across the street while we were making it and looking at Michael Shannon, the great

Chicago actor who played the security guard. I think Tom, Penélope, and I, and even Cameron Diaz and Kurt Russell all wanted people to know that they were passionate about this cover album. So, we went around the world and talked about it.

I was scared to death of going to Spain. Alejandro's movie was a hit in Spain. Penélope's the star of both movies. I didn't know what would happen when we got to Spain. There was a party the first night with all these Spanish directors. Do you know what they wanted to talk about? Billy Wilder. They had read this book that I had done on Billy Wilder, and we ended up having this amazing night talking about Billy Wilder.

What's Next?

I'm working on an ensemble comedy drama with about twelve main characters, and the idea is to fully create a world inhabited with people that you know incredibly well. I want it to be two hours, and when the movie ends, I want you to feel like you've just met a new gang and your life is better for knowing them. Seeing them in all stages of fallibility and happiness, and, so far, that's how it's turning out.

Making Movies Is Tough

It's hard to make a movie. It's the greatest job, but it's a hard job. Most directors that I've talked to would pay for the opportunity themselves. For me it began with writing, because writing is so much a part of the filmmaking process. You're always writing. You're writing on film. It's about writing on the page, and it's about the opportunity you get to put it on the screen. I want to be remembered for writing about people. And if there was an ounce of humanity in the stories that I was able to tell, I'm the happiest guy in the world.

I'm honored that some people feel that there's an element of spirituality to some of the stuff that I've done. As Billy Wilder says, "You must sugarcoat that pill." They swallow it before they even know what they have swallowed. I don't really think of it in that kind of mechanical way, but what I do know is that when the lights come up after you've seen a movie, you sometimes go out and look at the world differently.

Cameron Crowe Filmography

Say Anything (1989)
Singles (1992)
Jerry Maguire (1996)
Almost Famous (2000)
Vanilla Sky (2001)

Awards and Nominations

Academy Awards, USA

Almost Famous, Best Writing, Screenplay Written Directly for the Screen, 2001

Jerry Maguire, Best Picture (nomination shared with James L. Brooks, Laurence Mark, and Richard Sakai), 1997

Jerry Maguire, Best Writing, Screenplay Written Directly for the Screen (nominated), 1997

Australian Film Institute Awards

Almost Famous, Best Foreign Film (nomination shared with Ian Bryce), 2001

Boston Society of Film Critics Award

Almost Famous, Best Director, 2000

Almost Famous, Best Screenplay (tied with Steven Kloves for *Wonder Boys*), 2000

British Academy Awards

Almost Famous, Best Original Screenplay, 2001

Almost Famous, Best Film (nomination shared with Ian Bryce), 2001

Broadcast Film Critics Association Critics' Choice Awards
Almost Famous, Best Screenplay, 2002

Chicago Film Critics Association Awards
Almost Famous, Best Screenplay, 2001
Almost Famous, Best Director (nominated), 2001

Directors Guild of America
Almost Famous, Outstanding Directorial Achievement in Motion Pictures (nominated), 2001
Jerry Maguire, Outstanding Directorial Achievement in Motion Pictures (nominated), 1997

Empire Awards
Almost Famous, Best Director (nominated), 2002

European Film Awards
Jerry Maguire, Five Continents Award (nominated), 1997

Golden Globe Awards
Almost Famous, Best Screenplay—Motion Picture (nominated), 2001

Golden Satellite Awards
Vanilla Sky, Best Original Song (for the song "I Fall Apart," nomination shared with Nancy Wilson), 2002
Almost Famous, Best Director (nominated), 2001
Almost Famous, Best Original Screenplay (nominated), 2001

Italian National Syndicate of Film Journalists
Almost Famous, Best Director—Foreign Film, Silver Ribbon (nominated), 2001

Las Vegas Film Critics Society Awards
Almost Famous, Best Director, Sierra Award, 2000
Almost Famous, Best Original Screenplay (nominated), 2000

London Film Critics Circle Awards

Almost Famous, Screenwriter of the Year (nominated), 2001

Online Film Critics Society Awards

Almost Famous, Best Screenplay, 2001
Almost Famous, Best Director (nominated), 2001

San Diego Film Critics Society Awards

Almost Famous, Best Director, 2000
Almost Famous, Best Original Screenplay, 2000

Southeastern Film Critics Association Award

Almost Famous, Best Original Screenplay, 2001

Writers Guild of America

Almost Famous, Best Screenplay Written Directly for the Screen (nominated), 2001
Jerry Maguire, Best Screenplay Written Directly for the Screen (nominated), 1997
Fast Times at Ridgemont High, Best Comedy Adapted from Another Medium (nominated), 1983

Young Hollywood Award

Dream Director, Young Hollywood Award, 2001

The Films of David Cronenberg

David Cronenberg was born in March of 1943 in Toronto to a journalist father and pianist mother. Early on, Cronenberg submitted fantasy and science fiction stories to magazines. Although none were accepted, he received encouraging letters from editors urging him to keep writing.

He entered the University of Toronto science faculty, but, after a year, switched to English language and literature, graduating in 1967. While at the university, he became interested in film and produced two shorts in 16 mm, *Transfer* and *From the Drain*. His first films in 35 mm were *Stereo* and *Crimes of the Future*, both shot in the late 1960s. In these works, Cronenberg established some of the themes and preoccupations that would characterize much of his later work.

In 1975, Cronenberg shot his first commercial feature, *Shivers* (aka *They Came From Within,* or *The Parasite Murders*), which became one of the fastest-recouping movies in the history of Canadian film. His next film, *Rabid*, starring Marilyn Chambers, went on to make $7 million on a production investment of little more than $500,000, providing Cronenberg with an impressive track record after just two pictures by 1977. He then directed the drag-racing film *Fast Company*, inspired in part by his own passion for cars and racing.

Cronenberg lives in Toronto and, when he can, prefers to make his films there.

> *Very often, directors step out of their involvement with the story through the course of the day of shooting. David never does. He keeps himself in utter isolation around the monitor. It's not a coffee klatch. It's not social. It's not a place where you read the paper. It's a place where he is involved exclusively in the story. He seems to have that level of*

involvement all day long, no matter whether we're in between shot or we're in between setups. For me as an actor that's a relief because I don't feel so alone.

Holly Hunter—Actress

The Conversation

My father was a writer, and I used to fall asleep to the sound of him typing on his various typewriters, including, I think, the first IBM Selectric ever to be in Canada, because he was quite a gadget freak and very interested in the latest, whatever it was. I really always assumed that I would be a writer. I think I really aspired to be an obscure novelist, and those were the books that I read often. But, of course, as a young kid, I also read a lot of science fiction, and there were a lot of magazines that I just lived in. *Galaxy, Astounding Science Fiction,* and a magazine called *Fantasy and Science Fiction.*

I felt that to begin my career as a novelist, I should write short stories, and science fiction just seemed very natural for me to do. So I wrote several short stories and sent them to various magazines and got the rejection slips and did all of that. The highest point, I think, was when I was sixteen and I actually got a personally written rejection slip from *Fantasy and Science Fiction Magazine* saying, "This came quite close, please try again." I never did. I never wrote another short story. I don't know what that all means, but I'm kind of surprised to find myself being a filmmaker. Actually, it was not anything that I had ever imagined when I was a kid.

Naturally, I saw movies all the time. Not the way kids see them today. Of course, there was no videotape, no DVDs. But every Saturday, there was a kind of a lemminglike stream of kids that would be going to the various neighborhood theaters. I would see everything that was there for kids to see. In those days, you could see a double bill. You could see two movies in one day, plus news, plus cartoons, plus funny comedy shorts and all kinds of things. I would see things like Hopalong Cassidy and the Durango Kid, the kind of series that I loved as well as pirate movies. I loved them all. But it was like the air that you breathed, you know. It wasn't special in the sense of "Oh my God I'm about to see a movie." It was just there all the time; the way television is for kids today. And so, I no more thought that I would be involved in making those movies than I thought I would be involved in making automobiles.

Movies were not being made in Toronto at that time. Unlike someone growing up in L.A., you didn't see film trucks on the street. You didn't have friends whose fathers were in the film business. There was no connection with movies at all. They came from somewhere else, just like automobiles came from somewhere else. And, of course, being a racing enthusiast, I knew that in England, for example, people did make cars. They would make race cars. They would aspire to become car manufacturers. Individuals could do that, just the way people could aspire to that if they grew up in Hollywood. But in Toronto, those things were very far away. So it wasn't until I was in my mid-twenties that I could actually make a movie myself.

A Canadian filmmaker at the University of Toronto, named David Sector, made a film, and I saw it. It was called *Winter Kept Us Warm*. The title is a quote from T. S. Eliot's *The Wasteland*. I remember it got a good review in some French magazine that was considered the ultimate sort of critical journal for world cinema at the time. I remember being absolutely astonished to see a movie that had my friends in it as actors and that it had locations that were places that I walked every day at the University of Toronto. That was an incredible, shattering revelation for me. It meant that you could have access to filmmaking, and that had never occurred to me before.

Today, every kid who's ten has already made ten films or twenty films or has at least videotaped them, knows about movies, reads the magazines, and sees the behind-the-scenes documentaries. None of that existed then. Movies were a very mysterious process that was very secret. No one knew anything about it.

My real inspiration was the New York underground film movement and underground filmmaking in general. Because, once again, it said you can have access immediately. Go get a camera, go get a tape recorder, and that's what I did. I wasn't thinking that I would be a filmmaker. I still wasn't thinking of that as a career.

I was only aware of a few schools that taught this stuff. There was Ryerson Technical School, which still exists in Toronto. You could learn what they called RTA—Radio and Television Arts. At the time, it was to train technicians for the CBC [Canadian Broadcasting Corporation] television studios. And there was UCLA Film School. I knew some kids who had gone to one or the other, but that was beyond my reach in terms of money and everything else. But I didn't want to do that anyway. I wanted to just do it myself, on my own terms, and so I'm completely self-taught. I literally looked up "camera" and "lens" in the encyclopedia to start trying to figure out how it all worked. So, as a result, it was sort of on-the-job training for me.

In Canada, if you're an artist or an aspiring artist, you often do look to the government for support. It obviously doesn't work this way in all countries, but in Canada, the government is a kind of a benign presence at times in the arts. The Canada Council was designed to help artists of all kinds in many fields by giving people money when they're at the beginning of their careers and also when they're mature and looking to do some specific and difficult project. I remember applying to the Canada Council for a grant and being told that there was no cinema category. Cinema was not an art as far as the Canada Council was concerned. They actually advised me to apply as a writer. So I invented a novel that I would write. I had to get established members of the writing community to give an appraisal of my project. In fact, I found a couple of people who were quite excited about it. Then I applied and I got $3,500, which basically supported me for a year and allowed me to buy film stock, and I went and made my first movie, which was called *Stereo*.

The next year, the Council had a cinema category. They were very responsive, but moviemaking in Canada was still not being considered a reality. As far as filmmaking being an art, there was Federico Fellini, and there was Bergman, and no one would deny that they were film artists, but in Canada the government didn't think that filmmaking was accessible to its citizens at that point. I got to make shorts for the CBC to support myself, because I was determined not to do anything but make movies. At this time, the bug had really hit me.

Transfer (1966)

Rafe Macpherson.

Transfer was my first film. I wrote a script, which to me was a very natural thing to do because I had been a sort of a practicing aspiring writer. I got some friends together, and I wrote a short little sketch about a patient who keeps returning to a psychiatrist because that relationship with his psychiatrist is the only one that has any meaning for him. But there's a surreal aspect to it as well, because it takes place in a snowy field. They're sitting on chairs in an empty field in the winter, and it was very cold. I shot it myself, recorded the sound and edited it. I did all that stuff. I made all the mistakes and was very stubborn and did it all myself. There was a wonderful woman named Janet Good who had a company called Canadian Motion Picture Equipment rentals, and she would rent cameras that were kind of battered and didn't work all that well. I would hang out at her place near Carlton Street and learn how to take cameras apart, how to load film magazines and stuff. I learned a lot of lore just hanging out there hour after hour. That was as close to a film school as I ever came.

From the Drain (1967)

Stefan Nosko

From the Drain was my second film. It was basically kind of a Samuel Beckett sci-fi thing. Two veterans of some obscure war sitting fully clothed in a bathtub talking to each other about the various kinds of biological warfare that had been waged, and eventually a plant comes up from the drain and strangles one of them. I haven't seen it for many years, so you'll forgive me if I'm a little sketchy on the details. That was a slightly longer film—about fifteen minutes long. My filmmaking was getting a little more sophisticated. I give myself a break logistically by keeping what I was doing contained. *From the Drain* was easier to shoot because it wasn't outside and didn't have windnoise and all those things I didn't know about. Once again, I shot it myself. I cleaned the lenses myself. I loaded the film magazines myself. There was no one else around technically to help me.

I was very fascinated by 35 mm. It was the professional gauge of film. The problem, of course, was that 35-mm cameras were very noisy because they were all basically designed before the Second World War. I remember the first time a cameraman turned on a 35-mm camera for me. I thought it was going to explode. It sounded like a threshing machine, so noisy and so self-destructive. Of course, you couldn't shoot synchronized sound with that. You have to get what was called a blimp, which would cover the camera and deaden the sound. It seemed incredibly archaic to me, even at the time. I couldn't believe that this was the real professional technology, but it was. That is, you had to put a big padded case around this camera to keep it from being noisy because, of course, in the old days, when those cameras were designed, there was no sound, so sound was not an issue. I shot two that we called features because they were over sixty minutes long, and I knew that film festivals would accept films as feature films if they were, say, sixty minutes long.

Stereo (1970)

Ronald Mlodzik; Tania Zolty; Jon Lidolt; Jack Messinger;
Paul Mulholland; William Haslam; Stefan Czernecki.

Crimes of the Future (1970)

Ronald Mlodzik; Tania Zolty; Jon Lidolt; Jack Messinger;
Paul Mulholland; William Haslam; Stefen Czernecki.

The first one was *Stereo* and we shot it in black and white. The second one was *Crimes of the Future,* shot in color but with no synch sound. It was all voiceover that was added later. It was a dreamlike narrative spoken by various characters in the piece.

The soundtrack of *Stereo* was incredibly simple. It was really only one track with narration. In *Crimes of the Future,* I actually expanded to two tracks. There was total silence in between the narrative. I didn't realize that I had stumbled onto one of the most powerful and maybe unknown taboos in filmmaking—silence. Everybody thinks something's gone wrong with the projector if it's suddenly silent.

There were screening rooms in Toronto called the Backstage I and II. I remember screening *Stereo* for the man who was programming those theaters. The opening shot of *Stereo* was actually kind of elaborate. It involved a helicopter that descends from the sky and brings the main character down to a mysterious set of buildings, which, in fact, was Scarborough College. It had just been built and was very modernistic at the time. It was a visually spectacular shot for an underground film that cost about $3,000. The guy asked me where the sound was. I told him it was coming, and he got up and walked out, and that was it. That was my screening. It was the first of many disasters in my films. I realized that the world of underground filmmaking was one thing, but the real world of films was another. When you actually charge money for someone to come and see the movie, well, that was a whole other thing. So that's why I had two soundtracks on *Crimes of the Future*. A narrative track and a music-and-effects track on the other.

On Commercial Filmmaking

I had to decide whether or not I was going to cross the line and become a commercial filmmaker. That is, I would use other people's money to make my movies, and then I would actually be paid and could make a living. It wasn't an obvious transition for me, because I wasn't sure that that's really what I wanted to do. I spent a year in the south of France, very close to the town of Cannes, where the Cannes Film Festival is held each May. After spending time in this small town with friends, writing and sculpting and feeling that I would write my novel there, I was attracted by the magnet of the Cannes Film Festival. I thought I should go down there and check out what that was. I knew that not only was it a very famous film festival but also was a very famous film marketplace. So, if you're interested in film commerce, that's the place to get massive exposure. I went to Cannes, and I was absolutely horrified. It was such hype and such an erotic and intense activity with Rolls-Royces and Ferraris and yachts, the Carlton Hotel with a three-story cutout of James Bond on the front. I was so intimidated that I fled back to my little town, thinking, I just can't deal with that.

After a few days, the festival was still going, and I thought maybe I should go back. Maybe I should lighten up. So I went back down to Cannes and actually was allowed to use the office of the Canadian Film Development Corporation, which is now Telefilm Canada. They let me sleep there. Suddenly I got a completely different attitude. Cannes was kind of exhilarating. It was funny. There were, like, drug deals being done on the corners of each street, except that they weren't drug deals—they were movie deals. Deals being done by Bulgarians and Romanians and Russians and French and Greeks, all selling films to each other. And it was very fascinating and the community feeling there, there was a communal feeling. This was totally separate from the actual festival itself, where everybody was in tuxedos. I had no connection with that. But I was very excited by the film community itself, because amongst them were very-low-budget filmmakers, sort of soft-core sex filmmakers, action filmmakers—all kinds of stuff. I felt a real sense of community with them. I think that was really the beginning of my possibly being a commercial professional moviemaker as opposed to an underground filmmaker.

Shivers (1975)

Paul Hampton; Joe Silver; Lynn Lowry; Allan Kolman; Susan Petrie; Barbara Steele; Ronald Mlodzik; Barry Baldaro; Camil Ducharme; Hanka Posnanska; Wally Martin; Vlasta Vrana; Silvie Debois; Charles Perley; Al Rochman.

When I came back from the south of France, one of the first things I did was start motorcycle racing, which didn't work out very well. I still have scars from that. I also have scars from the other thing I did, too, which was writing my first script for a movie called *Shivers*.

There was a very interesting Canadian filmmaking company called Cinepics, which operated out of Montreal. They had emerged as one of the first independent moviemaking bodies in Canada. They were making soft-core sex movies that were very romantic and very funny, with a political edge. That interested me very much, because that seemed to me the only place in Canada that I could go with my strange little science-fiction horror script. I took it to them and met John Dunning and André Link, whom I consider to be my mentors in terms of filmmaking because they were the first to really guide me in how to make and market movies. They were very interested in my script because they were interested in breaking into the U.S. market. Their sweet sex films had a market in Europe, but they really had no market in the United States. They knew that low-budget horror films in the Roger Corman style did have a market. They were very interested in my script, but they were not totally interested in me as a director, because I could only show them *Stereo* and *Crimes of the Future*. And they weren't really going to trust me with one of their sex movies.

I eventually went to Los Angeles with a friend, Norman Snider, who later cowrote *Dead Ringers* with me in L.A. I thought I might have to move to L.A., because nobody in Canada understood what I wanted to do. I mean, there was no history of horror or science-fiction filmmaking in Canada. So we went to L.A., and I rented a red Mustang convertible. We were stopped by the police. I mean, we had all the great, most perfect, L.A. experiences. We went to a party. There was cocaine. I'd never seen that before. I went to visit Roger Corman, who was out getting a root-canal job. But I met some other people there who said that they would absolutely make my movie. They read it, and they got back to me the next day. It was amazing. Completely unlike what my experience was in Canada.

I looked up a friend, Lorne Michaels, a Canadian who had ended up moving to the United States. Lorne was producing *Saturday Night Live* and was doing a Lily Tomlin comedy special. I visited him at his home in Malibu. Living next door to him was actress Barbara Steele, who was a horror-film queen. While I was on the beach one day with Barbara, I met a bearded young man named Jonathan Demme. He had just directed Barbara in a film called *Women in Chains,* or *Caged Heat,* I can't remember which. I told Jonathan about my script, and he told me that he had read it. I was completely shocked. I couldn't believe it. This guy on the beach at Malibu had read my script, which I had only sent to people in Montreal—what was going on? He told me that someone at Cinepix had asked him to direct it. That was my introduction to another part of moviemaking as opposed to filmmaking. I was very shocked. I assured Cinepix that I would not let anybody else direct my script. Jonathan said it was obvious that someone at Cinepix felt that they would do an end-run around me. They knew I needed money. They knew I had no job. They would buy the script from me. They would get Jonathan Demme to direct it. They would get Barbara Steele to be in it.

I went back to Canada thinking this was the end of it, only to hear from Cinepix that the CFDC had decided to invest in *Shivers* after all, which they would regret later, as it turned out. The movie would happen in Montreal, because with that money it suddenly all made sense financially for Cinepix to take a chance on me directing the movie. The fact that I was a Canadian was very important for the government money to be invested.

So, suddenly, like, Jonathan Demme was literally out of the picture.

I made *Shivers* in Montreal, and it was an incredible experience. As it turned out, Ivan Reitman, who had connected with Cinepix and had not yet moved to L.A., was producing it. Ivan was a friend from the underground filmmaking days. We had belonged to the Canadian FilmMakers Co-op together, and now he was producing this movie. I was suddenly a professional filmmaker. I remember sitting around a table with my crew heads not knowing what any of them did. I had no idea what a production manager did. I had no idea what an assistant director did. I had no idea what a props person did. I vaguely had an idea what a wardrobe person might do. An art director—had no idea—because I had done all that stuff myself. I had fifteen days to learn how to do it, because that was the shooting schedule, plus two pick-up days. It was trial by fire, you know. You've got two hours in the morning to do eight pages of dialogue, and then we go and kill the security guard, then in the afternoon crash the cars, blow up the house, and do the special effects with the creature coming out of the mouth. That was my on-the-job training for moviemaking. It was exhilarating and fun and insane.

As I recall, the movie cost $385,000, and I think it made $5 million. It was the first movie that the CFDC had ever invested in that actually made money back. But it almost brought them down. It almost caused them to be dissolved. There was an article written in a very influential magazine called *Saturday Night Magazine*. A very influential Canadian film critic and publisher who wrote under the name of Marshal Delaney wrote the article. But everybody knew it was Robert Fulford, who was one of the editors of the magazine. He said the movie was pornographic and obscene and hideous and an atrocity, and you the taxpayer should know about it because you paid for it. I was shocked, because I had invited Bob Fulford to the screening. He had said good things about them, or at least about *Stereo*. I thought he would understand the connection between those and *Shivers*. He was horrified when he saw *Shivers*, absolutely horrified.

I remember telling the head of the CFDC, Michael Spencer, that only a hundred people read *Saturday Night Magazine*, why was this such a big deal? He told me it was the wrong hundred people. There was a time when nobody was talking about anything else in the House of Commons in Ottawa except *Shivers* and government money going into pornography or whatever. It caused such a big stir that it took about three years before they would even dare to put money into my next movie, which was *Rabid*. Unfortunately for them, that film starred the porno queen Marilyn Chambers.

At the time, I had never heard of David Cronenberg, but it was great for me, because it was one of my first films where I was going to get to actually play a character other than myself.

Marilyn Chambers—Actress

Rabid (1977)

Marilyn Chambers; Frank Moore; Joe Silver; Howard Ryshpan; Patricia Gage; Susan Roman; Roger Periard; Lynne Deragon; Terry Schonblum.

It's very difficult to say where the ideas for my films come from. Sometimes, it's a character, or it can even be a title or an image. It could be a conceptual thing. I've gradually come to realize the body is the first fact of human existence for me. So my imagery tends to be very body oriented. I think I'm interested in transformation as well, but not in an abstract spiritual sense or at least not at first, but in a very physical sense. *Rabid* was about the spread of disease, and in a way *Shivers* was as well. How a whole city is finally almost brought to its knees by a sexually transmitted disease. *Shivers* basically had the same plot, only it took place in one high-rise apartment building.

Even though *Night of the Living Dead* had been successful by that time, most horror films were still vampire movies, set in some imaginary centuries past with capes and vampires and torch light and so on. A modern horror film was still rather unique, and difficult to sell. So, in a strange way, I suppose *Rabid* was an amplification of the themes that I was beginning to develop in *Shivers*, both in its narrative style and also in terms of imagery.

Casting Marilyn Chambers as the lead in *Rabid* was really Ivan Reitman's idea. A woman in the lead in a horror film was a tough sell at that time. But I think it was a good idea, all things considered. I had really wanted Sissy Spacek. I had seen her in *Badlands* with Martin Sheen and thought she was fantastic and I wanted her. No one was very enthusiastic about that idea. By the time we were shooting *Rabid*, of course, she had made *Carrie* and was now not only hot as an actress, but also hot in the horror genre. It would have been an incredible coup if we'd had her as a lead in our movie, but that's the way the breaks go. Ivan's reasoning was that we had all gone to Cannes together for *Shivers*, and we had seen how difficult it was to distinguish our film from all of the others. Ivan and I used to walk along this very beautiful, palm-lined boulevard along the Mediterranean in Cannes putting up stickers everywhere on those palm trees. At night, the city officials would come and take them down. The next morning, Ivan and I would go out and stick them all back up. We saw that to get distributors from all over the world to come to your screenings to see your movie was a very difficult thing. If you had a star, of course, it would make it easier. But we were all making low-budget films. We couldn't afford a star, and, of course, no legit Hollywood star would be in our movie. We had Barbara Steele for *Shivers*. We got her because she had been out of movie making for some time and had just gone through a divorce and wanted to work again. She was the star of our first film. Who was going to be the star for *Rabid*? It could be Marilyn Chambers, who had made nothing but absolute hard-core porno films. But she was very famous because she had also been a model who ended up as the Ivory Snow girl. So her appeal was as the beautiful blond girl next door who would do these amazing sexual things. But she did have the sort of girl-next-door kind of looks. Ivan got in touch with her people, and it turned out she was very interested in doing a straight movie that wasn't porno. Ivan suggested we test her and said if I didn't like her, we wouldn't use her. I couldn't argue with that.

She auditioned and she was good. She was actually good. She could act, and her presence and everything would obviously work well for the movie. We ended up making the only straight movie that Marilyn Chambers ever made.

Fast Company (1979)

William Smith; George Buza; Nicholas Campbell; Don Francks;
Robert Haley; Claudia Jennings; David Petersen; John Saxon; Cedric Smith.

I had written the script for *The Brood*, which was a very intense personal experience for me. I had trouble getting that film made. I was offered another film called *Fast Company*, which was about drag racing. This was the first script that I was offered that came from somebody else. I had been a racer in the 1960s, when I raced cars and motorcycles. I loved racing, and I loved the mythology of racing, and drag racing was close enough to that. It had its own mythology. It had its own wonderful imagery as a very American kind of racing. With drag racing, you find out who the winner is in six seconds. It's not like LeMans, where you have to wait twenty-four hours to find out who the winner is. Six seconds, you've got it, and it was very American. It could be very juicy in its imagery, in its metaphor and its meaning—even though it was not a horror film, and I wasn't going to try and make it into a horror film or anything like that.

I ended up cowriting and directing that movie, which is perhaps my least-seen movie even though I have great affection for it. It had a wonderful cast of actors who were considered good, solid B-movie actors, like John Saxon and William Smith and Claudia Jennings (who was a *Playboy* Playmate of the Year and had been in quite a few movies since then). It was much more American than anything I had ever done. It took place in America, although we shot it all in Edmonton and Calgary. It was a very interesting experience for me also to be shooting someplace other than Toronto or Montreal. I met a lot of technical people on that film who I have continued to work with over the years. It had B-movie aspirations. It wasn't trying to be an art film, but there are some lovely things in it that I'm still really very proud of and have great affection for.

Fast Company was the first movie that I actually got the chance to shoot in a studio, as opposed to everything on location. With *Shivers,* we couldn't afford to build anything, so we were dependent on people's apartments to be the apartments of our characters. In *Fast Company,* we built the trailer for Bill Smith's character, Lonnie "Lucky Man" Johnson, because the racers all traveled in big semi-trailers. We actually had a trailer that was on springs, and you could jiggle it and it would look like it was moving. This actually was more difficult to come to terms with than the funny cars that they raced, although those were difficult to deal with as well. Those cars could be more temperamental than any actor could. But dealing with the space within a set was a new challenge for me, and it was the hardest thing that I had to deal with. I had to believe the set was real. When you're on location, you don't have that problem. Suddenly, I had to invent the life within the trailer and deal with the space, because one of the strangest and most unexpected things for me about filmmaking was dealing with space. Moving through it, cutting it up into cubes, having to deal with the three-dimensionality of it and moving people relative to each other and to the camera. There was elegance there and a meaning, and we could feel when it was awkward and wrong, but you couldn't always feel it when it was right. It was just something you had to learn.

The Brood (1979)

Oliver Reed; Samatha Eggar; Art Hindle; Henry Beckman;
Nuala Fitzgerald; Cindy Hinds; Susan Hogan; Gary McKeehan.

It's really the only film that I think of as being remotely autobiographical in the traditional sense. When the film came out, I used to amuse people by saying it was my version of *Kramer vs. Kramer,* which had been a big hit. I still believe that even though *The Brood* had creatures that kill and all kinds of fantastic dreamlike things in it, it presented a certain emotional charge, and it was much more realistic than the Hollywood version of a divorce. *The Brood* did have stars who were a level above the actors that I'd been working with before—although, frankly, in terms of the experience on the set, that means nothing, you know. I mean, if an actor is difficult and acts like a prima donna, then that's what you've got on the set.

Oliver Reed and Samantha Eggar were the leads in *The Brood.* Oliver in particular had quite a sensational career, which reached a high point perhaps with the movie *Women in Love* and *The Devils*, both Ken Russell films. Samantha Eggar had been a star of the *The Collector,* and her career had kind of dipped for various strange reasons, which I later discovered. I was really surprised that she agreed to do this movie, because it's a very strange and difficult role. She practically doesn't ever move in the movie out of one spot.

Without it actually being a Samuel Beckett piece, there is that element in it. Very horrific in some ways, because she has strange growths on her body, and she's kind of a horror diva in this film. But she did accept the role, and I was happy about that.

I was very intimidated by Oliver, because he had a reputation as being a very, very naughty boy. He was known to be very explosive and violent. Someone who did just outrageous things in public after he had gotten very, very drunk. The first time I heard that Oliver was in town was when he had been in a restaurant, had taken off his trousers, thrown them over his shoulder, and walked in his underwear across Avenue Road to the other side of the street. He was promptly arrested for indecent exposure. He had only just arrived and was already in jail. I thought, Oh my God, this is going to be a complete disaster. But, when I met him, it was like meeting Laurence Olivier. He was shy and polite. He was incredibly elegant, articulate, and very sweet.

And so it proceeded with the film. I think he just loved the script, and he loved what we were doing, and he felt that it was serious and that it was careful, and we were being artistically honest and a whole lot of other things. He was perfectly proper through the whole shoot, as was Samantha.

The Brood was not really a calculated thing. I knew, of course, that it was a horror film and that it could be sold as a horror film. It really demanded to be made, and I wasn't really thinking about where it would fit in with my other films. In fact, that's never really been much of an issue with me. I've just always assumed that because filmmaking is a very personal act for me, there will be enough of me in the film to justify its inclusion in my work. I just don't want to think in terms of whether a particular film is good for my career, much to the dismay of some agents. Often, there's been talk of something being good for your career, even though it's not good for you. As though the career is just this dog that you walk down the street or something. So, I never really worried about any of my films in that sense. Each film, hopefully, presents challenges to me that I have not experienced before. If you remade your own movie, it would not be the same movie. It would be something else.

> *David is, like, capricious and he's also not gratuitous. He is a moral cat,*
> *you know. He wants to know how the soul balances itself out. Some-*
> *times the soul awakens into horror and this horror must be expressed,*
> *not necessarily acted on, but expressed, and David expresses it.*
>
> *Peter Weller—Actor*

Money, Money, Money!

The increases in the budgets of the movies that I made weren't a concern to me up to a point. It wasn't a question of macho posturing that you now have made your first million-dollar movie, and now you've made your first two million-dollar movies. I was never very pragmatic about it. What I was concerned with was did the budget allow me to do what I had to do in a reasonable way? Can the movie at least pay for itself given that this is the budget? Those are the aspects I considered when I was thinking about budget, and I was always forced to think about the budget.

The Canadian film industry always was a little hothouse environment that was quite different from the American film industry or the English, specifically because of the tax shelter era in the 1970s. Our circumstances in

Canada were different. For example, one of the most difficult parts of making the movie *Scanners* was that the money was there before the movie was
there. It was tax-shelter time. Around October, all the dentists, doctors, and
lawyers would realize that they desperately needed a tax write-off. Most of
the year, crews were not working because no one could get a movie financed.
Suddenly, in November and December you could make a movie because the
money was there, but it had to be spent before the end of December in order
to qualify for a write-off for that year.

Scanners (1981)

*Jennifer O'Neill; Stephen Lack; Patrick McGoohan;
Lawrence Dane; Michael Ironside; Robert A. Silverman;
Lee Broker; Mavor Moore; Adam Ludwig.*

I remember riding my motorcycle to Montreal. There were no flights because
a Russian satellite was going to fall somewhere in Canada. I rode my motorcycle to Montreal to talk to a producer who wanted to do a movie with me
quickly, because suddenly the money had appeared and had to be spent. I
gave him a couple of ideas sitting in a bistro, and he picked *Scanners*. I had
two weeks' prep on that movie. It should have been three months.

It was a very difficult film, because there were a lot of special effects. A lot
of explosions, a lot of car gags in the middle of real streets. I remember reading in the 1960s about a famous Dutchman. The man drove a hole in his
forehead because he felt that, because of the pineal gland and the third eye
of Eastern religion, that would unleash psychic powers that would transform
him and make him telepathic or make him superhuman in a some way. Ap-
parently, he really did take a drill and drill a hole into his forehead, and didn't
die, and walked around, and people knew him. That certainly was part of
how I generated my concept of telepathy and scanners.

There were other things that came together to create *Scanners*. The
Thalidomide disaster, the drug that produced deformed children that had
been pronounced safe by various governments. The film was a nightmare to
make—right from the first day of shooting, when two young women died because we were shooting by the side of the road outside Montreal. People were

stopping to look at us because they could see the cameras and lights and so on. Suddenly, we heard a huge crash and metal crumpling and I turned to see a truck climbing up on top of a Toyota because the traffic had stopped in front of this truck. He had been watching us and didn't stop and he ran right over the top of this small car. Our grips jumped the chain-link fence to get onto the highway, dragged these two poor young women out, and laid them on the grass. They were very blue and purple, and they were dead. That was our first day of shooting.

I don't think I've ever been so cold in my life, even when we were shooting *The Dead Zone* outside in the winter. And there were all kinds of tensions amongst the crew and the cast, and it was just overall a very, very difficult shoot. I even ended up almost breaking my nose. We were setting up a shot where a car is supposed to hit a wall. I went with the cameraman and the stunt driver just to do a test run, and I noticed some fluid on the ground when we got in the car. I didn't realize that, of course, it was brake fluid. The stunt driver was strapped into his seat belt but I wasn't. I can tell you that no matter how much you brace yourself you cannot stop yourself from hitting something in a moving car. You really need those seat belts and air bags because I saw it coming. We were only going maybe twenty miles an hour, but we went into a brick wall and I just went forward, hit a light clip with my nose. When I got out of the car, my nose was streaming blood. Just at that moment, my wife appeared on the set, pregnant with our second child and towing along our first child. Suddenly, they see me covered with blood. Everybody is running around screaming. These incidents just went on and on during the shooting of that movie.

I was writing it from four o'clock to seven o'clock every morning, because there was no script. We were shooting out of sequence, and it was a very complex plot. I was trying desperately to make it work, but we were only able to shoot what I was able to write for that day. You normally prepare weeks in advance. An ordeal by fire more than a trial, by far, and yet it turned out to be my first really successful film. It was the number-one film in North America, amazingly enough, and considered by many to be a horror classic.

> *I got cast in that film because, I think, of the popularity of Blondie and the amount of exposure that we had at that time. I think David really felt some kind of kinship to the punk-rock scene.*
> Deborah Harry—Singer-Actress

Videodrome (1983)

James Woods; Sonja Smits; Debbie Harry; Peter Dvorsky;
Leslie Carlson; Jack Creley; Lynne Gorman; Julie Khaner;
Reiner Schwartz; David Bolt; Lally Cadeau.

Videodrome was one of those movies that was partly an image and party an experience I'd had. I remember as a kid watching black-and-white television. My father was very late in getting a television set into the family. He was a bibliophile. We had walls literally made out of books, because they were piled up everywhere.

But TV was sort of the enemy to begin with. We ultimately did get a television set, and I watched it all the time, and I watched it very late because my metabolism has always been night-person. So I would watch until there was no more TV. I remember we had a television aerial that would rotate. You had a control, and when all the local stations went off the air, you could pull in some very strange American stations. There would be a lot of static, and the sound would go in and out. They would be very tantalizing, and there would be images that you wanted to be sexual or extreme or something, but you never knew whether you were projecting your own fantasies onto what you might want to see or whether you were really seeing those things. That really was a central image for me of *Videodrome*—forbidden images coming to you from a distant place.

Most of my films have been what you would call independent films. They never have been studio films. Money has always been a big issue. And finding the right actor and the right star in the same person was difficult, because I was always more interested in the actors than the stars—partly because my movies tend to be strange and not immediately attractive to mainstream actors, so you're looking for actors who have kind of an edge. Actors are interested in doing difficult and strange things, knowing that I can't pay them a lot of money.

I can't remember exactly who came up with the idea of Debbie Harry for *Videodrome*. She had done a movie or two, which I watched. It was suggested that perhaps she would work very well for the role of Nicki Brand, partly because of her stage persona as part of the rock group Blondie, and partly because of her looks and her actual physical presence and her potential as an actress. I met her and auditioned her, and I thought, you know, this could work. It's also exciting to discover somebody. Debbie was very famous at the time. I mean, she was the Madonna before Madonna, and I liked her very much. She was very bright, and she had an amazing face and wonderful voice. But she was very inexperienced as an actress, and we knew that it was going to take time. At one point, she asked me if everything she learned as a performer was useless in movies. I told her it was worse than useless—it was destructive. I really had to go over the entire acting process: how to not use too much expression in a close-up, how to move differently than she did on stage as a rock star—all that stuff. So it was a learning experience for both of us, but a lot of fun because she was terrific and a lovely to work with. She was a bright, spunky girl, and that was Debbie.

The Dead Zone (1983)

*Christopher Walken; Brooke Adams; Tom Skerritt; Herbert
Lom; Anthony Zerbe; Colleen Dewhurst; Martin Sheen;
Nicholas Campbell; Sean Sullivan; Jackie Burroughs.*

I can't remember who approached me about *The Dead Zone*. The Stephen King novel had been very successful, as are most of his novels. That was the first time that I'd ever had to consider adapting a novel. I turned it down, and, some time later, I was at a party in L.A., and Debra Hill was there, and she introduced herself. I knew that she had done work with John Carpenter. She said to me, "I know you've been asked this before, but *The Dead Zone* is now with Dino De Laurentiis, and I'm producing it and I'd really like you to do it." I said, "Okay, I'll do it." I was very surprised myself that I'd said that, because I had turned it down once, and I cannot for the life of me remember what the circumstances were when she asked me, but I don't believe I was particularly desperate for a project. I don't remember what I was writing at the time. It was after *Videodrome*, although I might have been asked the first time even before *Videodrome*, I can't remember.

The Dead Zone was my most American movie, I suppose, in that there was no Canadian investment in it; therefore, it didn't matter how many American actors we had, although it was totally shot in Canada, in Ontario. It was a very intense and interesting experience working with people like Chris

Walken and Martin Sheen. This was very exciting for me and not really possible if you're financing a movie that has to have a certain amount of Canadian content, which is just part of the game in terms of financing a Canadian movie. The French and English have the same rules, as well as many other countries. Suddenly, I had all of America to choose from in terms of actors, and that was very exciting for me. I had a different pallet of acting talent to work with, and we got some of the absolute best in that movie.

It was wonderful to hear Martin Sheen say, "You don't know how good you've got it here in Canada. I don't think you'd enjoy shooting in L.A., because you've got the best I've ever seen right here." I've always been curious about what it would mean to shoot in Hollywood on a studio lot. I still have not done that. But it was good to hear from Martin Sheen that perhaps I wouldn't enjoy it at all because artistically it would not be a better experience. *Dead Zone* wasn't an easy shoot, but it was a lucky shoot. As lucky as *Scanners* had been unlucky. We got breaks with the weather. We got breaks with explosions. We got breaks with all kinds of things.

I had at first noticed Chris Walken's work in *Next Stop, Greenwich Village*. Chris was stunning in that movie, which was about the 1950s Greenwich Village bohemian life. He then won an Oscar for *The Deer Hunter* and had become quite an amazing presence on the American scene. A very unexpected and dangerous and unique kind of actor, and I had no idea what to expect. When I met him in a New York hotel, he walked in the door, and in about two minutes, we were laughing like mad. He was so funny, and we both had the same strange sense of humor, and by the end of it, I felt as though I had known him for many years, and we were very excited to do the movie together. He was just a wonderful, serious, real actor, but with a wonderful, wacky sense of humor and a great sense of fun.

Brooke Adams also had been an American actor who had risen to some prominence and had been seen in quite a few interesting movies. She had just a wonderful, open, innocent kind of screen presence but with all kinds of subtlety behind her eyes. I was very excited to get the two of them together. I thought that the combination of Chris and Brooke as the star-crossed lovers was magical. Not that Brooke is necessarily a rural person, but I needed a kind of innocence and small-town openness and naiveté and vulnerability. That was not what Chris was noted for, of course, and I really wanted to bring that into the mix. It was also interesting because I'd never made a movie that wasn't very urban before. *Fast Company* had some stuff happening out in the prairies, but this was particularly melancholy small-town New England, and to me, Brooke was the center of that. She was the center of all the longing and the loneliness and yearning, and we were lucky to have her.

Just having Stephen King's name in your movie meant that you had a very broad audience appeal, broader than anything I'd ever done. Stephen King movies like *Carrie* were very successful, but then there had been some other movies that were not so successful. I know that Stephen King himself had not been so happy with what had happened to his work when it got to the screen, and he was involved to a certain extent in *The Dead Zone*. He did not write the script, but he did come to a screening, gave me notes and so on, and I was very happy to have his input. I think the movie could have been a much bigger hit than it was. Many people absolutely adore and love that film. I know for a fact that Martin Sheen told me that Bob Dylan was obsessed with the movie.

I had never done anything like that, because I'd never done anything that had taken place in America before. I'd always set my films in Canada, basically. So it had the potential to be much more mainstream because of those things. Because of what it dealt with, because of America, because of the politics and so on. I think there were distribution problems with it, and I began to realize that you have to be very lucky to have a film that realizes its potential. There are so many things that can happen on the way that have nothing to do with the movie—corporate politics, internal struggles in a studio or a distribution company. All of these things were happening at Paramount at the time, and they really, really did interfere with the release of the movie. I think by all rights it should have been my biggest hit, and it was not.

The Fly (1986)

Jeff Goldblum; Geena Davis; John Getz; Joy Boushel; Les Carlson; George Chuvalo; Michael Copeman; David Cronenberg; Carol Lazare; Shawn Hewitt.

I was approached by a man representing Mel Brooks's company, Brooks Films. He came to Toronto to talk to me about doing a remake of the movie *The Fly*. Now, I had not really liked the script that they'd sent me very much. But, it had some wonderful, brilliant rethinking of the original movie, which I'd seen as a kid. We knew at the time that the original was not a great movie. People who think of it as a modern classic are kidding themselves.

It was pretty tacky in some ways. But it did have some stunning moments that everybody remembers.

I resisted for a while, but Mel Brooks is very charming and very persuasive. I had adored Mel Brooks's films, so I was predisposed to being interested in working with him. When they accepted the fact that I felt that I had to rewrite the script completely, they didn't have any problems. We sort of established the parameters of what the film would be. That it would be very horrific. That we would not hold back. That it would be very intense and be very extreme and that I could rewrite it. Then I agreed to do the movie.

I was rebounding from a year of doing rewrites for *Total Recall*. It was a Dino De Laurentiis project, and we had wanted to work together again after *The Dead Zone*. But after a year, it was apparent that I wanted to make a different movie from everybody else who was involved. It was kind of devastating, because I'd really never had a film fall apart that way. Every script that I had written had gotten made into a film. Once again, in my naiveté I thought that this was the way it worked. Little did I know that it's much more the other way around, because you almost never get your script made. So I was out of money and feeling very despondent, but I really wanted to make sure that that wasn't the reason that I was doing *The Fly*. I was really concerned that it not be a kind of rebound love affair that would be a disaster.

I started rewriting the script and really fusing my ideas with the screenwriter's ideas. The two of us had no qualms about sharing the screenwriting credit. I got very excited about the project, and I realized that it would be as much me as anything I could ever do myself. Even though it was a remake of a well-known film. Even though I had not written the original script. Even though I had not generated the project myself. And so, as it turned out, *The Fly* became my biggest hit. It was the number one film in North America for three weeks, and it got great reviews. It's very unusual to have a horror film that's a hit that gets wonderful reviews, even in the *New Yorker*. It was really three people in a room, and it was a story about two eccentric people who fall in love. One of them contracts a hideous, deforming, wasting, fatal disease. The other one watches while that disease takes its course, and she helps him commit suicide, and that's the end of the movie.

Now, it was very clear to me that if you tried to do that as a straight, mainstream kind of drama, you would never have gotten it financed. Much too dark, much too depressing, and yet it was protected by the horror-sci-fi genre. That darkness was on one hand invisible and on the other hand desirable within the genre, and I realized at that point that a lot of the moviemaking that I had done had been protected by the genre label. You know that it was all right to do this stuff if it was just going to be a horror film. But, if you were doing a serious drama, you could never get away with that. It just endeared that category of filmmaking to me even more as I gradually began to realize what it had done for me and other filmmakers as well.

Suddenly the movie is this huge hit. I was in L.A. when it was number one, so I had the experience of walking around L.A. and having studio heads who I had never met come up to me and congratulate me and be all glowing. I had that experience, you know, for what it's worth.

Jeff Goldblum and Geena Davis, who was his girlfriend at the time, got along beautifully well and worked so great together. Very congenial and bright people to work with. I loved the intensity of it, the claustrophobia of it, not having any idea of how well it would work for a big audience, but for me it was working beautifully. I loved the sexuality of it and the sadness of it and the humor. The special effects are always difficult, but it's an understood difficulty. It was difficult to light and difficult to get them to work, but Jeff was so good at acting through the rubber. We had gone to several actors who were very interested in the part but who were intimidated by having to wear fifty pounds of rubber.

As I've done some acting myself, I now realize even more how bodily acting is. How physical it is. In directing, you are disembodied. No one cares if you've got a cold, zits, or herpes, so it doesn't matter as long as you can say "action" and "cut." But to an actor, the body is the main tool that they have to work with. If you cover it up with rubber, then how can you get through all that and through the lens to your audience? That is an actor's concern. Jeff was totally non-intimidated by that. He adored the challenge. That could have been a very difficult aspect of the film, but it really turned out to just be one of the normal pragmatic problems that you have in making a film that has a lot of special effects.

Getting back to Geena for a moment. We were having trouble casting the woman opposite Jeff. I was concerned about physical things because Jeff is very tall. He's about six-foot-five, and it's a real compositional problem if you have an actor who works with him who is, say, four-foot-nine. It's not insurmountable, but nonetheless a problem. Then, just to match Jeff's eccentricity as an actor, the texture that he brings to the film, I needed an actress who could match that and could match his level of acting and his sense of humor. A lot of suggestions had been made about who could play opposite him. I had to audition some actresses I wasn't happy with at all.

I knew that Jeff's girlfriend was Geena Davis, but she was not that well known. She was primarily known for a very funny TV series that she did and also was well known for a couple of scenes in *Tootsie* with Dustin Hoffman. Finally, Jeff got around to saying (and I think he wanted to hold back), "What about Geena Davis, you know, my girlfriend?" I suggested we fly her up and audition her, because I had watched the things that she had been in, and I was starting to feel that she might do it, and she might be perfect for Jeff. And she was tall, and, I have to say, this was an added bonus. She came up, and she was so funny and so great, it was just obvious that she should be in the movie with him. The only problem with the two of them was that they had been together so long and would sing duets together and had sort of this secret kind of humor together. She was like Jeff's sister at the beginning. I mean, she had the same mannerisms and I very often had to tell her to do it the Geena way. She was a very good mimic and, without realizing it, was often doing an imitation of Jeff. That was sort of a strange problem to have.

I'd never worked with actors who had been a couple before, and I knew that there were many possible problems. What happens if they break up in the middle of the movie and so on and so on? But it turned out to be a delight, with only that very minor problem that needed adjusting to make it work.

Determining What Makes a Good Story

George Bernard Shaw said, "Conflict is the essence of drama." No one wants to see a movie where everything is great, and everybody is nice, and everybody just has a great time. I mean, we might want to live like that, although I sometimes wonder if we really do. So, for me, the beginning premise of drama is conflict, which to me only has significance if it's revealing, it it's got metaphorical weight, if it's provocative, and if it's difficult. Does it lead me to explore things that I wouldn't explore if I weren't doing this movie or writing the script? So that sort of takes out the traditional domestic drama away from me in terms of something that I feel very stimulated by. You have to find the socket that you personally have to plug into. I often feel, literally, that I'm walking around with the plug, looking for the socket, you know. Where's the juice, where's the electricity going to come from? Often, you plug into somebody else's socket that works for them, but it doesn't work for you. So, I never tell people what they should do, but I know that it's an individual process in terms of finding those things. That leads me to movies like *Dead Ringers* or *Crash*.

These are things that I find work. It's sort of like hitting on all cylinders instead of just a few. It means you've got a V-12 engine, and all cylinders are firing.

Dead Ringers (1988)

Jeremy Irons; Geneviève Bujold; Heidi von Palleske; Barbara Gordon; Shirley Douglas; Stephen Lack; Nick Nichols; Lynne Cormack; Damir Andrei; Miriam Newhouse.

Dead Ringers began for me with an article I saw in a newspaper—a very small little article whose headline said, "Twin Docs Found Dead In Posh Pad." I'll never forget that. I read the article, and I said, they've got to be kidding. I mean, this is so perfect. Somebody is going to make this into a movie. Then years went by. Many other articles were written about it, including one called "Dead Ringers," which appeared in *Esquire*. A novel appeared, called *Twins*, which was based on the Marcus twins, who were twin gynecologists and who were found dead together in their posh pad from drug overdoses and other things. It was a grotesque and fascinating story. Again, the years went by, and nobody was making this movie, and finally, I thought, I'm going to make this movie. So, the process began, which was maybe a twelve-year process before I found someone who was willing to back this project. (It was Joe Roth and Carol Baum, two producers who have since gone on to great acclaim, Joe Roth as a studio head and Carol Baum as a movie producer.) .

I asked a friend of mine, Norman Snider, to write the screenplay. Obviously, it was very closely based on the material we had on the real twins. However, I didn't want to be bound to have to be biographically correct, because I wanted the freedom to fly off the handle with metaphors and characters that were not real and not have to worry about being bound to the real story. Norman wrote a first draft. I think, ten years later, I wrote a second draft, combining some things of mine with Norman's draft. Ultimately, we got the film financed.

Dead Ringers was a difficult film from a perspective that was new to me, which was the financing aspect. I ended up taking credit as a producer in the film, because I found myself doing things that I'd never done before. At lunch, when, normally, I would take a nap, I was on the phone to Rank Films in England, asking where's the bloody money. The financing of that movie was so complex that I've completely suppressed it. I can't summon it back up. It was like juggling a hundred balls in the air and dropping, constantly dropping, them and filling in with other ones. I was very much involved in trying to get that movie together. There was a moment when we had the sets built, $350,000 worth, and the money disappeared. There was great pressure from the people who owned the studio space that we had the sets in to take those sets down so that they could rent the space. I knew that if we took those sets down, the movie would never happen, because we would have had to add that $350,000 to the next person's budget. So we ended up renting out those sets to commercials and begging people to shoot around us. I think we had parties there just to pay the rent on the studio and to avoid taking the sets down. It was that extreme. Those sets stood for months and months.

I couldn't get an actor. That was the other problem. This was not totally unique. You would think that a serious actor would be interested in playing twins that were very realistically portrayed.

I went to literally thirty of the finest American and Canadian actors, and they all turned it down for all kinds of strange reasons. One couldn't get past the word "gynecology." I mean, no way a macho American actor is going to play a gynecologist. One said that to play these twins would drive him over the edge of madness. You know, one said, I don't have two characters that can exist in my head simultaneously. These are names that you would recognize if I told them to you. They all said no. The first non–North American actor that I approached was Jeremy Irons, who said he was interested. I could have cried. I probably did, with gratitude, just to have a real actor say he was interested in playing this role. I flew to England, and I met with him, and we had a great time. Then I came back, and it looked like he might do it, and then there was no money. The project was going to be postponed. I ended up having to phone him again maybe six months later to try and get him to do it. Of course, he was saying, "Well I've kind of cooled on the idea." My heart was breaking.

I had to fly back to England. I had to seduce him and talk him into doing it again. Then he got excited about it. Finally, the money came together, although it was constantly falling apart while I was shooting. So, this was a movie in which I suddenly had to worry about all the finances. I had no protection like I had with *The Fly* money. So, because of that and because of the difficulty of getting my lead actor, *Dead Ringers* was very, very difficult.

The technology didn't really exist to do the kind of twinning effects that I wanted to do. We actually had to invent some. I've never really been excited to use the latest technology or to say that this movie is lit totally by candlelight or to do every shot with a zoom or with a Steadicam. That's not where I find the excitement. I'm quite happy to just use well-established technology. But in this movie, we actually did have to invent some of our own technology, which then was rented out by Panavision, because they helped us develop the twinning effects that we were doing, like moving shots where Jeremy was talking to Jeremy. We would have to shoot one side and then we'd have to shoot the other side. We were using motion-control cameras, and we needed a playback system that could show us the split and see if it was working. We'd have to move the split as they moved. It's very complex. It would all be done by computer now, but we were just before that era. So, we had to be innovative even in a technological way.

We never doubted that we were making a great movie. Everybody felt that we were making a fantastic movie, and the movie was looking fantastic, too. Jeremy was being incredible, and Geneviève Bujold was always being her amazing, fantastic, emotional self. There was no doubt that we were making a very special movie. We all knew that once it got going. But it was getting the first foot of film rolling through the camera that has never been harder for me than on *Dead Ringers* and it took at least twelve years to accomplish.

Jeremy was suddenly faced with the actor's problem of how to play these twins. They are realistic in that they are very similar to each other, and they're not the good twin and the evil twin. I mean, yes, there's one that's slightly stronger and more confident and one that's not. That is very normal in twin psychology. We had done a lot of research into twinning the twins. I'd seen every movie that had twins in it or twins visual effects. But Jeremy has to do the acting thing, and it's not easy. He started to get a little bit afraid. He made many suggestions about having separate dressing rooms for each character and doing very radically different hairstyles for each character. I said to him we couldn't afford two dressing rooms on the movie, and he couldn't have his hair sort of funny for one twin and funny another way for the other twin. It didn't take him long, though, being the pro that he is, to settle down and find on his own means of doing it and doing it well. He would have to do one half of a scene and then go off and get dressed and come back and do the other half. I had to treat him as two separate actors. I couldn't shoot all of one twin one day and then shoot the other twin another day. We couldn't do it that way. It was too clumsy, too awkward, too time-consuming, and therefore too expensive. Later, he told me some of the ways. With Elliot, he would stand on his heels, and it would give him a quite different posture. With Beverly, he would stand on the balls of his feet, which would give him a kind of slump—

that kind of defeated posture—along with very subtle differences in the hair. He got so good at it, finally, that he would just be one and then the other and then the other and the other, back and forth. Crying as Beverly in one moment and, ten minutes later, arrogant and unsympathetic in the same scene as Elliot. It's a phenomenal acting job beyond what you see on the screen.

When we were doing movie splits—that is, where the camera is moving, and the two twins are moving, talking to each other back and forth—he would record the first dialogue with another actor. When he did the second half, he would actually have an earpiece in his ear, playing back his dialogue from the first part of the performance, because the rhythm had to be exactly right, otherwise the two characters would be talking over each other and not responding. So, he wasn't actually responding to another actor. He wasn't even acting with himself, he was acting with nothing, you know. So difficult to do and so brilliantly done, to the point where people felt that it would be a gimmick film, and three minutes into the movie, that was all completely forgotten. There's no question that the Oscar he won for his next movie (*Reversal of Fortune*) was very much based on the perception of what he did in *Dead Ringers*. Which is why Jeremy thanked me, amongst others, for his Oscar for a movie that I had nothing to do with.

> *I thought to myself, you cannot make a screenplay of* Naked Lunch *unless you are going to make some fifty-million-dollar animated film, because it's a surrealistic film. It's overtly sexual and really graphic in its moral depiction of social horror. How are you going to make a movie about this? But David did.*
>
> Peter Weller—Actor

Naked Lunch (1991)

Peter Weller; Judy Davis; Ian Holm; Julian Sands; Roy Scheider; Monique Mercure; Nicholas Campbell; Michael Zelniker; Robert A. Silverman; Joseph Scorsiani.

One of the literary influences that I had as a young man was William Burroughs. Another was Vladimir Nabokov. I sort of found myself as a budding novelist imitating either Burroughs or Nabokov and sometimes both, which would be a kind of an estranged mutant creature, I must say, as a literary fig-ure. So there is always the desire, then, to somehow fuse with or connect with, in an artistic way, someone who has influenced you as an artist. The desire to make a movie basically out of a book that you loved or that had a big influence on you. To return to that influence and sort of dive to the depths of it and to reveal things about yourself. Why was I attracted to that material in the first place? Burroughs, of course, lived a totally different life from me. I mean, given that we're both North American white males, we couldn't have been more dif-ferent, but something about his writing, aside from its brilliance, was very at-tractive to me. Very liberating, very exhilarating, very dangerous, and I shared that enthusiasm with Jeremy Thomas, who is a producer I met at the Toronto Film Festival. Jeremy said, "You know, I think you should make a movie out of *Naked Lunch.*" I thought that was an insane idea, because *Naked Lunch* is some-thing most people would have considered not suitable for a film for many rea-sons. Burroughs—bringing Burroughs to the screen—what a strange idea.

At some point Jeremy offered to introduce me to Burroughs. So I met Bur-roughs in New York, and I was surprised to find a man who is extremely po-lite and actually rather sweet. He was quite different from his known persona and his exploits in his life. I became very fascinated by him and, gradually, the idea that I should make *Naked Lunch* became inevitable. You know, it wasn't even a decision. At a certain point, I was doing it. I wanted, once again, to establish the rules of engagement with Burroughs. I wanted to use incidents from his real life in the movie. I wanted to use others of his writ-ings, besides just *Naked Lunch*. Not in a literal way but incidences, metaphors, images. Burroughs was totally agreeable to all of that. He was very not-protective of the details of the work. He felt that his life and his work were one thing and, therefore, it was completely legitimate for me to use biographical elements in the movie. He understood that movies were not novels, and that it was going to be a different thing on the screen, and so he was very congenial. Eventually, I found myself making the movie.

On Film Critics

I was doing *M. Butterfly* when a lot of the awards were happening for *Naked Lunch*. So I was happily cocooned in another film project, which is something I like because no matter how many nice things people say about your movies, it's never nice enough. It's never completely right. I don't want to sound like a curmudgeon or an ungrateful filmmaker, but I have a very strange relationship with film criticism in general and with film criticism of my own movies in particular. If it's bad, I hate it, and if it's good, it's not good in the right way. It's so rare that you get a critique of your film that you feel is accurate and so revealing. It has happened once or twice, but it's more often the case that even the good reviews make you sick to your stomach because they're so wrong, even when they're saying good things. You are grateful for the good things because in marketing terms it's good, and in terms of word of mouth it's good. You're happy that somebody saw the movie and liked it enough to say something positive, but if I could avoid ever reading criticism of my movies, I would be a happy person, even though you can't avoid it because you have to market your film. You have to promote your film.

If you don't read reviews, people will tell you what the reviews were, as is happening even in this particular interview. So the good part of it is that you take all praise with huge grains of salt. I've never had the problem of ego inflation because of good reviews or good response to a film. I'm always suspicious of it. I always have qualms about it. It's not what makes me feel good about my moviemaking. That's probably the way it should be, frankly. I've had the experience of having a great review for one movie and having the same critic completely destroy the next film. Then you feel personally betrayed. You know, people say, don't take it personally. Well, of course you take it personally. You're making the films personally, and an attack on those films has to be received personally. There's no way to avoid it. You meet film critics socially. They want to be your friends, even though they've given you negative reviews, and to me that's very perverse. That's very strange. There's something unhealthy, unreal, and inhuman about it. It's an odd relationship then that I have with film critics, never mind the criticism. So, it's not my favorite aspect of filmmaking.

M. Butterfly (1993)

Jeremy Irons; John Lone; Barbara Sukowa; Ian Richardson; Annabel Leventon; Shizuko Hoshi; Richard McMillan; Vernon Dobtcheff.

I was beginning to realize that it was taking me, like, three years between movies—especially if I was going to write them myself or generate the project myself. I thought that put sort of a very specific and small number on my future as a filmmaker. So I thought I would try the traditional thing, which is to sort of ask my agent to tell me what's around, knowing me and knowing my tastes and what I might be interested in. I told him to look for a script that I wouldn't write and perhaps a script that I couldn't write. If I was going to do this, I was not really going to want to do a sci-fi or a horror film, something that was similar that I've done in the past or what people think I might do. I was looking for something that would be fresh and be a challenge in a different way.

Ultimately, my agent told me about the *M. Butterfly* project. I'd heard of *M. Butterfly*, because it was a very successful play about a French diplomat who had fallen in love with a Chinese woman who turned out to be a man. That sort of reminded me of how I had discovered the *Dead Ringer* twins—the same kind of intriguing newspaper article, although, of course, somebody else had discovered it and had made it into a play. So I agreed to read it and then found myself in a very interesting position for me, which was that here I was, interested in a script that nobody else was interested in me for. In other words, there was a list of directors who were being considered, and I wasn't on that list because I was not anybody's idea of somebody who could direct a movie based on an award-winning play. So I had to win that prize. I had to defeat the other filmmakers and take over that project myself.

Finally, I was on the list of potential directors, and I had to meet the producer, David Geffen. I met the writer of the play, David Henry Hwang, who had also written the screenplay. I gradually managed to convince everybody that I was the one who should direct that movie. It was, of course, David Geffen's project. He had been involved in getting the play to happen, and so he was the one who was going to do the movie for Warner Bros. But it was basically always a David Geffen production. That was all very interesting for me, because it was a game I hadn't played before. I'd never been in that position before. Suddenly I found myself making the movie. Part of the attraction of me directing, I think, was that everybody thought Jeremy Irons would be terrific casting for the lead in the movie. Since I had a relationship with Jeremy and so on and so on, this made me attractive as the director.

Sure enough, Jeremy was interested in the project and interested in working with me again, but he'd already turned it down. He had seen the script and he'd seen the play. He wasn't particularly crazy about the play or his understanding of what the movie might be. I had already started to rewrite the script. Not in the normal sense that I had done with *The Fly*, but just shortening it. I felt it was too long, so David Hwang and I collaborated on it. He did his own rewrites based on what I had talked about and our agreement that the movie would be a different creature than the play. David was very willing to do that. He was very interested in experimenting and trying something else. He knew that we weren't going to try to do a direct translation of the play to the screen, which I think is always an illusion anyway. It's always a transformation, whether it's a book or a play. The medium is so different that it's going to change and twist everything out of shape. It's better if you accept that and go into it with strength rather than to be surprised later. So there were many things different about the movie than with the play, and in the end I was very happy with the movie.

It was a fantastic experience making the movie, because it was really the first time that I'd shot anything outside of Canada. Quite a few scenes were shot in China and in Budapest, which was standing in for Paris. Many people shoot in Budapest, which was originally designed to be a mini-Paris. It's much cheaper to shoot there for all kinds of reasons. So, many people shoot in Budapest as a stand-in for Paris. And the shoot in China was fantastic. I'd never had to move an entire production with all the crew and all the logistics and all the actors to another country. Especially a country as far away and as different from Canada as China was. And yet it was a glorious experience shooting there. I was the only person who got fat there. Everybody else found the food a little difficult to take. It's not what people think of as Chinese food in North America. But I put on twenty pounds there.

It was very hot and sultry in Beijing, in the eighties all the time, shooting at night in the streets. People would come out in the middle of the night to watch us. I found myself with a little Chinese girl sitting on my lap watching the monitor as I was shooting scenes. There was such a feeling of urgent change and a sense of danger, of course, because the Tiananmen Square incident had already happened. We were worried that when the anniversary of that event came along that perhaps there would be trouble. But the Chinese were wonderful, and all the people that we met were fantastic. The Chinese crew that we worked with was just terrific. It was an incredible challenge and a sort of archetypal movie experience shooting on such an exotic location. There are filmmakers who will only shoot on exotic locations. They want danger and they want to shoot in the Amazon, you know. That's not where the excitement came from for me, and yet it was incredibly stimulating and a wonderful experience. A huge part of what M. Butterfly was for me was shooting in China.

I think, if the film had been made three or even five years before it was, that it would have been quite a substantial success critically and possibly financially as well. While I was editing the film, I saw a little movie called *The Crying Game*. I said to people at Warner Bros., I think we're in big trouble because this movie, *The Crying Game,* has some elements that are so similar to some of the things that *M. Butterfly* deals with. I think it's really going to take the wind out of our sails, and I wonder what we can do about it. Well, they were not the slightest bit worried—they'd say, "Well, it's just a little film and nobody's going to notice it" and so on and so on. But I knew. I actually stood up in front of a gathering at the Directors Guild of Canada when presenting *M. Butterfly,* and I expressed again my concerns about *The Crying Game*. Sure enough, *The Crying Game* turned out to be a huge success. It won Oscars and made a lot of money. People actually thought of *M. Butterfly* as kind of the Chinese *Crying Game,* only not as good. I knew from the beginning that we were really doing something else because we understood from the outset that John Lone, who plays the female character in *M. Butterfly,* is not a woman. It's not structured the same as *The Crying Game,* where you have an actor who's never been seen before who really is a wonderful female impersonator, and that's really what the strength of that other movie is.

Then there's that surprise at the end. We weren't trying to fool anybody. The whole idea of *M. Butterfly* was the lead character knows that he's fallen in love with a man, but he can't accept that. He can't be homosexual, so he's making him be a woman. The two of them together are creating this new reality, both sexual and emotional, which is to me a more complex and interesting thing than what *The Crying Game* was doing, although it was very successful doing its own particular thing. But, the two things were confused, and the movies were reviewed together, to the disadvantage of *M. Butterfly*. Then, to make matters worse, a movie called *Farewell, My Concubine*, a Chinese movie about homosexuality in a Peking opera, came out at the same time, and it was also very successful and won prizes at Cannes and so on. Timing is everything, isn't it, except you can never control it.

David's interests always lay in exploring extremities, particularly where sex and violence are concerned. He doesn't hold himself back from the audience as a filmmaker. He is relentlessly interested in extremities of behavior and exploring the moral stance and exploring the moral code.

Holly Hunter—Actress

Crash (1996)

James Spader; Holly Hunter; Elias Koteas; Deborah Unger;
Rosanna Arquette; Peter MacNeill; Yolande Julian; Cheryl Swarts.

I have to blame Jeremy Thomas once again for *Crash*. Jeremy is, of course, best known for *The Last Emperor*, which won many, many Oscars, including one for himself. It is certainly his most successful film as a producer. He and I were both attracted to extreme writing and groundbreaking writing, and he asked me if I'd ever read J. G. Ballard's book *Crash*. I hadn't read it, and in fact I hadn't read any of Ballard, although I'd heard many things about him and his writing. He said, "You know, I really think you should do *Crash*." So I started to read the book, and I got about halfway through, and I had to put it down. I think I didn't pick it back up for another six months because it was so disturbing in so many ways. I thought, I can't make this. I could never make this into a movie. Then I picked it back up and finished reading it, still thinking I could not make this into a movie. Jeremy came to Toronto for something and asked me what I thought about *Crash*. It was then that I told him that I thought I really wanted to make the movie.

That was another instance where, somehow, that damn book had just gotten its hooks, like a little parasite, into my intestines and took up residence there and demanded to be dealt with. I still couldn't say that I loved the book, but I knew I had to make the movie. Then I met Ballard, who turned out to be a delight. He's a wonderful, sweet guy—raised his children himself when his wife died very young and is just a lovely guy. We had some great conversations together, and he was hugely supportive of the movie from beginning to end. When I sent him the script, he actually came to Cannes to be part of the festival. He was a fierce warrior in defending the movie when it was attacked.

The movie was a terrific experience to make. It was physically difficult, because it was shot at night, and it was cold. But other than that we had a talented, great group of actors who were very devoted to doing the movie. It was the same feeling as with *Naked Lunch* and *Dead Ringers*—we were making something unique and something special and something mind-blowing and very worthwhile. We all loved each other—the actors, the crew, everybody.

From the beginning, *Crash* was a controversial project even before I wrote the script, which I avoided writing for a long time. When I started to write it, I thought that I would have to adapt it the way I did with *Naked Lunch*, that I'd have to involve other things and perhaps biographical elements and so on. But, in fact, the script almost wrote itself. It happened very easily and it was a true distillation of the book. Quite different from what happened with *Naked Lunch*. My agent at CAA was horrified. He begged me not to do it. He said it would destroy my career, and he asked me to do *The Juror* with Demi Moore and Alec Baldwin instead. He thought that was the right career move. Shortly thereafter, I got another agent and another agency. My agent was a lovely guy and was only hoping for the best for me, but he didn't get it. He didn't understand that *Crash* was a career move for me because that's the career I wanted. As it turned out, *Crash* undoubtedly did do better things for my career than *The Juror* would have done. That film was a flop of a movie in the end.

For over a year, in the English press, I started to feel like Princess Diana. I understood firsthand the hideousness of the English press. There was not a day that went by that there wasn't some mention of *Crash*. They called it the *Sex and Wrecks* and many other little wonderful epitaphs. Not a day went by that it wasn't mentioned in some radio show, television show, or newspaper article. I really got an education there. It was always defended by all of my cast and Ballard himself. In fact, the film was the first Canadian film to ever be the number-one movie in France as well as several other countries.

For me, if a film is working, it's a complex, organic creature with a life of its own, and it's not anything like a message. It's a much more complex animal than that. It's not a letter. It's not an agenda. It's not a proposal. It's a philosophical endeavor. It's a philosophical exploration. For me a film is a way I conduct my philosophical investigations. It's how I delve into my own responses to life and to society and to technology and to every aspect of life. It's almost not relevant to say, "What's the point of a movie?," or "What's the meaning of the movie?," in a very simple way. Because I found that if you do it right, without trying to be evasive, a movie will mean an infinite number of things to many, many people. You hope it affects an infinite number of people over time. Of course, *Crash* is about sex and death, and it's about the erotic element, but it is also about mortality. It is about how sexuality is transforming, as I think it is right now.

Sex is not what it used to be, you know. We don't need sex anymore. We can create babies without sex. So, what is sex? It's up for grabs. It's up for reinterpretation. I mean, sex has always been many other things. It's always had a political element and a power element and a social element and an aesthetic element. Now, we're in a position where sex is demanding to be reinvented. So, if you combine all of those things, you start to get the feel for what *Crash* might be about. I have to say that the movie is not the same as the book. Ballard and I have had wonderful moments sitting in front of an audience disagreeing about what the book is about and what the movie is about. For Ballard, *Crash* was a cautionary tale about the dehumanizing aspects of technology and the strange position that put sexuality in. I'd say to him that I didn't think that was correct. I think that his impulses in writing it preceded the idea that it was a cautionary tale. I think labeling it as a cautionary tale is a defensive position to take. I think a lot of people who see the movie also accept that there's something strangely attractive while also repulsive about the lives that these people are trying to create for themselves. So *Crash* is also an existential move because it discusses the necessity to invent your own reality. That reality is not a given thing. It's something that must be created and invented, and a lot of energy has to be expended sustaining the new reality that you've built. I think everybody does create his or her own version of sexuality or reality.

The script for *Crash* was very explicit and very direct. There wasn't anything hidden. Any actor who is drawn to that material had to know what he was going to get into. We offered the lead to James Spader, and he was very excited about it, and he wanted to know who the other actors were going to be. He said, "After all, I'm going to have sex with all of them, aren't I?" I knew he was the right guy because there's no point in dragging an actor kicking and screaming into a movie like *Crash* if he or she is inhibited, repressed, shy about their body, or whatever. They all had to know what they were getting into. They all had to be prepared to traumatize themselves if need be.

They all had different reactions to the different scenes. But, basically, my technique was an extension of what I do anyway, which is to be completely open and honest with my actors about what's going on. When I first started directing actors, actors were sort of the enemy, because they were the unpredictable creatures. They were the bulls in the china shop. I didn't really understand where they had to come from to do what they did. They didn't understand me either. They didn't know that I didn't have the time or money to allow them to get up from the chair and go to the window and say the line there. I couldn't afford to light the window, you know. I didn't realize that you could tell this to an actor. That you could say, "I can't afford that. Can we find some other wonderful way to do this line of dialogue with you still sitting in the chair, because that's all I can afford to do." When I gradually realized that actors could be your collaborators on many levels and that you didn't have to hide things from them and manipulate them, that made it possible for me to do movies like *Crash*, where I had monitors everywhere for the actors to look at. I would show them the takes that we had just done so that they could see what they looked like if that's what they were worried about. I mean, I've always been very open about letting actors look at monitors.

Some directors are very protective of that. They don't want that. They're worried that an actor will get into some kind of neurotic loop where he tries to change his performance because he doesn't like what he's seeing. I let anybody see anything they wanted. So I made a little protective shell around the set for them and for me, too, where we could do things. We could try things. We could be silly. We could be embarrassing, and we would all know what we were doing. That's really how I handled it, and it worked beautifully.

> *The films that he creates stay with you forever, you know. They're just extremely his own, and they make you feel things. It's all coming out of his imagination, which is just powerful and extraordinary.*
>
> Jennifer Jason Leigh—Actress

eXistenZ (1999)

Jennifer Jason Leigh; Jude Law; Willem Dafoe; Ian Holm; Don McKellar; Callum Keith Rennie; Sarah Polley; Christopher Eccleston; Kris Lemche.

eXistenZ come out of a fascination with technology, which a lot of people have seen as one of my major themes, sort of paranoia about technology, but I don't feel that at all. I feel the playfulness and the curiosity, and, yes, of course, there's always a sense of danger about something new that is powerful, and that includes technology. But I don't consider myself really a paranoid person at all.

Ironically enough, *eXistenZ*, which in some ways is very much about technology, has very little technology in it. For a sci-fi movie about game-playing, it is very devoid of high-tech stuff, and that really comes back to my love of the body as metaphor. All of the technology in *eXistenZ* is organic; it's physical, and it's human, and people plug things right into their spines. The machinery and the game-playing modules are all organic. They're actually animals themselves. And yet the film on many levels is a discussion of technology, the way that we absorb all technology into our bodies. I mean, we use our technology for sex. You're not going to go far before you're filming sex, before you're filming a naked woman if you're a man. It happens with videotapes. It happens with any new technology. We immediately incorporate technology into our sexuality and into our bodies and sometimes in a very physical way and sometimes in a more difficult-to-see, metaphorical way. But we do it, nonetheless, and that is why the movie *eXistenZ* looks the way it does, which is to say, extremely low-tech. In fact, one of the rules of engagement for this movie was that the tone of the movie would be developed through subtraction. There were no television sets, no computers, no computer screens, no telephones, no running shoes, no suits and ties. I mean, just subtraction, and a lot of the things that we were subtracting were technological things that you would expect to see in a sci-fi movie. It's always a struggle when you're doing a sci-fi movie dealing with people's expectations of what sci-fi will be. What movies have just been popular? What has been in the past, the retro things? And so I tried to sort of destroy all that by subtracting things from the movie that you would expect to find there.

eXistenZ started as an MGM project, and it would have been my first true studio movie. *The Fly* was really Brooks Films for Fox, but not a Fox film. *M. Butterfly* was with Geffen Films for Warner Bros., and even *The Dead Zone* was Dino De Laurentiis for Paramount. There have always been other entities between the studio and me. MGM was looking to resuscitate itself, and my former agent, Mike Marcus, had become head of MGM. He suggested we work together. I proposed to him a science fiction movie about a game artist who was on the run for her life because she was being condemned for what she'd created. Mike was very interested, and I wrote a draft of the screenplay. In fact, I wrote a couple of drafts.

They gave me notes in the normal studio manner. The notes were very intelligent, actually, but some of them I really couldn't comply with because their purpose was to really push me in the direction of making a movie that I didn't want to make. So I incorporated in subsequent drafts those suggestions that I thought would help me make the movie I wanted to make. Unfortunately, we reached a point where they wanted me to go further with their ideas. But then I would be making their film, not mine, so why would I agree to do that? I just did not use what I felt didn't work and that was the end of it.

Suddenly, I wasn't making a studio movie again because it was picked up by Alliance, the Canadian company that had made *Crash* with me. I was making what in effect was an independent movie again. That's really the genesis of *eXistenZ*, because that script that I had, which, as I say, did incorporate some of the MGM suggestions, was the script that we ended up shooting.

It's very difficult for me to get any perspective at all in terms of my other movies and how people perceive movies in general. Some people have felt that *eXistenZ* was like a sequel or remake of *Videodrome*. Certainly, I can see the connection between the two movies. There's no doubt about that.

One of the things that I would love to be able to do would be able to walk into my own movie never having seen it before and knowing nothing about it. Now, perhaps, when I get a bit more senile, I will be able to do that. I'm hoping it will be a great experience. Of course, you could look at your movies and hate them all, so that would be the bad part. It's impossible, really, to see your movies objectively. I must say that someone who grew up on *Videodrome* probably wouldn't find *eXistenZ* that bizarre. The truth is that a lot of my movies have had influences, I'm happy to say, and so there's a whole generation of filmgoers who've grown up on my movies and have been influenced by my movies. It really depends on who's doing the talking.

To Create or Not to Create Something Original

I used to be very rigid and rigorous and arrogant about feeling that you must write your own stuff and it must be original. But I had such a good experience with *The Dead Zone* that I began to realize that it's a very difficult philosophical question to decide where you end and the rest of the world begins. I mean, really, you can't really quite find that point. You know, you absorb the world, and the world absorbs you. I feel that, in a sense, that nothing is original and in another sense everything is original. So you find that point within yourself where you don't feel that you're compromising anything—that you feel that you are mixing your blood with the project, and then it is you. It's as much you as your children are you. It doesn't have to be something that you thought of, that you woke up thinking you wrote yourself, that no one else had any input into. Only each individual can decide whether he's selling out, collaborating, betraying his own talent, or whatever. No one else can tell you; only you can tell yourself.

An Acting Job Now and Then

When I was starting making underground films, my friends and I would all act in each other's movies because we couldn't afford anybody else, and we were a very congenial group. I had had some experience acting and had done a little bit of theater. I did high school plays and things like that. But, I never really did any sort of movie acting until John Landis asked me to play a role in *Into the Night*. Now, John loves Hollywood and loves the whole process of moviemaking and movie history, and it just always has given him a real kick to put directors in his movies as actors. He does this all the time. I agreed to do it because it meant I would fly down to L.A. and I would actually act in a real movie. That is to say, a Hollywood movie. The film starred Michelle Pfeiffer and Jeff Goldblum. John asked me to play a small role but with some complex dialogue, playing the role of Jeff Goldblum's boss. I thought I had prepared, and when I stood up to say my lines, suddenly, my heart was beating so hard that I couldn't hear. I couldn't hear John say "action" because I was about to faint, I think. I was so nervous because it wasn't an underground film and there were all these paid professionals expecting me to be a paid professional and not to blow my lines. But I had a lot of fun doing it.

I was terrified and was very fascinated about standing ten feet away from where I normally stand as a director, because that distance might as well have been miles. You're on the same set, you're in the same context, but what you're doing is so completely different from what you do as a director. I thought, I kind of like this. It really is a challenge. It's not easy, and maybe I'll learn something valuable from it. So, whenever anybody offered me a chance to act, I would do it. Most notable, I think, was Clive Barker, who asked me to play the third lead in *Nightbreed*. I actually spent three months on location in London acting in that film. That was very difficult, because I had not at that time even shot a movie on location, never mind had to live as an actor on location. It's a very strange life to be out of your context and be waiting by the phone. You can't do a lot of things, because they might need you on the set. I had to learn how to be an actor. I spent most of my time writing the script for *Naked Lunch* when I was in London. I found that I got very weird and introverted, and I was eating out of cans because I didn't have the energy to make food and I was alone. I've not really ever done another role outside of Toronto. The thing is, I don't really want to do that. I'm just not serious enough about being a professional actor to do that. But I have done quite a few roles in Toronto, where I could go home to my own house at night and sleep. It does a couple of things for me. The first thing is it makes you more sympathetic to actors in the sense that you understand what an actor needs and what an actor does and where an actor comes from. I understood what it is to sit there in front of the camera and to do that stuff. It's very different from imagining what it would be like. The other thing is that, when I'm between movies—and it tends to take me two or three years between movies—I feel not like a filmmaker anymore. If I'm being a writer, I feel disconnected from the film process entirely. To act, to be able to go onto a set, see crew members I know and actors that I've worked with before, I suddenly feel more like a part of the filmmaking community. It's important for me to sustain that feeling that I am a filmmaker.

He has a vision that's very much his own. He will not shy away from it ever, whether people like it or not, and I admire that.

Brooke Adams—Actress

The Wonderful World of Filmmaking

The wonderful thing about moviemaking is that it has all these sequences that flow into each other but are very unlike each other. Writing is the first thing and is the primal thing. Then you go into preproduction, and that's a different thing. You go into casting, and that's a different thing. Shooting is its own little world. Editing is almost like writing in that it's sort of contemplative, and it's not quite the time pressure normally that you have, except you have other people around, and there's technology involved. And then, the sound mix, which is perhaps the least understood aspect of filmmaking. All of those elements are critically important, and they all have different tones and modes. You're in a completely different mode for each of them. I love them all, and they are all in their own way equally important, because you can make or break a film at any one of those stages.

Writing is difficult because it's the primal act. It is the leap from nothing to something. It is always the most difficult for me, anyway. While I'm making a movie, I'm a moviemaker, and then I have to relearn how to be a writer. I literally have to remember how to type because I don't even type while I'm making a film. Believe me, it's very hard to get back into being a writer. I'd say that for me writing is the hardest because it's the loneliest job of all. You only have yourself to generate it, whereas when you're making a movie there are always other people around. You can absorb their energy. There's pleasure and pain involved in every segment of moviemaking. Perhaps that's what makes it so attractive.

David Cronenberg Filmography

Transfer (1966)
From the Drain (1967)
Stereo (1969)
Crimes of the Future (1970)
Tourettes (TV, 1971)
Letter from Michelangelo (TV, 1971)
Jim Ritchie Sculptor (TV, 1971)
Winter Garden (TV, 1972)
Scarborough Bluffs (TV, 1972)
Lakeshore (TV, 1972)
In the Dirt (TV, 1972)
Fort York (TV, 1972)
Don Valley (TV, 1972)
Programme X, TV Series, (TV series,
episode "Secret Weapons," 1972)
Shivers (1975)
Peep Show (TV series, episode "The Lie Chair," 1976)
Teleplay (TV series, episode "The Italian Machine," 1976)
Rabid (1977)
Fast Company (1979)
The Brood (1979)
Scanners (1981)
Videodrome (1983)

Note: Since this interview took place, Cronenberg has directed *Camera* (2001) and *Spider* (2002).

The Dead Zone (1983)
The Fly (1986)
Friday the 13th (TV Series, episode "Faith Healer," 1987)
Dead Ringers (1988)
Scales of Justice (TV Series, episode "Regina vs. Logan," 1990)
Naked Lunch (1991)
M. Butterfly (1993)
Crash (1996)
eXistenZ (1999)
Camera (2000)
Spider (2002)

Awards and Nominations

Amsterdam Fantastic Film Festival
eXistenZ, Silver Scream Award, 1999

Avoriaz Fantastic Film Festival
Dead Ringers, Grand Prize, 1989
The Dead Zone, Critics Award, 1984
The Dead Zone, Grand Prize (nominated), 1984

Berlin International Film Festival
eXistenZ, Outstanding Artistic Achievement, Silver Berlin Bear, 1999
eXistenZ, Golden Berlin Bear (nominated), 1999
Naked Lunch, Golden Berlin Bear (nominated), 1992

Boston Society of Film Critics Awards
Naked Lunch, Best Screenplay, 1991

Brussels International Festival of Fantasy Film
Videodrome, Best Science-Fiction Film (tied with *Bloodbath at the House of Death*), 1984

Cannes Film Festival

Spider, Golden Palm (nominated), 2002
Crash, Jury Special Prize, 1996
Crash, Golden Palm (nominated), 1996

Catalonian International Film Festival

eXistenZ, Best Film (nominated), 1999
The Brood, Prize of the International Critics' Jury—Special Mention, Best
    Casting for Feature Film, Comedy, 1981
Rabid, Medalla Sitges en Plata de Ley—Best Screenplay, 1977
Shivers, Medalla Sitges en Oro de Ley—Best Director, 1975

FantaFestival

The Dead Zone, Audience Award, 1984
The Dead Zone, Best Film, 1984

Fantasporto

Naked Lunch, Best Film, International Fantasy Film Award (nominated),
    1992
Dead Ringers, Best Film, International Fantasy Film Award (nominated),
    1989
The Fly, Best Film, International Fantasy Film Award (nominated), 1987
Scanners, Best Film, International Fantasy Film Award, 1981

Genie Awards

Camera, Best Live Action Short Drama (nominated), 2002
eXistenZ, Best Motion Picture (nomination shared with Robert Lantos and
    Andras Hamori), 2000
Crash, Achievement in Direction, 1996
Crash, Adapted Screenplay, 1996
Crash, Golden Reel Award (shared with Robert Lantos and Jeremy
    Thomas), 1996
Crash, Best Motion Picture (nominated), 1996
Naked Lunch, Achievement in Direction, 1992
Dead Ringers, Achievement in Direction, 1988
Dead Ringers, Achievement in Direction (shared with Norman Snider),
    1989
Dead Ringers, Best Motion Picture (shared with Marc Boyman), 1989

Videodrome, Achievement in Direction (tied with Bob Clark III, *A Christmas Story*), 1984

Videodrome, Original Screenplay (nominated), 1984

Scanners, Achievement in Direction (nominated), 1982

Scanners, Best Original Screenplay (nominated), 1982

Los Angeles Film Critics Association Awards

Dead Ringers, Best Director, 1988

National Society of Film Critics Awards

Naked Lunch, Best Director, 1992

Naked Lunch, Best Screenplay, 1992

New York Film Critics Circle Awards

Naked Lunch, Best Screenplay, 1991

The Films of Mike Figgis

Born in Carlisle, England, Figgis moved to Nairobi, Kenya, when he was a baby. He lived there until his family relocated to Newcastle, in the north of England, when he was eight. As a teenager, he started playing trumpet and guitar with various rock 'n' roll bands, one of which was the R&B group Gas Board, featuring British pop star Brian Ferry.

Moving to London, Figgis studied music for three years and began playing with The People Show. The People Band made one album for Transatlantic Records, this being produced by Rolling Stones drummer Charlie Watts.

In 1980, Figgis left The People Show to concentrate on writing and directing theater, as well as to break into film. He formed his own theater company, The Mike Figgis Group, and began creating multimedia productions, which included extensive use of film. Some of his earliest projects, including *Redheugh 1980*, *Slow Fade,* and *Animals in the City*, won awards for their innovative blend of live action with music and film. This first caught the eye of England's Channel 4, which then financed Figgis's first film, *The House*, which starred Stephen Rea.

Stormy Monday was Figgis's next film, which marked his emergence into full-length features. Figgis wrote, directed, and scored the movie that was wet in Newcastle's steamy jazz club world and boasted an impressive cast, including Melanie Griffith, Tommy Lee Jones, and Sting.

As many "downs" as "ups" have marked Figgis's career. His penchant for making the films he wants to make his way are well known, and he will fight for his vision every time. The result is that his films are never boring and always challenging.

> *Mike is a great director because he has a musical sensibility. You know, someone once said that all art aspires to the condition of music and the*

*music has rhythm, it has shape. If a film has rhythm and shape, then
you have a successful film. I think Mike understands that intrinsically.*

Sting—Singer-Actor

The Conversation

My father's family, the Figgis family, is Irish colonial. They moved out to
Nairobi in the early part of the century because my father and his brother and
sister were all born in Nairobi. My father was a pilot during the war, and
then, after the war, he studied law for, I think, probably about six weeks or
something, or maybe a little longer. But like a lot of people who had been in
the war, he was overly mature at the age of twenty-four or twenty-five, and
he was a heavy drinker like a lot of people from that kind of background. We
eventually moved on to Kenya. So my memory of it is a pretty decadent
memory—a lot of drinking and a lot of parties and a lot of happy-valley kind
of behavior, as well as a lot of hysteria. In Africa it was also the time of the
Mau Mau, the African Independence Movement, and everybody was armed
to the teeth and was very paranoid. When I first started making films, I was
intrigued by the idea of making a film about that period of being a child in
Africa. I then became so disgusted by the research about how badly we'd behaved there in terms of just stealing land and all the rest of it that I decided
not to make a film about it. But one of the interesting statistics was that during the entire Mau Mau crisis, as a child, I had a sense that it was this huge
bloodbath, that thousands of white colonial people were being killed. In fact,
it was something like twelve. There was a large number of fatalities through
marital squabbles. Quite a lot of people shot each other, I think.

I remember spending a lot of time with my sister alone in a huge house
with a huge garden. There were incidents where my brother was attacked by
a hooded cobra, which spat in his eye. I remember the cobra very clearly. We
spent a lot of time by ourselves. And I remember. By the time we moved back
to the north of England, my English was almost my second language. England seemed to me like a very cold and inhospitable and exotic place, you
know. I remember seeing snow for the first time when I was about seven or
eight years old.

Initially, we lived in Carlisle, and then we moved from Carlisle to New-castle, which are the two towns in the thinnest part of Great Britain—in fact, the two opposite ends of what was called the Roman Wall, or Adrian's Wall. Carlisle is the on the west side, and Newcastle is on the east side. They're only sixteen miles apart.

When I was a child, I guess one of the biggest influences on me was the fact that my father was, to put it mildly, obsessed with jazz. He had this in-credible collection of jazz records—ten-inch and twelve-inch LPs. Unlike a lot of children, I didn't really have much contact with him. You know, when you want to impress your parents, you choose the thing that you think they might want you to be, and, as it happens, I adore jazz. It really has become part of my life. But I know that initially it was through wanting to have some-thing in common with my father. He played the piano. He wasn't a trained musician, but he played jazz piano and improvised. That was really my first experience with music.

When I was eleven years old at school in Newcastle, they were giving out the instruments, and I fought hard to get the trumpet. My idols were Louis Armstrong and people like Henry "Red" Allan. That's all I wanted to do, was play the trumpet, and I played in the school band. I used to put jazz records on and play along with them, and it was a very positive way for me to have a relationship with my father. So he and I played together and improvised to-gether. He played the piano, and I played the trumpet. One of the things I re-ally regret is that I remember he had a very early eight-track tape recorder. I know that he recorded the first time we played together. I remember it very clearly, and it was a huge moment in my life. Somewhere along the way, the tape was either thrown out or lost, and I've never been able to find it. I'd love to find it and hear it again. My father was only fifty-four when he died, and I would say that, for most of our relationship together, one of the few ways that we used to communicate was just by talking about jazz.

Once a Musician, Always a Musician

Because I studied music, if I had to give myself a job description, I would probably still describe myself as a musician. The music continues to be re-ally important to me in the way that I make films. I think I realize now that I am informed musically about structure. With something like *Time Code*, for example, it's really a piece of music, but it just happens to be a film. It's structured like a string quartet and so on. The great news about this new digital revolution is that now the equipment is so much smaller and so much more accessible that it's possible for me now to do the entire score for the film in my office, you know. With a good microphone and a good computer recording system, I can do it all on a system called ProTools.

I have a friendship with and am associated with a number of really good jazz musicians, and some younger musicians who also cross over into contemporary music. My son, who is a DJ and a musician, works with me, and I incorporate some of his ideas as well. And that's what I love about the way films are made now. There isn't a huge division technically between the different crafts of filmmaking, like cinematography, sound, music, and editing. The systems sort of married all that together in a good way.

My career has involved quite a bit of luck. One could define luck by having the ability to be in the right place at the right time with the right idea. A lot of it has to do with having the ability to observe what's going on around you and say, well, here's an opportunity. I made my first film around the time that Channel 4 in Great Britain opened this new and very innovative film channel that was actually looking for new talent. Now, the idea that people were looking for new talent in Britain was revolutionary in itself. Up until that point, the BBC and ITV and the traditional routes to becoming a filmmaker were very closed and very difficult to get into unless you belonged to a certain kind of group of people, which I didn't. My background had been theater. But, going back to the beginning, I trained as a musician. This was towards the end of the 1960s, where in London it was a very, very open artistic community. There was a lot of crossover.

I joined an avant-garde jazz band called The People Band, a free music ensemble. They worked with an avant-garde theater group called The People Show. I started doing performances that involved music and drama and some improvisation. The musicians and the performers had a falling out. I mean, they radically fell out, violently fell out, by which time I found myself being more sympathetic in a way to the performance side of things. As a musician, I was intrigued by the possibilities of the music within that dramatic context, so I chose to stay with the performers. I left the music ensemble and I became the musician in this theater group. Then there was sort of a Mickey Rooney–Judy Garland fight within that group. Two of the performers just walked out before a very, very important gig at the Royal Court Theater in London. And it was, like, "Mike, you know, you're on stage tonight." I was pushed out onto the stage at the Royal Court Theater in front of Mick Jagger and all kinds of trendy media types, you know. But within five minutes I was hooked. I thought to myself, this is what I want to do. I want to be an actor. I want to be a performer. I want to stand in front of a lot of people and make a fool of myself. I just loved it.

Segueing Into Film

For the next ten years, I stayed as a member of this ensemble, which toured the world—America, South America, Poland, Yugoslavia, and Scandinavia. During these performance-art pieces, these improvised theater pieces, I played music, and I was also an actor, and through that I became quite naturally interested in film and how film was really just an extension of that whole tradition of performance.

I then tried to become a film student at the National Film School. My interviewing panel consisted of David Puttnam, Ozzie Morris, and other luminaries of the British film establishment, and I had a terrible interview, and we clashed almost immediately. There was a very deep suspicion of anybody coming from the theater who wanted to make films, and I probably was pretty rude right back at them. I'd sent them a show reel, which was like silent, Super-8 home movies. I also sent them a tape I'd made of a collection of very impressionist sounds and things that I'd made over a ten-year period, because I was also a sound man, and I used to make performance tapes. Well, the board ran the film and the tape together at the same time as if they were connected to each other. They'd done that to save time. I found that to be the most insulting thing that ever happened to me; that they couldn't take the time or have the courtesy to at least listen to them separately. I was pissed off with them about that, and, on top of that, I had a terrible interview, and I didn't get into the film school. Now, I was even more determined to make a film. I got a theater in Amsterdam to give me £5,000 to make my first 16-mm, forty-minute film with sound, which I incorporated into a theater performance piece. I had the same live performers on stage as in the film. I also had live music as well as music in the film.

Eventually, I left The People Show, and I formed my own company, The Mike Figgis Group. I did three very, very complicated mixed-media pieces, which incorporated film, slide shows, live music, taped music performance, opera, and all kinds of things. It was incredibly ambitious, much more ambitious than any film I've ever made, I have to say. And it was technically more challenging than any film I've ever made as a pure film. These pieces were quite successful, and I toured them around Europe to all the prestigious theater festivals. I used that time also to develop and learn as much as I could about filmmaking. Because of budget constraints, I was working on 16 mm and not even Super-16 mm. And I was shooting a lot of Super-8 mm stuff as well, along with some tentative forays into video. But I was not impressed by video at that point at all. It was pretty cumbersome, and I love celluloid. Like any aspiring filmmaker, it really was a love affair and a desire to get down and dirty with celluloid. I loved the idea of cutting film, and I really was in love with the idea of what you could do with film. I have to say I was happy to be making films in that context. I was very happy. I always used to say that for me the greatest cinema event would be to be watching a thriller in a cinema and for a spotlight to come up in the middle of the audience and have Boris Karloff sitting three rows in front of you. He turns and smiles at you, and then the lights go out again. What's the Woody Allen film I'm trying to think of, where the guy comes off the screen? Mia Farrow is the waitress who was in love with Jeff Daniels. It'll come to me in about ten minutes. [The film referred to here is *The Purple Rose of Cairo*.] That was great, the ability to cross the line of the suspension of disbelief. People lost the ability to differentiate between what really took place in reality and what took place on the screen, because it was that relationship between the subconscious and reality. Between dream state and waking state. To me that's what's interesting about film; it does allow the audience to go into a dream state. That period for me was experimental, where I was discovering things every time I tried something or discovered something new about film. That was very important to me.

The House (TV, 1984)

Diana Hardcastle; Nigel Hawthorne; Ingrid Pitt; Stephen Rea; Dudley Sutton

The first film I made as an official film was called *The House,* and it was for Channel 4 in London. They were looking to give people who'd never made a film before an opportunity to get in there. So I went in with a little film that I'd made for the theater on the basis that with a little bit more money I could film the parts that had been theater. I could sort of cobble together a one-hour film by using the existing footage and adding some more footage. It turns out they were underwhelmed by this concept and this idea but were sort of vaguely intrigued by what I was doing. I remember in the meeting, David Rose, who was the chief film commissioner for Channel 4 at the time, said, "You know, we're commissioning new work. Do you have any new ideas?" And I said, "Well, actually, yes, I do. I do have an idea for a film," which was a complete lie. I had an idea but never thought of it in the terms of a pure film. But I was also, you know, not stupid. I knew that this was an opportunity and that this is what luck is. Someone asks you a question like that, you'd better have an answer.

My advice to any young filmmakers is always have a notebook handy. Always have an idea that doesn't have to be graphic, just enough of a description to whet the appetite of someone who may or may not be in a position to commission work. So, he said, "Do you have anything cooking?" I said, "Yes, I do," and I pitched this idea, which was simply that England, as we recognize it as a map image, was not surrounded by water but was surrounded by landmass. We recognize the shape of England, but it's surrounded on its northeastern border by Lithuania, Estonia, Latvia, Prussia, and Russia, making it completely landlocked. The opening sequence was a cartoon of the map. As you pulled back, you started to see all the other countries. And it said, "1880." In fact, we had just invaded Latvia. Latvia had signed a pact with Russia, which had counterinvaded, and we were about to be completely overrun by Russian soldiers now linked to Latvian soldiers. That drama took place on New Year's Eve in a country house on the border between the north of England and Latvia. "And," I said, "that's the idea." And they said, "Okay. We'll commission it." Then I had the problem of writing it, you know.

I then wrote this kind of surrealistic piece about the Brits as a landlocked nation. And, again, through good fortune, I managed to get a cast, which included Stephen Rea and Nigel Hawthorne and some pretty well-known British character actors. I had the immense good fortune to have as my cinematographer the great Roger Deakins. I ended up with this pretty heavy-duty group of people around me, and that was my first film, shot standard 16-mm film. It was ravishingly beautiful to look at, with very, very ambitious locations. The exteriors were shot in the snow, very near where I had spent part of my teenage years growing up in the north of England.

For the interior of the house, I was looking for a partially wrecked, classically beautiful country house. I went into a photo exhibition one day and saw these beautiful photographs of what I thought I was looking for. I rang up the photographer and said, "You know, there's this house that you photographed." And he said, "Yes, but this is really the most overpho-tographed house in Great Britain, you know. Every rock video in the world has been shot there. But there is a house in the north of London that I think no one knows about, and it was designed by a famous architect whose name was Nash. It's one of his first houses in London, and it's in a very derelict state." It turned out to be about five minutes from where I lived. I went to look at it, and it was absolutely perfect. By a strange twist of fate, it reemerged in my life again when General Augusto Pinochet was arrested in London. He was receiving treatment in a private hospital, which turned out to be the same house that went from being derelict after I used it to becoming a private hospital. So I then had this incredible location for my first film, exactly what I needed.

I need to go back a bit. When we finally got the financing together for *The House,* I went to Walter Donahue, one of the editors at Channel 4, and told him I needed to have a script written, and he said, "Why do you need a writer?" I said, "Because we need a script." And he said, "Well, why didn't you write it yourself?" And I said, "Oh, I just wouldn't know how to write a script." And he said, "Well, why don't you just have a go at it. Try and write the script, and if it's terrible, we'll find you a writer. But, you know, you seem to have a clear idea of what the film was about, so try putting it down on paper." So I did, and no one said it was terrible, and we just proceeded. But I remember being daunted by the idea of attempting to write a script. I re-member having to borrow scripts from other people just to see how they were laid out. How do you write a script? What's the secret language and what does *cut to* and *fade to* mean? In reality it takes about an hour to learn that stuff, but I didn't know that then. But these things can be very daunting.

What I did was lay it out as a theater production, where I tried out all the ideas on stage using Super-8 mm projections and all kinds of things like that. I brought the people from Channel 4 to see it as a kind of work in progress that eventually would become the film. Then I realized that I had shot my-self in the foot because when it came to budgeting the film, they said, "Well, so you're just going to videotape your theater performance?" And I said, "No, no, no. This is a blueprint. This is not it, you know." But unfortunately, or fortunately, the sort of work in progress, what I considered to be the blue-print, became a very, very successful theater show called *Slow Fade.* It got the best reviews I'd ever had in the theater and was a sellout when it came on in London at the ICA Theater. It was a sellout in Amsterdam. It was only through the intervention of Jeremy Isaacs, who was a great influential head of Channel 4 at that time, and later on the head of the National Opera, who finally said, "I'll give them the money." So we went ahead and finally got enough of a budget to shoot it on film.

So that got the show on the road, as they say. And then I found this beautiful location, and I found these terrific actors. And everything was just perfect, and I was in heaven. I was going to be a real film director, and we went into preproduction. I felt confident and competent, and then came the first day of the shoot, and I turned up on the set; I was very, very happy. There was this buzz of activity all around me. We had created a nineteenth-century sort of fantasy England. Everybody was in the most amazing costumes, and the wardrobe was incredible. Couldn't have been more perfect, until the awful moment where everybody sort of drifted into the first location.

The producer wisely had decided that one of the first scenes we would shoot was the most complicated dialogue scene in the entire film. It involved probably ten, twelve actors, all talking, all in a dining room with a blazing log fire with a beautiful snowscape outside. And then someone said, "So, what do you want first?" My mind went completely white, and all rational thought vanished, and the only thing I experienced was intense fear and paranoia. I suddenly looked around, and everybody in the room was just staring intently at me with a sort of quizzical look on their face. I could not think of a single thing to say, because, in truth, I didn't know what to say. I suppose I assumed that by osmosis or something, something marvelous would happen. It was the first realization that a director's job is to tell people to do things that they will respect, but instead I went totally blank, and I don't know how long that moment lasted. I do recall it felt like an eternity but, in reality, was probably thirty seconds or a minute at most. I literally couldn't think of anything to say. Then, a tremendously kind act took place from Nigel Hawthorne, who, incidentally, is one of the nicest people on the planet. I think he sensed exactly what was going on. And he said, "Well, I mean, I've got the first line of dialogue. I assume that I'll just sort of walk in. I'll warm my back on the fire and then Stephen's got the next line. You'll probably be covering this in a wide shot to start off with, and we'll do the close coverage later on." He talked through what was going to happen, allowing me the respite, because people were looking at him while my brain regathered its thoughts, and I said, "Yes. That'll work really well. And then we'll go into some coverage." I had very little idea what coverage was, you know.

So we started preparing, and once the wheels started turning and we shot our first take, I was okay again. I had my confidence back, or I had my brain back. Gradually, over the next couple of days, I started to build up some confidence in my own ability to lead that many people, and by the end of the shoot, I was fine. I was confident. I sort of knew what I was doing. I then did a storyboard of every single line in the film, similar to what I had been doing in the theater, but that moment on that first day of that film I'll never forget. I now have the courage to say, "I don't know." There are times when I made films when someone would say, "What do you think?" And I'll go, "You know, I haven't a clue."

When we did *Miss Julie,* we did a scene that just didn't work. And I just said, "You know, I have no idea why this isn't working, and I don't know what the alternative is. So, I think we should stop and have a cup of coffee and let's think about this." I've arrived at a point when it's okay to say you don't know. But, by God, that first moment was terrifying. I'll never forget it.

The film got a lot of attention, ironically, from David Puttnam, who I had these huge fights with when I tried to become a student. We both tactfully pretended that we'd never met each other before. He said, "You know, that's a wonderful film you made. I would like to commission a feature film. Do you have an idea?" and, of course, I now knew that you always have an idea, and I immediately said, "Yes."

> *He's an original thinker. He's an original guy. Most of his ideas are new,*
> *and he believes in the value of originality and not merely the illusion*
> *of originality, but the actual thing.*
>
> Tommy Lee Jones—Actor

Stormy Monday (1988)

Melanie Griffith; Tommy Lee Jones; Sting;
Sean Bean; James Cosmo; Mark Long; Brian Lewis.

I had written a short called *Mindless Violence,* which I tried to get the British Film Institute to pay for. It's a twelve minute short, which took place in this very exotic postindustrial location in Newcastle, where I'd grown up. It's a great, Americanesque sort of city with shipyards and a lot of heavy industry. I never managed to get the finance together for that. So I said, "Yes, I've got this idea for a gangster movie in the north of England." The only other film that's ever been made there, which has become a cult film, is *Get Carter*, with Michael Caine, which was remade by Sylvester Stallone. The original with Caine is really an incredibly good genre gangster movie. But nobody else had ever shot in Newcastle, and I knew it backwards, of course, because I had grown up there. So [Puttnam] said, "Okay. I'll commission a treatment." That was the end of that. I mean, I never saw David Puttnam again. I did four or five different treatments. They were never read. I never got any feedback. I never got any money. I went back to teaching, and I was kind of in despair over really getting a real film made.

One day, I was in the middle of London, and I was in the back of a Dumpster, because I was teaching film to students. I noticed this Dumpster was full of old reel-to-reel tapes, and they all seemed virtually new. It was outside a TV commercial's house, so they'd obviously just thrown out stuff that had been used once. I thought, well, this is a criminal act to throw this out. I backed my car up to the Dumpster, and I actually got in the Dumpster, and I was unloading all the tapes. Suddenly, I heard someone say, "Mike. Hello." I looked up, and it was this guy Nigel, who had produced my first film, *The House*. He said, "What are you up to? How are things?" I said, "Well, I got this one idea." To cut a long story short, he said, "Well, let me read it," so I sent it to him. He rang me up the next day and said, "Look. I think it's a good idea, but there are far too many ideas in this." I had fallen into what I call the first-film syndrome, where you're paranoid and you think you might never, ever, ever, ever be asked to make a film again in your life. So every idea you've ever had you cram into the script. There were at least twenty subplots. "And," he said, "if you take out the three particularly annoying subplots, I think there's a movie there. And I'll produce it for you." And that became *Stormy Monday*, my first full-length feature film.

There's something great about the practicality of a particular situation and how do you deal with it. It becomes part of the craft of what you do to the extent that you become fiercely proud about your participation in the structure of something. One of the things that really distressed me when I came into filmmaking was how lax and laid back it was. People didn't really take responsibility for anything outside of their fairly narrow responsibilities, you know. When you start making films you are usually working with a low budget, you know. If you are capable of writing and you are capable of doing the music, you're a pretty good bargain. So, if you say, "You know, well, Mike Figgis, he wrote, directed, and scored *Stormy Monday*," it's great for me. But the practical reason for all of that was that I was one-stop shopping along with a one-stop fee as well. Those elements that normally are quite expensive within the budget become free, basically. They say, "Okay, we'll pay you this much, and we'll happily take all of your services."

I guess if you make a mess of any one of those things, the next time you make a film, people say, "Well, I only like him as a director." I remember the first review I read for *Stormy Monday*. I was in the Hyatt Hotel on Sunset Boulevard, in L.A. By accident, I saw the review in *Variety,* and it was a stinker. It said I was an ex-promo director, which I wasn't. I was an ex-rock musician, which I wasn't. It just said this guy should stick to music. The scores were reasonably good. Cinematography's good. The rest sucks. That was my first ever legit review of a film. I was staying on, I think, the ninth floor, and I remember looking out the balcony thinking, maybe I should jump. I'm thinking, is this the end of my career?

As for the leads in *Stormy Monday*, well, to put it bluntly, they are now very, very respected, and they have big names. Very expensive names, to put it even more bluntly. At the time, Melanie Griffith had done *Something Wild,* and she got great reviews. She hadn't done *Working Girl* yet and hadn't become a huge star. Tommy Lee Jones had done brilliant work in *The Executioner's Song* but, again, wasn't a huge star. Within the acting community there're always those actors that one really admires. As a fledgling filmmaker, it comes as a great shock when you come to America for the first time to start casting. I was amazed that these people will come and work with you if they like the script. The thing that I found most flattering was that they were prepared to trust a first-time director. It never ceased to amaze me that they were willing to go to the north of England, to an industrial town, and make a film with a first-time director. I was so impressed by their faith, I guess.

My favorite story about *Stormy Monday* is that one of the reviews called it film noir, the haunting loneliness of those wet, windswept streets. The reality is I'd written the street scenes as being throbbing with life and neon signs. I think I had just seen *Blade Runner,* and I thought, that's how I wanted my streets to look. And then Nigel—the famous Nigel who found me in the Dumpster—at a preproduction meeting said, "Mike, there is a problem with the budget, so you have a tough choice to make. You can either get rid of the throbbing streets that are throbbing with life or we can just lose another section of the film entirely. But you can't afford both." So the throbbing streets took a dive, and we had these windswept, hauntingly lonely streets instead. But I never wanted hauntingly lonely. I wanted throbbing, you know. So when you translate hauntingly lonely and you put it with a saxophone in a minor key in a jazz idiom and you get Roger Deakins to shoot beautiful, dark photography, it suddenly becomes film noir, you know. Melanie was wearing a low-cut dress—that was noir, too.

I think the truth is, when you're making a film or you're doing a piece of music, you just have an idea, and you think, what is the best way to serve this idea? You know you don't set out to do a film noir kind of piece. It just turned out that way.

> *It was interesting. A British director was going to direct a film on police corruption with the LAPD. I wondered what was going to happen here. And sure enough, Mike did more than most American directors would have done.*
>
> William Baldwin—Actor

Internal Affairs (1990)

Richard Gere; Andy Garcia; Nancy Travis; Laurie Metcalf;
Richard Bradford; William Baldwin; Michael Beach; Katherine Borowitz;
Faye Grant; John Kapelos; Xander Berkeley; John Capodice.

One of the things I do admire about the studio system in America is that they do have openness about new talent. So I suddenly found myself in Los Angeles being invited to all kinds of studios to discuss my film [*Stormy Monday*] and for people to offer scripts and so on. I briefly got involved in a film called *The Hot Spot,* with a dream cast. I was about to make the film with Sam Shepard, Uma Thurman, and Anne Archer when it all collapsed for reasons of incompetence. It had nothing to do with the actors. I'd done a script for that, which I did a reading of in the National Film Theater about two years ago. I was surprised by how good it was, and I regret not having made that film. Dennis Hopper directed a version of it with Don Johnson, which was very different from the way I would have done it. During that period of trying to kind of keep that going, I got hold of a script called *Internal Affairs,* written by Henry Bean. I was horrified, to say the least, by the blood and the body count in the film. But there was something about the structure that I thought was unique and very, very disturbing.

*I can't remember Mike ever making a choice that was based on what
the audience was going to think or feel. We both felt we should take the
film as far as we could, and we did.*

                                                    Richard Gere—Actor

I went in for a meeting and met the producer, Frank Mancuso Jr., at Paramount Pictures, and I decided to go for it. I think I ended up having six,
seven, eight meetings over a period of months and months and months. I
went back to England, and then I came back again. I thought I had gotten the
film, and then I didn't get the film. Andy Garcia was already attached, and I
started pushing the idea of Richard Gere. That met with a lot of resistance at
the time. After a long struggle I did secure the right to make the film and was
approved by the studio and suddenly found myself working on my first
American film. But you have to understand that as a Brit it's a very different
world here in L.A. There's something very, very exciting on the one hand
about being a director on a film in Los Angeles with all these Americans running around and cop cars and all that. The film was about the LAPD and cor-
ruption. Shooting it was a slightly out-of-body experience, I have to say.

I remember shooting this action sequence in a warehouse with real SWAT
teams shooting fake bullets and cars skidding around corners and sparks flying off. People were getting shot and fake blood was flying around. We had
two second-unit directors, and I was basically told to just let them shoot it
because these guys supposedly knew about this stuff and how to shoot it. I
remember watching them shooting it, thinking this doesn't actually look very
good. I mean, two cars, when they skid around corners always had sparks
flying off them. And surely, if they fired that many bullets, everybody would
be dead. And every time anyone had a gun, they were shooting. It was sort
of orgasm for these special-effects guys, you know. I remember, as we were
wrapping that particular section of the film, the ground was littered with car-
tridge cases from these automatic weapons.

Then we looked at the footage, and the producer and I had the same
thought; it wasn't very good. We had to reshoot the whole thing. This time, I
directed it and said, "You know, don't fire your guns so many times." I tried to
work on the acting more because the first time we'd shot it the whole scene
was like a bad TV sequence where it was just about the action and there was
no emotion at all. Actually, in the finished film, it's a very strong scene. It's a
very good scene for both Andy Garcia and for Laurie Metcalf, and I think it
adds the tension. I remember getting in the stunt car with this amazing stunt

man and driving around and skidding around this course with a camera in there to see the point of view. But you realize that regardless of what the scene is in the film, you have to get in there and direct it. You can't let somebody else direct a second of your movie if you're really serious about making films.

I have always believed that the director's job is to cast well. Once you've cast your parts well, then you have to marry yourself to the actor, particularly with a difficult performance like the portrayal of the character of Dennis Peck. You really have to push and push and push. If you have an actor who is psychologically as complex as Richard Gere, it's a gift. He is a performer that has the ability to really play the two characters in an interesting way, to be believably likeable and attractive and then terrifying in terms of his ability to be very evil. Thankfully, Richard and I got on very well, and he became a friend. I really do admire him as an actor. We worked together on another film that wasn't quite so successful. He's a very old-fashioned actor in some ways. He can deliver that amazing charm, as he did in *Pretty Woman*. But I also think he's one of the most complex actors around, and I think he's somewhat underused, to be honest. I worked with him on *Internal Affairs* at a time when he was down on his luck. He was down on his status and perhaps wasn't being given the respect that I think he deserves. So it was a good, healthy time for us to be working together, because I was an up-and-coming director, and he was an up-and-coming actor, actually, with not a lot to lose, you know. I think he was very well prepared to really go on a journey with that character.

Let me get back to Richard Gere for a moment. When we were shooting the film, one of the tricky things was dealing with the evil side of Richard's character. You know Richard is a Buddhist and so had a very specific approach, which was, "I'm an actor, so I'll do this. But it's acting and this is not me." This is something that comes up a lot with actors, where each actor has a different approach, a method, or a nonmethod, and so on. I liked working with Richard because he could utterly concentrate on what he was doing. And then I'd say, "Cut," and a couple minutes later, we could talk about something else. Other actors are much more intense, and I, too, sometimes find it quite difficult in a sense of, you know, it's a job. I like being able to contain and compartmentalize this function that we do and so on.

We were shooting a scene downtown L.A., in a really tough neighborhood. We had two actual drive-by shootings where our cops basically said, "Just hit the ground." It was a scary atmosphere, which was appropriate. When I watch the film now, I recognize certain scenes that were shot in certain areas of town that are very real to me—particularly, the scene where

Richard has to ultimately kill his partner played by Billy Baldwin. The two of them stop to investigate a suspicious car. Richard knows damn well that there's an assassin in the car. Billy opens the door, and he gets horrifically shot and blown onto the police car, and then the guy who shot him drives away. It's a very complicated scene. Then Richard discovers, to his horror, that Billy Baldwin is still alive. By this time, he's already called for a support team to come in. He can't let Billy Baldwin live, so he has to kill him. This is a helluva scene for an actor to do, because you got to play all kinds of emotions. In my opinion, it is one of the best scenes in the film, because it's so disturbing. But by the end of it, in a bizarre kind of way, I feel sorry for him because he's in hell. He really is in hell by the end of this scene. The look on his face is one of a man in hell. The scene is actually quite Shakespearean.

In this same scene, Richard actually kills one of the assassins as part of his plan. Richard has to shoot him through the head. We rehearsed the scene. I remember saying to the stunt man, who was also an actor, "You know, when Richard shoots you, I'm sorry you can't really have a death scene. He shot you through the head, so you just drop like a stone." The stunt guy wanted to do a bit of a performance, you know. I've seen enough footage of stuff in Vietnam and all the rest of it to know that death is often very undramatic. Particularly when the bullet goes right through the middle of the head. So we were rehearsing the scene one more time, and Richard put the gun to this guy's head. I said, "Action," and Richard shot him, and the guy was kind of making a lot of movement and I went, "Oh, cut," and I'm thinking to myself, "I thought I told you not to overact." Then suddenly there is that awful moment when you realize that things are not quite right on the set. I go over and the guy is actually hurt. What happened is that the gun was a recoil action and automatic. Richard's been told by the experts to put the gun to the man's temple and pull the trigger and has basically cold-cocked him because the gun is recoiled and the metal has basically banged the guy in the head. It knocked him out, and now he's on the floor. Now, that's the most vulnerable part of your skull and you can actually kill someone with not a lot of pressure with a piece of metal by doing that very thing.

Richard was so upset he went to trailer and said, "I'm not gonna work anymore. This is absolutely outrageous. I'm an actor. We pretend to do these things. We don't actually do them. I almost killed this guy and this, this happened because of advice that was given to me that was incorrect, and we can't fool around on this level. Human life is too precious." One of the trickiest things I've had to do was to go into Richard's trailer and convince him to come out and finish the scene, because in my heart I agreed with everything he said. I thought it was an outrageous mistake, too. Why do we have experts on the film if the result is that we hurt someone when it could be avoided? It added to the scene a kind of—not that I'm proud of this—but it added a kind of level to this scene, which makes it even more disturbing when I watch it and remember what happened.

> *He has a point of view that's very much shaped by his experiences in his life and what his training is and what his sensibilities are. That's what makes him so unique.*
>
> Andy Garcia—Actor

I was also knocked out on the film. I did a cameo, and the stunt guy said, "Andy Garcia is going to throw you. He's going to shove you and you're going fall over. But don't worry about where you're going. Just let your body go and we'll be there and we'll catch you." They were dressed up as guests in this restaurant. So I said, "Okay. I'll just go for it," and I did. Andy pushed me really hard. The next thing I remember is opening my eyes and seeing everybody standing over me just saying, "Are you all right? Are you all right?" He pushed me straight into a concrete pillar and knocked me out and the scene is in the film.

Women & Men 2:
In Love There Are No Rules (TV, 1991)

Matt Dillon; Kyra Sedgwick; Ray Liotta; Andie MacDowell; Scott Glenn; Juliette Binoche.

That was a nice idea by HBO. It was a chance to do a short film that doesn't necessarily take three years of your life to do. This story was set in Paris, and I was basically told by HBO that this was sort of a director's medium. There's not a lot of money for the director, but you get to make the film that you

---

Women & Men 2 is comprised of three short stories directed by Mike Figgis, Robert Breslo, and Walter Bernstein. Figgis directed the segment titled "Mara."

want to make. HBO will respect the filmmaker, trust me, blah, blah, blah. So I agreed to do it, and I wrote the script. It was an adaptation of a Henry Miller short story from *Quiet Days in Clichy*. The original story was called "Mara," which was what we ended up calling ours. It was a story about a prostitute that bumps into Henry Miller, and it was a sweet story. I went to Paris and I started casting. It was like coming to America the first time—I got to meet all these amazing European actresses. I met with a number of wonderful actresses, one of whom was Juliette Binoche. Within about five minutes of talking with her, I thought, my, this is an amazing actor. I want her to do the part, and so she did it. Scott Glenn agreed to play Henry Miller. Jean-Francois Rabin was the cinematographer. He's the guy that had filmed *Betty Blue*. He is a fantastic cinematographer. We shot it all on the streets in Paris at night with a French crew. Had wine with our meal and all that, and it was the quintessentially romantic film experience.

I cut the film myself, which was a nice experience. And I scored it myself. I was very influenced by the music in this wonderful movie *Lift of the Scaffold*, which Miles Davis had done the soundtrack for in the 1950s. To me it's one of the seminal soundtracks. It's basically just improvised blues trumpet. So I did a little homage to that and did a kind of blues trumpet and created a kind of film noir kind of soundtrack. I flew on the Concorde to New York to show them the first cut. I took notes and went back and recut. Then they came over; they saw it again, and they loved it. They signed off, basically, and I gave them the movie.

A couple weeks later, I got a phone call from the producer saying, "You know what? We've taken your music off the film and recut it." And I said, "Well, then take my name off the film, too." I was then persuaded to leave my name on. I saw the film on television a couple years later and was very distressed to see how it had been changed. The score and the music were appalling, and I was just really hurt, because I had done it really as an act of love, and I had been told that this was a filmmaker's affair. The money was lousy to begin with, but I didn't care. I got to work with Juliette Binoche and got to make a nice little half-hour film. But I was really upset by the treatment I received. To this day, I'm shocked. But I have my cut on tape, and it's better than their cut, and I know that. I say that with no false modesty: it is better than theirs is. I was better at making the film than they were. I'm a filmmaker.

Life has a wonderful way of being a cycle that sort of pays things back. Years later, when I did *Leaving Las Vegas*, I got a very charming letter from the same producer, and he said, "You know, I loved your film. And I loved everything about it. The performances were great. I really loved the music." So, I wrote back to him and said, "I was delighted to hear from you, and it was particularly charming of you to say that you liked the music. I wondered if you were aware of the fact that that same music was the music you threw off the HBO movie, and I just recycled it note-for-note. Just took the same piece of music and put it on *Leaving Las Vegas.*" I never heard from him again, you know.

Liebestraum (1991)

Kevin Anderson; Pamela Gidley; Bill Pullman;
Kim Novak; Graham Beckel; Zach Grenier; Thomas Kopache.

I think *Liebestraum* was the most ambitious film I ever made. It was my third feature, my fourth film, and was done very much on the strength of the success of *Internal Affairs.* It went through funny stages, because I suddenly became very high profile for about ten minutes after *Internal Affairs* came out. That film got great reviews, and, from word of mouth, it got fantastic box-office response. I got messages from Sean Penn and people like that saying that it was an incredible film. People simply loved the film. People came up to me in restaurants. I've never had this experience in my life before. They just want to say to hello. And it could be people like agent Mike Ovitz or Michael Douglas, you know. I was kind of blown away by this.

So I'd written this film script called *Liebestraum,* and I actually had written the basic story in one night. It literally was a dark and stormy night. I was in a very, very isolated cottage on the Atlantic coast of southern England, and it was a dark and stormy night, and I was writing in my notebook. I wrote a kind of ghost story, and that became the basis for *Liebestraum.* It was about two affairs, a generation apart, and the mother that's never met her son before. I remember I was in therapy for a period just before I made *Liebestraum,* and I gave my therapist the script on my last visit. She wrote me a letter afterwards saying, "I think you should still be in therapy, you know. I think you've got more stuff to talk about. Please come back."

The film suddenly got a high profile. People started reading it, and they loved the script. It was very sexy and dark. Madonna was gonna do it for a while. All kinds of people were going to do it for a while. MGM finally picked the script up and gave me a fair amount of freedom. I shot the film in upstate New York with a relatively unknown female lead and male lead. But I had Kim Novak in the film, which was the thing that seemed to interest people the most when the film came out. The film was a complete disaster in terms of its economics, and got appalling reviews, and we got murdered at the box office. We had a limited release in Belgium, England, and the States, I think. It went straight to video in most places, if it went to video at all. It has become something of a cult film to the extent that somebody in the London paper the *Evening Standard* said they thought it was one of the ten best films of all time. So, you see, certain people loved it. It had its world premier last year in Italy, and I went. It was a strange experience.

I got a phone call saying, "Would you like to meet Kim Novak?" from the William Morris office. And I said, "Sure." I met her and thought she was an amazing woman. Her agent had given her the script, and she had read it and said, "I really want to play this part." So I said, "Okay." I mean, I met lots of other incredible actresses, too, including Mary Tyler Moore and Raquel Welch. But Kim Novak really wanted to do it. She stuck in my mind. I thought she was a very interesting person, and so I agreed to make the film with her. I don't know if I realized quite the amount of strength that I was going to need to make the film and to deal with Kim Novak, too, who is an incredible person, but she's so strong and so strong-willed. She has not spoken to me since the film came out. I don't think she liked the film.

I was forced to take out one of the scenes, and she was angry with me for that. She actually went into print to badmouth me. She wrote a letter to MGM saying, "You know, I'm the star of this film. I'm ahead of Mike Figgis. So, let's face it. You should fire him, put my scenes back in the film. That's your only hope of this film ever being a success." She may have been right, you know. But certainly, dear Kim, it wasn't my idea to take your scene out in the first place. It was forced upon me.

The film was released in America in a very, very truncated form. They took out the key scene of the film, which actually is the only scene in the film that would explain to an audience what the film was about. Unfortunately, it was a very, very important scene. It was a kind of sexually confrontational scene and it was a long scene. It's an entire reel of the film, and they just took the entire reel out. The film makes absolutely no sense at all without that scene.

But again, you know, someone said to me the other day, "You know, you make a film, it may not be a success when you make it. But it still exists as a film." Which means that through video, or DVD or whatever, people can revisit the film at some point. I find that very, very comforting. I mean, people come up to me and say, "You know, I finally saw *Liebestraum* on tape or on cable the other night, and I loved it." I'm sure a lot of people also hated it, and they presumably don't tell me. I loved the fact that these things that you work on, unlike theater, continue to have a life long, long after you finish them.

Mr. Jones (1993)

Richard Gere; Lena Olin; Anne Bancroft; Tom Irwin; Delroy Lindo; Bruce Altman; Lauren Tom; Lisa Malkiewicz; Thomas Kopache; Peter Jurasik.

It's a little-known fact that I did, in fact, write *Mr. Jones*. There was a certain point in the preproduction that I became aware of the nonsense that was going on about the script and the committees that were supposed to be involved in getting the best script. I mean, the classic cliché about studio film-making is the phrase, "Well, hey, we're all making the same movie, right?" Never was their a bigger lie than "Hey, we're making the same movie." I got very frustrated and I was very naïve. At a certain point, it was determined there were all these problems with the script. By then, I think, we had moved on to our fourth writer, and they were paying these writers a fortune. I suddenly thought, this seems silly because, you know, I'm a writer. I've now spent a month or two months thinking about this material. I've spoken to everybody about it. I seem to have assimilated all of the desires of everybody.

So I went out and bought a computer and bought one of those scriptwriting programs. I had never used one before. I rewrote the entire script from page 1 to page 102 over a weekend. I just locked myself in and rewrote everything and handed it in at the beginning of the week. I made ten copies and sent one to every executive and to the actors and said, "What do you think?" I was met by a deafening silence. Then, over the weekend I tried desperately to ring all the people I'd given the script to and just got answering machines and literally couldn't make verbal contact with a single person. The weekend was over, and we went back to work, and I couldn't get a response out of anybody. It was the weirdest thing. It's almost like, here I am telling you this story, but it's almost like a dream, like something that really didn't happen, but it did. The script was never mentioned again, like it never happened at all. Understand, I wasn't asking for any money. I didn't want to suddenly be the writer. I just wanted to fix the script. I've still got the script and it's really not a bad draft. It did address a lot of the problems, which subsequently are still issues in the finished film. But my writing a draft seemed to create a terror in people. So what we did was pretend that I'd never written the script and then we moved on to another five or six writers and proceeded to try and write our way out of trouble with the film.

It's a very tricky film. It's about manic depression. The problems with the film are best summed up by jumping way forward a year or two later, when the film was previewed and one of the producers came in and said, "Well, it's clear from the previews that the audience loved Richard Gere as a manic but they hate him as a depressive. So, why don't we just cut out all of the stuff that deals with depression? It'll be a shorter film, but let's make a film about manic. Because as a manic, he's terribly attractive." I mean, I heard things on that film that normally you think only are associated with people like Louie B. Mayer or whoever. "It's not the film you make today that's important. It's the film you make tomorrow." "Take a look at the trailer and you'll see the kind of movie you're supposed to be making," and so on and so forth.

I made the film with a great cast that included Richard Gere, Lena Olin, and Anne Bancroft. I have on tape—and I managed to steal a copy of this, but it is my right as a director to do that—of the first cut of the film. It's not a perfect film, but it contains stunning performances by Richard Gere. I mean he was absolutely stunning. And then it was butchered. This film took two-and-a-quarter years to get completed. We did reshoot after reshoot, until finally I was replaced on the film. One of my British colleagues, and I say that sarcastically, offered his very, very expensive services to reshoot the ending of the film. We cut the film, and then it was also then rescored with a new music track. I was also the original composer on the film.

I have never seen the finished product. I saw a version of it, and all the way through, I'd look at a scene and go, "My God." The studio tried desperately to make Richard Gere cute and attractive and to get as far away from the reality of what depression is and what suicide is. The whole point was about how manic depression is very closely related to suicidal tendencies. A lot of manic depressives commit suicide, and it's a very, very common disease, and it's a very important issue. It proved that Hollywood just shouldn't bother with important issues unless it's going to deal with them in a realistic way. I have a real problem when something as important as manic depression is emasculated and turned into a kind of love story. I mean, please, why bother making a film about manic depression in the first place? Why don't you just make another goofy love story? There's no shortage of goofy love stories. They seem to grow on trees in California. That was *Mr. Jones,* and it kind of finished me with the studios for a long time. I just didn't want to go there again.

The Browning Version (1994)

Albert Finney; Greta Scacchi; Matthew Modine; Julian Sands; Michael Gambon; Ben Silverstone; James Sturgess; Joe Beattie; Mark Bolton; Tom Havelock.

I'd been pretty beaten up by *Mr. Jones.* I really was humiliated, insulted, and very abused, in particular by Ray Stark, who was one of the producers on the film. He was a Hollywood legend, as they say. He and I engaged horns, and it was a battle that I was always going to lose. Sure enough, I felt very beaten up afterwards and was really wondering what to do next and where to go with my career. Ridley Scott approached me some years earlier and offered me *Thelma and Louise*, which he wanted to produce at that point and wanted me to direct. I wanted to do *Liebestraum,* so I declined the offer. Then he approached me again with *The Browning Version*, which I had seen almost by chance on cable, the original version of the film, which is exquisite and starred Michael Redgrave.

I read the script, and it was a good piece of writing and a very good adaptation. It was set in England, which I liked the idea of. And it helped that Ridley was a director that I respected. My career was going down the tubes, you know, and it was a work offer that I couldn't refuse. But I got beaten up a bit when it came to doing the deal. They said, "Well, you know, his status has fallen. We're not going to pay him this much money, and he can't have this privilege and he can't have that privilege. And, you know, we're doing him the favor." The one thing that really peeved me was when they said, "Well, we don't know if we can trust him financially because, you know, *Mr. Jones* went so far over budget." That really pissed me off because I'm an incredibly financially responsible director and producer. The budget problems on *Mr. Jones* had nothing to do with me. They were to do with the studio's insistence on all that reshooting. But you know, at a certain point in your career, you have got to learn humility, and you sort of keep quiet and say, "Okay. Well, I'll accept this."

I had contracted as being the director-composer on this film. One of the reasons I wanted to do it was because of one of my favorite actors in the world, and that is Albert Finney. It was finally the opportunity to work with that genius that allowed me to say yes to this project. We had an idyllic summer shooting the film in the most beautiful part of England. It's a strong piece of drama, and I thought Albert was incredible.

I delivered the film. I know that Ridley didn't like the film, and he made no bones about it when he saw it. He didn't like Finney's performance. He didn't like the way I directed it. So I kind of felt I was back in a very familiar territory in a way. It's like the abused director, you know. I had gotten to the point where my armor had become very, very thick. I just expected abuse, almost. I expected no one to really like anything, you know. I'd come to believe that being a director was just to soldier on.

I ended up back in L.A. with the film, because I had to show it to the studio. Sherry Lansing from Paramount Pictures was there, and Ridley was there, along with some others who I don't remember. I remember showing up in this huge preview theater at Paramount, feeling very alienated. I sat by myself. I remember that everybody brought Chinese food in because they hadn't had lunch. And I just thought, I see. I'm going to show my film, and it's like a TV dinner, everyone just watching and eating. I moved as far away from everybody as possible because the smell of this food I remember as being something that I really didn't want to be part of.

The film started. I watched the film by myself in this huge theater about a hundred seats away from anybody else, and I quite enjoyed it. I'd done the score. I'd done kind of a jazz score for it. When the film finished, I remember thinking, "Oh, well. I wonder what they thought of it. They probably hate it, you know." And then I began to hear this kind of strangled sobbing from behind. Sherry Lansing was sobbing and crying, and the other executives were sort of crying with her. You know, it's an interesting thing about running a studio. If the head of the studio cries, everybody cries. If the head of the studio laughs, everybody laughs. I mean, you know I'm right about that, right? I was being somewhat shocked by what appeared to be their favorable reaction. I remember catching the word "Oscar" and Sherry saying, "It's just the most beautiful film. Albert Finney is going get an Oscar. Everybody come to my office and we'll talk about this."

So, we went to Sherry Lansing's office with Ridley. It was kind of an odd situation because I knew Ridley didn't really like the film, and suddenly Sherry loved the film, you know. She was the head of Paramount! So, I thought, that's interesting. Sherry said, "It's not a question of *will Albert Finney get an Oscar? It's will he get this time or the next time?* We have to talk about when we release this film." I thought, this is very positive, and I agreed. I think he should have gotten an Oscar for that performance. It was a superb performance. He's a superb actor. And then she said, "But the first thing we have to fix is that dreadful music." She looked at me and said, "I know this is only temp score. We got to get a real composer." It quickly became clear from our conversation she had absolutely no idea that I was a musician and that I had anything to do with the score. Or, as my son pointed out later on, that perhaps one of the reasons that they were all sobbing and couldn't speak for ten minutes might have had something to do with the fact that the music was appropriate. I was promptly fired as the composer and Mark Isham was brought in to redo the score.

I had to sit with Mark and Ridley Scott and try and convey my musical ideas to somebody else altogether, which is a most strange experience, and then watch my score be replaced. The music of any movie in my opinion is the psychological fabric of the film, and I had to watch it be replaced by someone else, who now is speaking not just to me but also to the producer, and he's getting his notes from the studio, not from me. Again, rather like my earlier story about *Mara* and the HBO producer. The theme that I wrote for Albert Finney became the theme for *Leaving Las Vegas*, a much-lauded musical score. It was, I believe, in the Top 50 Album Charts for two years and was played at the Oscars in front of about 50 million or so viewers. Once again, there are small compensations. But I do, to this day, regret the fact that I wasn't allowed to complete the score, because it was, you know, just keyboards and temps stuff that I first showed them. I really felt that music was the key to Albert Finney's character. Now, I think Mark Isham did a reasonably good job, but I don't think he had as much information about the characters as I did. After all, I made the film. I just loved the fact that you can have someone sobbing, telling you that you were a genius, and, oh, by the way, you're fired as the composer. It's one of the many ironies of being a musician involved in the film.

> *When I first read Leaving Las Vegas, I was leery about the script because I didn't see any break in the drive, the relentlessness of it. Looking back I think what really serviced that movie really well was the sense of humor that Nicolas Cage brought to his character.*
> Laurie Metcalf—Actress

Leaving Las Vegas (1995)

Nicolas Cage; Elisabeth Shue; Julian Sands;
Richard Lewis; Steven Weber; Kim Adams; Emily Procter.

I was in postproduction on *The Browning Version*, which was about the time of the really big earthquake here, and it was a strange time to be in Los Angeles. A friend of mine by the name of Stuart Regen gave me a book to read. Stuart Regen runs a gallery here in Los Angeles and is a really, really great guy. It was one of those awkward situations that all filmmakers have experienced when a friend buys a book at the airport, says, "You know, you should read this. I read it on the plane, and I think it'll make a great movie." You always know that if people are reading it, it's already optioned by someone else or something like that. If it's not, it probably is no good to begin with. So he gave me this book called *Leaving Las Vegas* by John O'Brien, and I had it in my bag for months and months and months. I kept saying I must read that book. And Stuart would ring up and say, "Did you get a chance to read the book?" And I'd say, "Oh, no. But it's on my list. I'll read it this weekend," and I never did. Finally, I knew that the next week I had to go and meet with Stuart, so I finally forced myself to get the book out. And with dread, too, because I always feel it's sort of a waste of time and a waste of energy.

I started reading the book, and I would say that within five pages I started to sort of get a tingle and think, "Wow, this is so far removed from the standard Hollywood fare and from the sensibility of filmmaking in this town. It is a quintessentially American story, and I do love the American genre." I grew up reading Ernest Hemingway and listening to jazz, and I'm sort of absolutely impregnated with American culture. This book seemed like a classic to me, and I read it in one sitting. When I got to the end of it I thought it would be a great challenge. It's so dark and so sad. Structurally, it was so difficult because it's a very internalized novel. I didn't even know if it was possible to make a film out of it, but it certainly would be an interesting thing to try. I had the meeting with Stuart, and I said, "I think it's tricky stuff, and there's no way a studio will pay for this. So we would have to shoot this on 16 mm and do it as a really, really down-and-dirty, low-budget film. But I think it could be interesting." And he said, "I quite agree, you know." So we made a verbal agreement there and then that I would direct the film.

I think the trickiest thing I've ever had to do as a writer was to decon-
struct the novel. What I did was copy the entire novel. Then I made three
piles. I had a pile that said, "Could be something in the film" and then I had
a pile that said, "This doesn't work in the film." Then I had a third pile, which
said, "I have no idea how to get this into the film. But it's such an interesting
idea that I'll put it to one side." So, the first pile, which was stuff that I believed to be cinematic, I then constructed into a very short script, which had
big gaps in it. I then wrote transitions. Up until the time that we shot the film
I kept delving back into the interesting stuff. I gradually began putting as
many of those back into the film, often cheating in terms of the chronology
of how it was written in the novel but getting as much of O'Brien back into
the screenplay as I possibly could.

> *It turned out to be the most amazing auditioning experience I ever had*
> *because it was about the work. It was not about somebody watching me*
> *or somebody judging what I was doing. It was just Mike and me read-*
> *ing the entire script, scene by scene.*
>
> Elisabeth Shue—Actress

The first actor that I approached was Elisabeth Shue, who I'd met years
before in a casting session. I had almost broken her heart, I think, because I'd
offered her a role in *The Hot Spot* and then I ended up offering the role to
Uma Thurman. It was a period in Elisabeth's life when she also lost her
brother. He was killed in a terrible accident, and I think it represented a very
down period in her life. I always felt very guilty about disappointing her in
that way. But I always thought she was terrific. I remember meeting her at the
Farmer's Market and sort of offering her this role in *Leaving Las Vegas* and
saying, "Read this." So she was in way before Nick Cage, and I thought she
delivered a great performance in the film. I thought Nick was magnificent,
but I actually thought she deserved an Oscar for her performance. I think
that she almost enabled Nick's performance, not as an actor but as a character. Her framing of his character made the film accessible.

I finished *The Browning Version,* and it went to the Cannes Film Festival
and was in competition. I was trying to raise this small amount of finance to
make *Leaving Las Vegas* and getting nowhere. I remember just before
Cannes, going with my agent around, I think, to five different meetings in
L.A., visiting all the usual suspects. They'd all read the script. I think people were kind about the writing. They all said it was way too dark. At one

of those meetings, someone actually made jokes about alcoholics and things like that. I was running out of choices.

I went to Cannes because my expenses were being paid by Paramount to go there to do a lot of press for *The Browning Version*. I said, "Well, can we just pack everything into two days?" I wanted to liberate the other two days so I could go and hustle for money. So we ended up doing something like 140 television interviews in two days. We virtually did them one after another in this hotel room. It was a surreal experience. It's quite funny at Cannes, because you start with the CNN types and go on to CBS, BBC, and so on. Then, on the tail end of those interviews, you end up doing Moscow television or Peruvian television or whatever. There's a clear pecking order about who gets into the hotel last and first.

Then, I'd bought a couple days in Cannes, and I was on this amazing mission with my agent. We visited these magnificent yachts and sleazy hotel rooms where there's a back end to Cannes that people don't really know about, which is really the porn industry. You go into some of the lesser hotels, and you see very dubious videos playing and posters of naked women being tortured and God knows what, you know. You walk down the corridors in these lesser hotels, and all you hear are porn movies. We were going to some pretty shady people for money, you know, but they weren't interested. We ended up on this yacht with a woman called Lila Cazès from a French company. It was pretty bizarre. We had a polite conversation, and then she saw us off the yacht, and we shook hands, and she said, "I'll make this film," and she did. She and her company came up with the money. It wasn't a bed of roses, but they paid for the film, and we were in production a couple months later.

I had always been a huge fan of Super-16 mm film. In fact, to test out the aesthetic of Super-16, I shot a deodorant commercial in Cuba. I persuaded the commercial company to let me shoot on super-16 mm, because in Britain, TV commercials are often shown in the cinema. I knew this commercial was going to get a cinema screening. I remember going to the theater to see a Woody Allen film and suddenly, bingo, there was my commercial. I watched absolutely fascinated as it ran on this huge screen in the West End of London. And it looked pretty good. So, I felt confident about the Super-16 mm.

I never had the opportunity to play somebody who was in so much pain. Somebody who is so complicated, who had been very bruised emotion-

ally and yet she had this real courage and sense of strength about her that I really loved that allowed her to survive the world she was in.
Elisabeth Shue—Actress

As I think I said earlier, I believe the most crucial decision you ever make when you're preparing a film is the casting, and I was lucky enough to have an incredible cast. People really didn't know who Lisa Shue was, and when they found out, they were always, like, puzzled. They would say, "Do you mean the girl from *Adventures in Babysitting*?" And I said, "Yeah. She's going to play a hooker." Nick Cage had a funny following at the time, which was love him or hate him. I remember one company saying, "Well, we'd make the movie, but not with Nick Cage." I remember thinking, well, are you offering me a lot of money or something? Because this is a $3 million film, and Nick Cage is doing it for a hundred thousand dollars, you know. Who were you suggesting, Tom Cruise? I'm not the kind of a director that will suddenly fire an actor because somebody is saying the money is contingent on who I put in the film. I went into it with a blissful kind of feeling, or liberation really, which was that at last I was making a film the way I wanted to work. The way I used to work with small units and handheld cameras. I was also operating a camera for the first time. Declan Quinn was the cinematographer, and I was the second cameraman. We worked out a very nice choreography between the two of us. He was very generous in his letting me be the second cameraman, and we shot really quickly. I created certain ground rules, which is that we will designate two hours for this scene. It's not negotiable. We have to finish the scene in two hours.

There's this sequence in the film where Nick leaves his house in Los Angeles and burns all of his scripts and all of his photographs and then drives off in his car to Las Vegas. We'd allowed a day to shoot that whole sequence. It should have been a daylight sequence, you know, which was how it was supposed to be, with natural light. We were in California. But we took too long with the lighting, and it got dark, and we were told that our permit was about to expire. Now, if we come back the next day, my schedule would have been shot to pieces. So I suddenly got immensely creative and said, "Okay. Put 100-watt lightbulbs in all of the rooms. Kick the entire crew out and give Nick a radio mike and hide the tape recorder somewhere on the step, and we'll just shoot in one take." So I said to Nick, "Okay. Trash the house. Start a bonfire and we'll just keep shooting." So, I think, by that time I had left the house. It was just Nick and Declan Quinn and six lightbulbs, and it's a lovely sequence in the film. It worked just fine. It was a scene that was conceived somewhat out of desperation and necessity. But it characterized the way we made the film.

I had no expectation of any success for the film. I really didn't care. I remember coming over with a very bad VHS copy of the film and going to Nick Cage's house. The two of us, smoking a cigar and drinking brandy, watched the film. At the end of it, Nick said, "I think it's fantastic. I don't know if anybody will ever see the movie, but I'm really glad I made it." I felt fine about the film, too. Then, suddenly, MGM picked it up. They started to do little test screenings for press, and it suddenly started to grow very little legs. The turning point, I think, was when David Thompson saw the film and made an unequivocal positive response and said, "I think it's a masterpiece." His words, not mine, by the way. All of the doubters who had legs on both sides of the fence suddenly hopped over into the positive field and suddenly nearly everybody said they liked it, except one critic who said he kind of liked it. Then, when he reviewed my next film, *One Night Stand*, which he detested, and of which he said, "This is such a bad film, but it allows us to revisit *Leaving Las Vegas* and see the overrated piece of work that it really was." I love it when critics do double reviews like that, just in case you're feeling even remotely positive about something.

Leaving Las Vegas came out, and it was a hit and made money and on top of that got great reviews. It won tons of awards, culminating in Nick Cage actually winning an Oscar. The film was actually nominated for four Oscars, two of which were for the writer-director. It's only in the last period of time that I've actually been able to look back on that time and sort of appreciate it. It was, as they say, a cliché. It was a roller coaster. It's quite hard in this town to keep your perspective, because, suddenly, you make the film, which some said was my revenge on Hollywood. It was never revenge. It was just a filmmaker's pathetic attempt to get in touch with himself again and do good work. To suddenly find that your work succeeded, proving all kinds of theories that if you follow your instinct and if you make the film you want to make, that may give you success, rather than trying to fit into other people's idea of what a great film is.

I found myself in a situation where, for example, [shortly before the release of *Leaving Las Vegas*,] I'd gone into a major studio because I'd read a script about the fashion industry that I thought was rather kind of ironic and funny. I went in and basically pitched for that film, offered to do it in such a way that they could reduce their budget by 50 percent, and did what I thought was a pretty good pitch. During that pitch meeting I watched executives leaving all the time, saying, "I'm sorry. I have to leave now. It's been really interesting meeting you, but I have another appointment." I ended up with two executives from what had been a room full of execs. Then, hearing back from my agent, "Well, sorry, Mike. They're going to go in a different direction because they feel that you don't have a sense of humor, and they really need someone with a sense of humor for this script, because it's basically a comedy." Okay, fine. Then, literally four weeks later, after the movie comes out, getting a call from the same people saying, "Well, now we do think you're funny. I mean, we made a mistake. Would you like to come back in? We'd like to offer you the film now," by which time I had moved on, you know.

> *He's not really interested in chasing the same thing again and again. I think his idea with* One Night Stand *was something that was a little looser—I think maybe a little more fun in some ways.*
>
> Kyle MacLachlan—Actor

One Night Stand (1997)

Wesley Snipes; Nastassja Kinski; Kyle MacLachlan;
Ming-Na Wen; Robert Downey Jr.; Marcus T. Paulk;
Natalie Trott; Glenn Plummer; Amanda Donohoe.

I got a script titled *One Night Stand,* based on a two-page synopsis by Joe Eszterhas. I read the script and remember thinking it was kind of a porno script. I went in for a meeting with the studio, and I said, "The thing that fascinates me about this script is how would you possibly shoot it, because virtually every page has a description of a very, very explicit piece of sex, all of which would render the film pornographic. You'd never get a release for it. So how did anybody think this was ever going get made as a film?" Nobody there really had an answer for that. Then, they said, "Well, you know, what do you think?" And I said, "Well, I think it's unfilmable. I think it's an interesting idea of a one-night stand by a married man and the whole question of love within the confines of marriage and that whole thing, but I don't think it's coming out in the script." And they said, "Well, would you consider rewriting it?" Now, I'd been obsessed with another film called *The Woman Next Door*, Truffaut's penultimate film, which I think is a masterpiece. For years, I toyed with the idea of doing a remake of that, which I think someone's now doing, actually. I eventually decided not to make the film, because Truffaut's a bit of a genius, and there's nothing wrong with his film. So I let that go. But there were elements about the structure of *One Night Stand* that kind of had similarities to *The Woman Next Door*, and I thought it could be an interesting American story. So they asked me to do a rewrite.

I literally did a page-one rewrite, where I kept the idea of the principal characters, but that was about all I kept. I completely and utterly threw out the entire script and started again. I invented a new character, which was the Robert Downey character. After much casting, I put Wesley Snipes in what had originally been a role that I wrote for Nick Cage, but he didn't want to do it. Then Sean Penn was going do it, but then he didn't want to do it. And then there was John Cusack. I read with all of those leading white actors. Then, one night, as I was publicly bemoaning the lack of choice, I thought, what a pity this isn't a kind of a character that could be played by a black actor, because there's so many brilliant black actors out there. I heard my own voice, and then somebody said, "Well, why not a black actor?" That actor ended up being Wesley Snipes, because I think he's a fantastic actor. I went ahead and made the film with a very eclectic cast that included Nastassja Kinski, Ming-Na Wen, Wesley Snipes, and Robert Downey Jr., who was going through a terrible crisis in his life at that time. I don't think he would mind me saying he was a bit of a junkie at the time.

I made what I thought was going be a very commercially successful film, I have to say. I thought it was something that people would be able to relate to. It was about marriage and a nice, old-fashioned, romantic love story, too. It was far removed from Eszterhas's kind of erotic, quasi-porno movie as you can get. Eszterhas took his name off the script and disassociated himself from the project. I made the film, and it got absolutely slaughtered critically in this country. Wesley Snipes won the Best Actor Award at the Venice Film Festival the same year with that film. It got incredible reviews in England. But the American critics thought the film was beyond salvage. If you could find any of the quotes, please feel free to use them in this interview. I remember the day the reviews came out; I was at the Farmer's Market. I saw director Paul Mazursky and some of my friends there, a group of people that I sometimes have breakfast with. And they all just went, "I'm so sorry." I didn't know what they were talking about. I'd forgotten the reviews were coming out that day.

And they said, "Oh, you haven't seen the reviews." And I said, "Is the *New York Times* bad?" Paul said, "Bad, yes! But compared to *L.A. Times*, it's good." The film lasted two or three weeks at the box office and then just went away.

I think I often underestimate morally where the audiences are. And, ironically, an audience that can watch a film about alcoholism and a love affair between a prostitute and an alcoholic perhaps has slightly more of a struggle with a black-white love affair. If you look at American film in particular, I'd say black characters are still very marginally represented. They can be judges and doctors or hookers and pimps and drug dealers. But the reality is the majority of us aren't pimps or judges, you know. We're either working-class or middle-class people with middle-class and working-class ideas and problems. I don't think we see anything like enough multicultural casting in American film, because the actual culture is way ahead of the way it's portrayed in film.

Someone said to me afterwards, "You know, maybe one of the problems was that Wesley was a bit too cocky," and that incensed me. And I said, "Do you mean cocky for a black actor or do you mean just cocky?" Because in the film, the guy's a television commercial director, and if Sean Penn or John Cusack or Nick Cage had played that character, they would have been ten times more cocky, arrogant, swaggering, because that's what the character calls for. But I think you get uncomfortable when it's someone like Wesley Snipes. I think it does call into question a lot of value judgments about what we think film is, and the film's supposed to be on the cutting edge of social change. In fact, when it comes to social change, film is way behind—way, way behind. I think it also propagates all kinds of very bad stereotypes about ethnic minorities. It's not that healthy and it needs to get healthy.

Robert Downey Jr., is without a doubt one of the most talented actors I have had the pleasure of working with. I visited him while he was in jail. I'd been to see him three times and he was doing well. He's had a very, very tough time. I do believe him to be one of the most talented actors of his generation. I'd certainly work with him again tomorrow. I do genuinely love the film very, very much. I think it's one of the best films I've made on every level, and in particular because it has an incredibly strong ensemble, and everybody gives a strong performance. It's a very varied group of actors, and Robert Downey, I think, shines in his performance. Interestingly enough, he never once disappointed me in terms of his ability to act and to give a performance. I mean, in between takes he was difficult. He was a sick person, and I really had to look after him in many ways, and the people who worked for me had to look after him as well. But he never once gave less than 100 percent as an actor.

One of the great things about making *One Night Stand*, up until its release, was that I was working with a studio that allowed me to make the film that I wanted to make. It's my music and it's my cut, and New Line Cinema actually gave me enough of a budget to work with. That was probably because of the success of *Leaving Las Vegas* and the amount of credibility that that gave me at that time. So, for the first time in my career, I was able to work with an orchestra for the music score, with a hundred musicians playing at the same time. That was an out-of-body experience for me to be in a recording studio with so many musicians when I'd spent my entire life faking orchestral sounds and scrimping with budgets, because I never got paid properly as a musician. I was given full rein as a filmmaker on that film. It was a wonderful experience.

The Loss of Sexual Innocence (1999)

Julian Sands; Saffron Burrows; Stefano Dionisi; Kelly Macdonald;
Gina McKee; Jonathan Rhys-Meyers; Bernard Hill; Rossy de Palma.

When I first started making films, I had a foot in both camps. I was still working in sort of experimental theater, and I was starting to make low-budget films. I conceived an idea for a film called "Short Stories," which became *The Loss of Sexual Innocence*. It was based around the idea of the loss of innocence, the Garden of Eden, and Adam and Eve and biblical ideas about women and men. I imagined that I was going to do it partially on film. I was going to get a huge warehouse and make the film on very small sets and then do it also as a performance, with the audience on foot, being able to move from one short story to another because the film would be a collection of short stories. For anyone who's seen the film, it's not too difficult to understand that this was a tough project to raise money for, you know. I'd written it fifteen years before it got made as a film. In that period, I had regularly revisited the script, rewritten it, and gone out to try and raise money again. At one point I raised the budget and the ability to make the film here in Los Angeles. Then, at the very, very last minute, I lost the money through my own inability to adapt.

I had a lunch with a couple of producers. They said, "We love the film. We have a very large studio that we have a distribution deal with. They've read the script. They like it and they think it's very interesting. But they want you to change one thing. In your script, Adam and Eve are portrayed by a black actor and a white actress. We would like you to change it. We would like Adam to be white and we would like Eve to be black. Do you have a problem with that?" To cut a long story short, I said I did have a problem with that. I said, "Do you have a problem with it the other way around?" They said, "Yes, we do." And I said, "Well, thank you for lunch," and that was the end of that. It was literally down to the Wesley Snipes thing. They didn't want a black actor to play the first man on Earth. So, I put it back in the drawer.

Then, after *One Night Stand*, I was going through a period where I had a lot of projects on the back burner. I thought, you know, unless I actually concentrate on this script, I think it'll never get made. So I made a decision that this was going be my next film, come rain or come shine. I have sort of evolved a system where, if you presell certain territories in Europe, you can raise enough for a low-budget film, so I did it that way, and in doing so I own the film. It wasn't a huge box-office success, but it did create a certain amount of interest. The critics savagely trashed it, for the most part. The word "pretentious" was the dominant, most common word in most of the headlines of most of the reviews, which is interesting, because it's clearly an art-house film or what would be called an art-house film. It's not a mainstream film, and there does seem to be a real nervousness or fear amongst mainstream film critics for anything that's not mainstream. Almost like they feel affronted or insulted by it and feel they have to savage it.

Time Code (2000)

Xander Berkeley; Golden Brooks; Saffron Burrows;
Viveka Davis; Richard Edson; Aimee Graham; Salma Hayek; Glenne
Headly; Andrew Heckler; Holly Hunter; Danny Huston; Daphna Kastner;
Patrick Kearney; Elizabeth Low; Mía Maestro; Leslie Mann; Suzy Nakamura;
Alessandro Nivola; Zuleikha Robinson; Julian Sands; Stellan Skarsgaard;
Jeanne Tripplehorn; Steven Weber; Laurie Metcalf.

When I used to do theater stuff and mix all that together, on one of the pieces that I did, I split the stage right in the center. I built two identical sets. I dressed each of the sets differently, so one was in a slightly different time zone than the other. I had two actresses doing exactly the same movements as each other some of the time, sometimes coinciding, sometimes not. I've always been kind of obsessed and interested with the idea of chance and coincidence and of real-time drama, you know. When I was a student, I loved short stories about coincidences and about fate.

One of the scenes in *Miss Julie*—the love scene, actually—I used it in the film as a split-screen sequence. It's the same scene shot from two different angles, and there were no cuts. I was intrigued by the psychology of what you get on the screen with this. I can't explain why I think it's potent. I just think it is. And so it was after we finished the film, I was writing in my notebook, and I was speculating about split-screen and the idea that now video cameras exist where you can shoot for two hours, if you want to, on the same tape. I just wondered to myself if it would be possible to shoot an entire feature in one take using these split-screen techniques? Because I knew now that audiences are so used to the idea of getting visual candy all the time in the form of cuts that if you're not going to use cuts, you're going have to give them something else. You are going to have to give them as much of a visual feast as possible.

I then came up with the idea of four screens running at the same time, same story, and no edits. Gradually, I came to the realization that all four cameras are telling the same story from a different angle and different point of view. And so, initially, as an exercise for me to find out for myself, I wrote a basic plot—a four-camera scenario. I wrote the story specifically for this technique. Originally, I was going to shoot it in London and do it as a very low budget, sort of a one-day event. Shoot the film in the morning, invite an audience in that evening to watch the film as a kind of a live film event.

I happened to be in L.A., and I explained those ideas over lunch to the head of Sony Pictures. It wasn't a pitch, and I wasn't looking for money. I wasn't looking for a studio to back me, or anything like that. Just as a "Hey, what do you think of this? It's an idea. I'm going do this in London." And he said, "Well, you know, all of the studios right now are fascinated by digital technology and what that medium means to the studios in the future. What do you think about coming and doing this in Hollywood, as a studio picture with low budget? Do it any way you want. You got final cut, obviously, because there are no cuts. But, would you consider the idea of doing it with us?" And so I said, "Well, yeah. I mean I'll have to think about whether the story will work here, but I'll consider it." So, to cut a long story short, I said yes. So, it was a very, very quick and potent and experimental sort of adventure. I loved it. I loved every minute of it.

When you say to actors, "Look. It's an experimental film, and it's on video, and it's not a big deal," it's not the same as saying it's 35 mm, and your co-stars are Tom Cruise or whoever. But when you're saying, "Look. There's an ensemble cast. You're all in the same boat and there's twenty-seven actors altogether and there's no script. We'll shoot it time and time and time again. It's kind of a workshop, basically, but with very good people," all of the actors [become] immensely enthusiastic about the idea of doing it. To be honest, originally, I was only going to shoot it three or four times. Then I realized as soon as we started working that the best way to develop these ideas was just to keep shooting. So we shot the entire film fifteen times in a ten-day working period.

We still live in a culture where, even though you shoot a film on digital video, you still have to project it on 35-mm celluloid. So, the challenge was to transfer the video imagery onto film. And secondly, because we were running, I think, something like 35–40 channels of audio live while we shot the film, you're looking at four parallel stories in which people are talking all the time. To find a way out of this maze, this verbal maze, meant doing a very, very sophisticated sound mix where you had cohesive sort of narrative coming through that a mainstream audience could understand. Because it was already enough of a technical challenge to watch four screens. So, the clarity had to come from the sound. That was the biggest challenge in the postproduction of the movie.

On Risk-Taking

I think a risk taker is someone who jumps out of an airplane at 20,000 feet with a small amount of fabric and some string. Or a journalist that goes to cover a civil war in Africa. Those people are risk takers. The only risk I ever take is that I might offend someone in the studio, or I might not get my money the next time around. Meantime, as an artist, if one could be so bold as to use that word, being an actor, I indulge my every fantasy and every desire on a recurring basis with some of the greatest talent that exists in our culture on every level. I would say film directors lead not a high-risk life, but a charmed life, you know. I once said that I think film directors are people that, were they not endorsed by the film industry, they'd be in prison for abuse because we ask actors to do such extreme things to indulge our ideas, you know. If we were not protected by cameras and the crew, we'd be arrested for all kinds of things.

A Bit of Philosophy to Live By

You have to make films for yourself first and foremost. If you're not challenging the explorer and the innovator in yourself, you're not really working
at your full potential. I think if you're not connecting with those things
within yourself that are challenging, then you're not really doing your job. I
mean, your job is to be innovative and to be fresh and to present ideas to an
audience in a way that will challenge them and push them. We're really not
in the popcorn industry here, you know. A lot of film directors seem to think
that they are. We're not in the service industry. We're not here to entertain,
full stop. Our work should be entertaining. But it should also be innovative.

Filmmaking is far too important of a genre to be linked with the food industry—for example, the popcorn, the soft drink industry, or the ice cream
industry. It's too important to be just a venue for selling bad music and so on.
And it has become such a kind of hall to the theater, a service industry to
other industries, that sometimes I despair about where cinema is going. So, of
course, if you were functioning well, it should, by definition, then be working well for an audience. But I do believe it is a catastrophic mistake to assume
that you make something for an audience first and foremost. I don't think any
painter would ever claim that he was painting for an audience. Or any great
writer would claim that he was writing for an audience, unless you're talking
about the kind of books that you pick up in an airport or the kind of paint-
ings that you buy at Woolworth's, where you just want something on the wall
because you're lonely. I don't think interesting art or creativity ever comes out
of a kind of desire to appease an audience. I really don't.

If you look after your health, I think you can maintain a reasonably high
standard of work for your entire career because, to be honest, the older you
get, really the more interesting your work should become. One of the problems, as Oscar Wilde said about youth, is that it is wasted on the young. I
guess what he was getting at is you have that energy and you have that sexual drive. You don't really know quite what to do with it. You know it's good
but it hasn't really got enough books in the library yet, you know. Some of
the best work that has come out of cinema has come from more mature directors. Therefore, it's almost like a duty to sort of try and maintain your
health and things like that so you can continue. The problem with filmmaking is that it is a very high-energy occupation. I do understand why people
retire now, because to maintain that degree of physical energy is difficult.
Like on *Time Code*, for example, I operated one of the cameras. One of my

real concerns before we started shooting was whether physically I could keep going for ninety-three minutes without falling down from holding that heavy camera. And that also requires a degree of concentration. Adrenaline is an amazing drug, but I was very concerned.

I think what I hope to have done by the time it's all over is a body of work that shows an interesting progression and shows a kind of passion and, if you like, a bit of an obsession with continuity. I have no interest in the end of the journey or the beginning of the journey. I think it is the journey itself that's fascinating. The kind of films that I've always loved have really been films about dropping in on a certain point of a journey and the ability to observe every human being in a way that's interesting for me and for other people as an audience. It is an ongoing obsession with other people, not with cranes, or Steadicam camera rigs or digital innovation. These are just tools. The fundamental obsession is other people.

Mike Figgis Filmography

The House (TV, 1984)
Stormy Monday (1988)
Internal Affairs (1990)
Women & Men 2: In Love There Are No Rules (TV, 1991)
Liebestraum (1991)
Mr. Jones (1993)
The Browning Version (1994)
Leaving Las Vegas (1995)
One Night Stand (1997)
Flamenco Women (1997)
The Loss of Sexual Innocence (1999)
Miss Julie (1999)

Note: Since this interview was completed, Figgis has directed *Hotel* (2001), a segment of *Ten Minutes Older: The Cello* (2002), a segment of the miniseries *The Blues* (2002), and *The Devil's Throat* (2003).

Time Code (2000)
Hotel (2001)
Ten Minutes Older: The Cello (2002)
The Blues, TV Series (2002)

Awards and Nominations

Academy Awards, USA
Leaving Las Vegas, Best Director (nominated), 1996
Leaving Las Vegas, Best Writing, Screenplay Based on Material from Another Medium (nominated), 1996

British Academy Awards
Leaving Las Vegas, Best Adapted Screenplay (nominated), 1996

British Independent Film Awards
Special Jury Prize, 2000

Cannes Film Festival
The Browning Version, Golden Palm (nominated), 1994

Directors Guild of America
Leaving Las Vegas, Outstanding Directorial Achievement in Motion Pictures (nominated), 1996

Flanders International Film Festival
Miss Julie, Golden Spur (nominated), 1999

Golden Globe Awards
Leaving Las Vegas, Best Director—Motion Picture, Golden Globe (nominated), (1996)

Golden Satellite Awards
One Night Stand, Outstanding Original Score (nominated), 1998

Independent Spirit Awards
Leaving Las Vegas, Best Director, 1996
Leaving Las Vegas, Best Screenplay (nominated), 1996

Los Angeles Film Critics Association Awards
Leaving Las Vegas, Best Director, 1995

Mystfest
Stormy Monday, Special Mention, 1988
Stormy Monday, Best Film (nominated), 1988

National Society of Film Critics Awards
Leaving Las Vegas, Best Director, 1996

San Sebastian International Film Festival
Miss Julie, Golden Seashell (nominated), 1999
Leaving Las Vegas, Best Director, Silver Seashell, 1995
Leaving Las Vegas, Golden Seashell (nominated), 1995

Venice Film Festival
One Night Stand, Golden Lion (nominated), 1997

Writers Guild of America
Leaving Las Vegas, Best Screenplay Based on Material Previously Produced
or Published (nominated), 1996

The Films of Frank Darabont

Frank Darabont was born in France in 1959, the son of Hungarian refugees who fled Budapest during the 1956 uprising. He emigrated to the United States as a child, and, after living in several locales around the country, he settled with his family in Los Angeles immediately prior to entering high school. After graduating from Hollywood High, he spent his early years in the film world as a production assistant and set decorator.

He first worked as a production aide on the 1981 film *Hell Night*, at which time he met another aspiring filmmaker, Chuck Russell. Together, they established themselves as screenwriters with the scripts for *A Nightmare on Elm Street 3: Dream Warriors* and the 1988 remake of the 1950s horror film *The Blob*. Darabont also shared screenplay credits on *The Fly II*, the sequel to David Cronenberg's 1986 classic.

He wrote seven episodes of George Lucas's TV series *The Young Indiana Jones Chronicles* and two segments of HBO's popular anthology series *Tales from the Crypt*, the latter earning a Writer's Guild nomination for the episode entitled "The Ventriloquist's Dummy."

The public first became aware of Darabont's name when he wrote and directed the feature film *The Shawshank Redemption*, based on the novel by Stephen King. That was followed by yet another adaptation of a Stephen King novel, *The Green Mile*. For his efforts on that film, Darabont collected two People's Choice Awards as well as a Broadcast Film Critics prize for his screenplay adaptation. He remains one of the six filmmakers with the unique distinction and honor of having his first two feature films receive nominations for the Best Picture Academy Award.

> *One of the most impressive things I learned about working with Frank is that he started off as a set decorator on a low-budget film. For somebody*

to begin working on films as a set decorator and end up directing films
that he himself has written is a stunning accomplishment as far as the
industry goes. It just means that Frank has always been some brand of
a filmmaker.

Tom Hanks—Actor

The Conversation

My parents are from Hungary. I was born in France. I have no real memories of France. I was just a baby when we came over on the boat. We first landed in Canada and then wound up going from Canada to Chicago. So Chicago was our port of entry into the United States. But I was very young. My earliest memories are really in Chicago.

Growing up was pretty fragmented. The parents split up, and I wound up living in I don't know how many places. My mother was always here, in Los Angeles. My father tended to move around quite a bit. And it gets wearying for a kid after a while. I'm sure there are a lot of people who have experienced that—every year is a new school, and every year is a new set of friends that you have to make and a set of friends you have to say good-bye to. I came to live here with my mother as of the age of twelve, so from then on, I've been sort of an Angelino.

I loved all kinds of films. Cheesy horror movies like *Count Yorga the Vampire* scared the hell out of me when I was twelve. At the same age I thought *Omega Man* was the best movie I had ever seen. It doesn't quite date well when you're an adult. But at the age of twelve, I think I saw it ten times. But not at the expense of more mainstream, or more ambitious films as well. I loved David Lean films. I loved John Ford movies as well as *Attack of the Mushroom People* at two o'clock in the morning on television if I could stay up that late on a weekend. I loved them all. I've always had sort of a special leaning, special inclination toward the genre of the horror and science fiction, things of the fantastic. My house is filled with vintage posters of *War of the Worlds, The Day The Earth Stood Still,* and *King Kong.* So you definitely see my taste reflected in my home. I don't know if you've really seen it much reflected in the movies I've directed, necessarily.

It's interesting to me that I wound up going in the direction I have, because, when I was younger, I thought I'd wind up doing more genre-type films. But when I reached the age where I had the opportunity finally to direct, I was interested in telling *Shawshank Redemption* as a story. From that, I was interested in telling *The Green Mile* as a story, which certainly has a fantastical bent to it. It's definitely got a genre, supernatural element to it. But it's really more humanistic, character-driven storytelling. So I don't know. You explain it, because I can't.

I'd always been interested in film. From the earliest age of having first seen a movie in a movie theater, I felt that that's what I wanted to do. At a young age, I didn't even understand quite what it is that filmmakers do, but I knew that somehow I wanted to be involved in telling stories. It was wonderful. It was something that I responded to very strongly as a kid and wanted to be part of.

My very first job in films was as a production assistant on a movie called *Hell Night* with Linda Blair, and it was really the bottom of the barrel in terms of low-budget horror movies. The way this came about kind of falls into the category of "listen for the opportunities when they come and don't be afraid to take those opportunities." I got a call from a friend of mine that I had gone to high school with, Steve Regal, who was at the University of Redlands. And he said, "I seem to recall you wanted to be in the movie business. Well, there's this movie shooting out here, and I understand that they're hiring PAs. If you come out, maybe they'll give you job." I said, "Great. Thanks, Steve." I hopped in the car with two other friends of mine, and we drove out to Redlands that afternoon. And I didn't even know what a PA was, but I figured hell, if they're going to hire me, I'll find out. It was getting dark so we drove around until we saw lights in the sky, which is where they were shooting. We drove to the set and jumped out and walked up to I don't know, a grip or somebody, and said, "Hi. We're here to be PAs." We were led to this trailer, and this guy who was the line producer on the show looked up and saw us and said, "Okay. Well, all right. Good. If you're willing to work for $150 a week, you're hired." And that was the first gig.

Now, the fun part of the story is that the guy who hired us, the fellow who was line producing that movie, was Chuck Russell, whom I subsequently became very, very dear friends with. In fact, years later, I was best man at his wedding, which is just kind of crazy. But after I worked for him on a couple of movies, he realized I had a very keen interest in writing. He was looking for a writing partner at that time. He was also sort of struggling to become a filmmaker himself, so we started writing together. That lasted for a period of some years. Then, finally, he got his directing break on *Nightmare on Elm Street 3*, for which I cowrote the rewrite with him. So, our careers have just kind of gone since then into some fantastic places.

I feel very lucky, very fortunate, and very blessed. But it also goes back to that phone call. It wasn't Steven Spielberg; it was Steve Regal calling to say, "Well, you know you can be a PA if you drive out to Redlands." All those opportunities are valuable. If I trace the path of my career, it goes right back to that, and being goofy enough to be willing to drive to Redlands and be a $150-a-week production assistant. So, I never turned down an opportunity, because I don't believe any of them are wasted. And no job that you do in this business is wasted effort.

The Woman in the Room (1983)

Bob Brunson; Michael Cornelison; Dee Croxton; Brian Libby; George Russell.

The Woman in the Room came about as a result of, well, what year would that have been? 1981, I think. I think this was after I had just worked on *Hell Night*. My friends and I—the same friends that worked with me on that film—thought we should make a film. We should make a short film, not a Super-8 mm film like we made in high school. (That was back in the days when 8 mm actually meant film. Now it means something else.) But we thought we should make a real 16-mm movie with real actors in it, et cetera. I had read this fantastic short story by Steve King, a very moving short story that he had written as a result of his own experience with his mother, who died of cancer. That's what this story dealt with. I sat down, wrote a little adaptation of this short story, wrote him a letter, and said, "Dear Mr. King, my goofy friends and I would love to make this as a short film." We never really actually expected that we would be given the right to do that. But Steve, as it turns out, has this wonderful philosophy about encouraging young talent. He has been known to grant rights for one dollar to student filmmakers or young filmmakers.

It took three years to make this thirty-minute short film. I mean we only shot for eight days. But the rest of it, mostly postproduction, I had to pay for myself, which I did by working as a prop assistant on commercials that summer. I put up most of the money to finish the movie. That's how the whole thing came about. It was a wonderful experience—a difficult experience, but really a very rewarding one.

> *I'm primarily a theater person, and I love working in the theater. In the theater, you have to project to the back row, and in film you can't do that. Frank kept saying to me, "A little less, Jim. A little less," which was very important and valuable to me and is the mark of a very good director.*
> *James Whitmore—Actor*

The Shawshank Redemption (1994)

Tim Robbins; Morgan Freeman; Bob Gunton; William Sadler; Clancy Brown; Gil Bellows; Mark Rolston; James Whitmore; Jeffrey DeMunn; Larry Brandenburg; Neil Giuntoli; Brian Libby; David Proval; Joseph Ragno; Jude Ciccolella.

I should point out that in 1989 I directed this cable movie for USA Network that was produced by a lady who was one of the producers on *Nightmare on Elm Street 3*. We were talking about trying to get something going together, and she was given the opportunity to make these cable films. It was a $2.5 million budget and a twenty-one-day shoot, and it damned near killed me. Talk about being buried alive. But I took that opportunity because it was a chance to get my feet wet as a director in a professional situation, in a professional capacity. When you're not making a short film with your friends, you're responsible for budget, and you get a sort of baptism by fire, as it were. I wanted to get more experience before tackling something more ambitious, like *Shawshank*.

I'm an enormous fan of Stephen King's work as a writer. I've read everything the man has ever written, just as a fan. I am an appreciative reader. Steve had been known by the public for a certain kind of story. The movies that were being made only reinforced this perception of him as the horror guy. And that's about the extent of it, right? I knew better, because I had been reading a lot of his stuff, these little gems of his, and *Shawshank* was one of those hidden gems. I was so captivated by the story. I was so touched by it and moved by it, I thought this would be a great first feature for me. If I could convey the same tonality of that story that he did on the written page, if I could convey it on film, we might actually have something here. That's why I asked him for the rights to it.

I kind of sat on that project for about five years before actually writing the script. I think that on a very real level I did that because I was waiting for my skills as a writer to match my ambitions for that screenplay. I'm not sure I realized that at the time, but I certainly realized it looking back on it. These were years where I was working as a writer constantly. I had blundered happily into this career where I just kept working and working. And every script you write, you get better. It's like playing the violin. Every time you pick the darn thing up, you get a little bit better. Finally, I felt ready to sit down and write this screenplay. And, indeed, compelled by the fact that as a writer, I had seen so much of my work get eroded—it didn't happen all the time—but by and large, the work got eroded by other directors. I thought, hey, I could screw up my work just as well as anybody else can. As Quentin Tarantino says, "It's mine to screw up now." By the same token, it's maybe mine to get right, to do better than the other guy did.

As soon as I finished the script, I took it to Castle Rock Entertainment. I didn't know anybody over there but I felt that if anybody in town, any studio or production company, really got the sensibility of that story, it would have to be them. I would have to credit Rob Reiner for that because of his film *Stand By Me,* which was also a Stephen King novella. In fact, it was from the same collection that *Shawshank* came from. It was a very delicate piece of character-driven material. And I remember, when I saw *Stand By Me*, I thought, wow, somebody really got Steve King, finally. So, I took it to them. They read it and were very taken with the script, and, from that moment on, were very supportive of the project and very keen to get it made.

Shawshank was shot in Mansfield, Ohio, which is just about halfway between Cleveland and Columbus. They had this magnificent old prison there, this imposing edifice and this mountain of rock and steel that happily had been vacated. Happily not just for us, but for the people who were incarcerated there. It was just an appalling place, and it had a date with the wrecking ball when we found it. Thankfully, we were able to work things out so that we stayed the demolition for a period of a year while we prepped and shot the film. The front part of that prison is still there as a historical site, but everything else was ripped down—the walls, the towers, the buildings in the yard, everything. So the timing was very fortuitous for us. Had I waited an extra year to write that script, I don't know where we would have shot it, because there's no other place in the world like the Ohio State Reformatory in Mansfield. Without it I'm not sure what we would have done.

I did have reservations about the narration in *Shawshank* here and there. When I was writing the script, initially, I remember very distinctly getting to the halfway mark of the script, on page 60. And I suddenly froze in place a little bit because I thought it was very popular back then to slam films with narration. It was the complaint du jour at that time. I thought, oh, my gosh, I'm really relying on a tremendous amount of narration here. Maybe I'm making a mistake. Maybe this isn't right. But I couldn't really imagine the movie any other way, because the voice of that character, the voice of Red, the Morgan Freeman character, was so prevalent in the story. It was that character telling us that story. I couldn't quite picture how to do the movie without that. Nevertheless, I was momentarily daunted.

I was rescued by Martin Scorsese, who in this sense was like a guardian angel. In the middle of writing, I remember a night I sat down and turned on the TV. I felt kind of worn out. *GoodFellas* was premiering on HBO, a film that I had seen the year prior and was knocked out by it. It's a masterpiece. But I had forgotten how much narration there was in it. I sat down, and I started watching *GoodFellas* again, and I remember thinking, wait a minute. This is nothing but narration. It's wall-to-wall, front-to-back narration. The hell with it! Who cares what people think? It doesn't matter what tools you employ. It doesn't matter what techniques you employ, as long as it's valid, in and of the piece that you're doing. What's the best way to get the job done? It really doesn't matter. There are no rules. It's what is instinctively correct to the storyteller, and, if it works, it works.

I think the biggest challenge in adapting Steve's story for *Shawshank* was, for starters, trying to cram all that texture in and not have a four-hour movie. But also I think of prose fiction and film being two different languages that require changes along the way. You're going to have to compress some characters. You're going to have to rebuild the architecture a little bit. And, indeed, there is a good bit of that in the movie. But to do that and still make it feel like the same story that somebody would read when they picked up the book, that was the challenge. Even when things change, as long as it felt like the same story, as long as it felt like the same author, as long as it felt like Steve's storytelling, I figured I was safe. That was, I think, my biggest challenge, or at least the one thought that I kept in the forefront of my mind at all times, was not to sound like somebody else. If I was injecting myself into the story, I had to do it in such a way where, if you just kind of squinted your eyes and blurred your vision a little bit, I'd look like Steve King.

The sequence when Andy, the Tim Robbins character, plays the Mozart record over the prison speakers, that's not a scene that exists in Steve's story. That scene was wholly invented by me. And yet it feels like his story. It was a liberty taken, certainly, but at least in such a way that it didn't wind up feeling like somebody other than Steve. The James Whitmore character, who was mentioned in one paragraph of Steve's story, actually became a very fundamental character for me. There was a lot of narrative invented around him, which provided me the thematic spine of the story. But in the end it all felt like Steve. I've had people come up to me who, like me, are rabid lifelong readers of Steve King's work and say, "Wow. That *Shawshank Redemption* was the most faithful adaptation we've ever seen." I always say thank you and I always think it wasn't that, actually. It was a lot of stuff we invented along the way, but what a great compliment. Because the job was to try and make it all feel like Steve. To tell his story in a way that it would feel like one piece.

I've been blessed with fantastic actors in all of my films. In *Shawshank,* Tim and Morgan were a very unlikely pairing. I don't know what compelled me to want to put those two actors together, because, on the surface of it, it seemed like we were definitely running the risk of not having the kind of chemistry those characters need. The happy result of that was something in my head just said, "I bet these guys are going to be really interesting together," and, indeed, they were. Together, they generated this phenomenal, low-key chemistry that is, I think, the core reason that the film works. If you didn't believe that friendship, if you didn't believe that unlikely pairing, if that chemistry wasn't there, the whole thing would have just gone south. But it was there, thank goodness. They provided that for me, these two very different actors, and two very different kinds of people.

Morgan is a very instinctive kind of an actor. He plays purely from the gut. He doesn't have to think about it too much. Tim is a very cerebral person, a very cerebral actor. He needs a lot of sort of intellectual input. He needs a lot of discussion about where he's going. Morgan needed none. As a director you're always trying to gauge what the actor needs from you, and you can be that kind of director for that kind of actor. It's not that one way is better or one way is worse, it's just different. You got to be a barometer. It was interesting being a barometer on that movie, because we had the two key characters in this relationship, and they were both opposite ends of the spectrum, both amazing actors. Both delivered amazing performances. Both were very rewarding experiences for me. But it was interesting. I was the bouncing ball. If I started explaining too much to Morgan Freeman, I'd see his eyes glaze over. All Morgan ever wanted to know is do you want to pause here? Do you want me to turn him that way? What do you want? Once he knew those practical issues, he'd just get in and do it. And with Tim there was a lot of the thematic meaning of this or that? Or what's the inner life of the character? It was really interesting.

I was surprised at how poorly the movie did and then how well it did. When we finished, I thought we had a pretty special little movie there. Our initial release of the film was not a successful release. People tend to forget that. For whatever reason, we couldn't seem to beg people to come see this movie. Perhaps it was the prison setting. Perhaps it was the fact that it was obviously not an action film behind bars. It featured two significant actors in it. But I think people thought it was going to be some kind of a downer. So they really didn't want to show up. Looking back on it, it was the Oscar nominations that saved us, ultimately. We very happily were nominated for seven Academy Awards, including Best Picture. So, when the entire world was watching the Academy Awards, they kept hearing *Shawshank Redemption* over and over during the course of the show.

When we came out on video, suddenly, there was this rush of attention toward it. We were the most rented video of 1995, and everything that *Shawshank* has become to people since really sprang from that. So I've always been incredibly grateful to the Academy for noticing the film. That really brought it to the attention of the public. Now, we're eight years after the fact, and it has really become something that people have embraced tremendously. That's enormously satisfying to me, because you don't ever want to make a movie to play in a vacuum. The reason we got into this business was to touch people's heart, to communicate with an audience. When an audience doesn't show up, it's like oh, man! I guess we screwed up somehow. In the case of *Shawshank*, we hadn't screwed up; it just took a while for people to get to it, I guess. It didn't have the obvious elements, I suppose, to draw people into a theater. It wasn't an event film. It was not an effects-heavy movie. Nothing blew up. So it just took them a while.

A lot of directors will fiddle with a script. Many make hash out of a good script. Those are the ones who don't have an appreciation of the nuance of language, who don't know what it is in the scene that allows an actor to get from one point to another. But with Frank, he creates the material; he creates the venue and knows instinctively where to go with it.

James Cromwell—Actor

The Green Mile (1999)

Tom Hanks; David Morse; Bonnie Hunt; Michael Clarke Duncan; James Cromwell; Michael Jeter; Graham Greene; Doug Hutchison; Sam Rockwell; Barry Pepper; Jeffrey DeMunn; Patricia Clarkson; Harry Dean Stanton; Dabbs Greer; Eve Brent.

After the nominations, a lot of offers came through the door. I guess we were still on that *Die Hard* rip-off cycle, because every other movie being made was *Die Hard* in a boat or *Die Hard* on a plane or *Die Hard* in a phone booth or *Die Hard* in a tackle box. I kept getting these offers to direct, and it was another *Die Hard* rip-off. I kept thinking, what was there in *Shawshank Redemption* that leads these people to believe that I'm the right guy for this? It was a very strange experience. But it's actually one of the reasons I didn't direct again for five years. Luckily, as I always joke, I have a great day job. Screenwriting has been very good to me.

There's a really perversely amusing thing in Hollywood, where if you don't want the job, they're willing to throw more money at you to say yes. If you do want the job, it's because your passion's there. You don't charge extra for the passion. If you're gonna hire somebody, wouldn't you want somebody who's really enthusiastic about what you want made? That's kind of how I think, but that's not the way they think in Hollywood all the time. It's very strange. I didn't direct again for five years until Steve King called me up one day and mentioned *The Green Mile* to me, and that's how that got triggered.

Reading the script of The Green Mile *was surprisingly like reading the novel. It was perfect, as close to perfect as a screen adaptation is going to be. The script was long, but actually had an economy to it that was equal to Stephen King's original novel.*

Tom Hanks—Actor

I did not get the rights for a dollar on *Shawshank*, but I did get them for a dollar on *The Green Mile*. Steve King was so delighted with the result of *Shawshank* that he approached me on *The Green Mile*, funny enough. He said, "You know, we ought to go back to that dollar deal. We'll do it for a dollar." The myth, of course, has sprung up that we got the rights to *The Green Mile* for a dollar, which isn't exactly the case. We got the option for a dollar. When the film was green-lit and went into production, Steve was given many more dollars to go along with that first dollar, as is appropriate. He's a best-selling author, and it's a marvelous piece of material. But his generosity in allowing us that option made for very little risk going in. It's not like we had to pay him a fortune in order for me to write the script and get the film green-lighted. Yeah, we got the option for a buck, bless his heart.

In the case of *The Green Mile*, I think the greatest challenge was really getting the key elements of that sprawling Stephen King tapestry of characters and narrative into a manageable length. There are some books that I just am nuts about. I won't touch them because I know that, by the time I finish adapting them, either they're going to be six hours long, which is completely unworkable, or I will have been forced to truncate them to the point where it's not even the same story anymore. I think *Green Mile* was just on the borderline of that in terms of the amount of story I had to tell.

I think it's okay to tell a story in three hours. It's not something you want to do every day. And, contrary to popular myth, that's the only time I've ever made a three-hour movie. At one point, I had hoped that it would be maybe a two-hour, two-and-a-half-hour movie. But it just turned into a three-hour movie. What can you do? At a certain point, the movie becomes its own thing. It makes its demands of you. It makes its polite requests of you. You have to listen to it. There's only so much hammering you can do on the thing before you force it all out of shape.

I think, in the case of *The Green Mile* people didn't mind it being a three-hour movie, for several reasons. One would be Tom Hanks, because Tom is a person that the audience trusts. They know that he's not going to waste their time. He doesn't do crappy movies. In a sense, he's almost the seal of approval for an audience, and they love spending time with him. He's got a very rare and unique gift that way. Let's also give credit again to Steve King, because once they got there and once they sat down in the theater, they got a story that was really compelling and put them completely into this world and intrigued them and kept them involved in these people's lives. That's Steve King. For those two reasons the running time of *The Green Mile* didn't seem to be that great an issue.

I remember that the studio was a little panicked when I said, "Guys, its going to be a three-hour movie. Ain't nothing I can do about it." But Castle Rock and Warner Bros. were just slapping their heads and saying, "Oh, my God. He's out of his mind. We have to stop him." Then we had our first test screening with an audience. I think we got the highest test scores in Warner Bros. history. So, suddenly, overnight, the running-time argument evaporated. They were perfectly happy to put a three-hour movie out there. To me it just goes to show that if the material is really sound, if you're going from a really solid foundation of the story, the audience will be happy to go along with you on the journey. Shortened attention spans don't necessarily do you in. I noticed that with a number of movies recently. *Lord of the Rings,* for example. It's incredibly compelling, and you're in that world. You're just there. James Cameron pulled it off with *Titanic,* which was three and a quarter hours long. The audience didn't mind because the rewards were great. It's not necessarily the running time so much as it is about what you do with that time. How each minute counts in that running time, because if you make the audience forget that they have a babysitter at home, or they're getting hungry, or whatever, if you can get the audience to pay attention to the screen and not glance at their watch, it's wonderful.

Fleetingly, I was concerned about doing another prison film. I had started my directing career with a prison film, and now I was doing another one. And I thought, "Well, this is a great way to maybe pigeonhole myself." But on the other hand I should digress and say I never imagined I would make one prison film, much less two in a row. I have to blame Steve King, because the stories that he wrote were too compelling and too moving for me to say no to them. So I thought, oh, what the hell. What am I going do, wait another five years for something else to come along that I can fall in love with? No. *The Green Mile* means the world to me. I have to make this movie, and if that backfires on me, fine. At the very least maybe I'll carve this really obscure niche in movie history as the one guy who always does Stephen King period prison movies. So I just kind of went blindly ahead with it and said, "It's a great movie. It's a great story to tell. Why worry about the surface details of that?"

I always knew that in *The Green Mile* we wanted to keep the effects contained in the more obvious scenes. I knew that those scenes with Michael Clark Duncan, where he's healing the warden's wife, or where he's healed Tom, for example, the supernatural effects would work in the movie. I always knew that we wanted to keep that at a minimum and get it done as well but as subtly as possible. I knew that we were always running a risk of yanking the audience out of the movie, out of the moment of the story to say, "Wow. Look at all these effects," but we never wanted to do that. We wanted to keep them right with those characters and give them just enough that it conveys the event. I think we hit pretty close to the mark.

Charlie Gibson, who's my effects supervisor, is brilliant. When I pulled those shots out of *Green Mile,* he said, "Oh, good," because Charlie's smart. He knows it's about the story; it's not about these wonderful effects that he's supervised. He said, "The less we have here, the more the story's going to stay preeminent and not shatter the illusion that we are creating." When I got my effect supervisor's approval on what I was doing, I knew I was along the right lines of thought.

Let me get back to Tom Hanks for a minute. Gosh, I love that man. What a blessing he was and is. He came to *The Green Mile* really very simply. I sent him the script. I thought, Tom Hanks is the perfect guy for this. I'd met him a few times before. He was a great admirer of *Shawshank* and said, "Look, if you got anything you want me for, ever, send it to me. Love to work with you." So I sent him *The Green Mile.* He read it, and I think he committed to the project within, like, twenty-four hours. It was a tremendously easy thing to get him, which only shows how committed he is to the material. He's not impressed by a big paycheck being waved in his face. What he's impressed by is a good script with a role that he feels he can play. Getting him onboard was really the easiest part of making the movie.

It was a long process casting Michael Clarke Duncan in *Green Mile.* I think he was the very first actor who walked in to audition. I think we have Bruce Willis to thank for that, by the way. He was working with Michael in *Armageddon* and was a fan of the book and heard that we were making the movie. Bruce pulled Michael aside one day on the set and said, "You got to read this. This is your part. You got to go in and read for this." So we got a call and we said, "Well, we'll look at anybody, because this is going to be a very difficult role to cast." It's hard enough finding a great actor, much less a great actor who happens to be of that size, or that ethnicity. It's a very narrow window of a talent pool there. So, Michael came in and was not great in his first reading. I think he was very nervous and, I think, in some measure fairly inexperienced.

We went for months through this casting process, looking at and working with other people. The thing I could never let go of with Michael was his essence, the person who walked into the room, that sweetness that he had, that gentleness that he had. He lingered with me. And I thought, okay, let's give this guy another run at it. Let's actually give him the tools. So we put him with acting coach Larry Moss, who's a brilliant acting teacher. Michael worked with him for like a week before coming in and reading for us again. And you know what? That second reading was pretty darn good. So he worked with Larry some more, and he came in again, and every time he came in he was better and closer to it. Whatever nervousness he had was being stripped away. Whatever artifice he had was being stripped away, and he was really wanting to just be that character. And boy, once he hit the set and once we started filming, he had all the tools and then some. He just was this character. He was this person. It was the most astonishing sort of quantum leap from first reading to a performance that you can imagine. We can credit Larry Moss with some of that, because he unlocked whatever it was that Michael had inside him. But the truth is, Michael had the talent and was ready to do it. It just needed to be guided a little bit. His performance blows me away. Whenever I see any part of that film, I think, oh, my God, did I get lucky when this man walked into the room? I'm lucky that I wouldn't let go of him. I'm lucky that I kept him moving him along in the process, because without him that movie would not have worked—even with Tom Hanks in it.

That wonderful character actor, Dabbs Greer, played Tom as an old man. He's been around forever, and he just keeps going on. I think, if I'm not mistaken, *Green Mile* was his hundredth feature film, and we won't even bother counting up the episodes of television that this man did. I remember when we first thought of using him, his health was not so good, which is one of the reasons, actually, that the bookends to *Green Mile* were shot later than the principal photography. By then he had bounced back and had dropped some weight, and he was hale and hearty and ready to go. (My first memory of Dabbs Greer, by the way, is in *The Terror From Beyond Space*. I'm betraying my childhood here of watching horror movies and science fiction movies on late-night television. He was one of the crewmen on this ship that was being plagued by this monster they'd picked up on another planet. Gosh, sounds like *Alien*, doesn't it? Dabbs was wonderful in that. I've always been a fan of his.) And thank goodness that he was still with us and he still is. He was able to marshal his talents at that age, which I thought he did brilliantly.

I hired him because I didn't want to do Tom Hanks in old-age makeup. That kind of thing is essentially incredibly distracting to an audience. They realize they're watching an actor with makeup on, and so they're out of the movie. I think it's easier for an audience to accept another actor in the same role if it is a huge span of time.

The mice in *Green Mile* did steal the show, didn't they? There was a tribe of little furry actors. I think we had twenty-four mice that we trained for this movie. And a brilliant animal trainer, Boone Narr, and his team, bred these mice for us. Each mouse had a little, slightly different specialty. You can't take one mouse and train him to do everything, but you can take one mouse and train him to turn left. Or take another mouse and train him to stop on a mark or whatnot. What they were able to get these darn mice to do was pretty phenomenal. I directed the mouse in all the scenes where you have principal actors, which actually limited my dealings with the mouse, I have to say. The real unsung hero there, aside from Boone Narr and his team, was Charlie Gibson, my effects supervisor, who shot about two months of second unit for me of just mice, getting the mice to do what needed to be done. They figured out sometimes some very clever tricks to create the illusion of certain things. We still have people who write us letters and say, "How did you get the mouse to roll the spool?" I'll never tell, but you're not going to get a mouse to do that naturally. Using some very clever little tricks here and there, and a lot of patience, they gave us that wonderful creature on the screen.

When you have material like *The Green Mile*, pace is always going to be a concern. As a screenwriter, you don't know where the pace is going live, really. You can only take your best guess at it. You don't really start to get a sense of it until you're editing the movie, until you got that footage, and you are actually editing, which I call writing the last draft of the script. That's when you start really honing in on pace and trying to get every scene to be as efficient as possible. Sometimes, you wind up dropping shots that you went to a lot of effort to get, just so that the scene would move on better. I figure if I'm getting anxious, then the audience will get anxious. So I want to build the momentum of what they're learning about the story and the characters as soon as possible and then just hope that the audience will come along for the ride. I guess if the story is compelling enough, they will come along for the ride. It's not a roller-coaster ride in terms of pace, by any means. But the story keeps the audience there.

My cinematographer David Tattersall and I really had a lot of discussions about how to keep that cell block set interesting. We wanted very much to approach every scene on that cell block in some kind of visually different manner—whether it was choice of lens in that we would shoot something with long lens versus a wide frame, whether it was a subtle bit of camera movement, whether it was the tone of the lighting, whether it's a sunny day outside or whether it's a cloudy day outside, whether it's nighttime, whether it's daytime. We always wanted to keep it slightly different so that it wouldn't visually oppress the audience. Hopefully, we did a good enough job that people didn't feel that they were trapped in there like we felt when we were shooting it.

In Delacroix's execution scene—Michael Jeter's character—we actually did hold back. It may not seem like it, but we did. Again, we were really going off of what Steve King had written, though what he wrote was far more horrifying in terms of specific details like the eyeballs coming out of the head and sizzling and all that stuff. We thought, we can't really do that because it's not really a horror movie in that sense. So we're going try to keep to the basic strokes of it. It seemed a bit farfetched until we actually started doing the research on historical executions that have gone wrong. That's when we realized that actually what Steve had written was really quite accurate. What you see in the movie is really quite accurate. There have been instances where the sponges weren't conducting the electricity properly and suddenly flames are shooting ten inches out of the guy's ear and that sort of thing. We were hoping to strike a balance with that. We wanted it to be horrifying enough to convey the horror of it, but not so horrifying that the audience would be compelled to turn away or to run out of the theater saying, "I don't want to see the rest of this movie because it's really appalling." It was a bit of a fine balance to strike. And, again, in the edit one always pulls back, even a little bit further than one had anticipated when filming it.

Subplots Are Important

The subplots of a film, those are very important to me, particularly when you have material as rich as Steve King's. Both *Shawshank* and *Green Mile* are very emblematic of the kind of writing he does. He tends narratively to weave this tapestry of plot and characters. It seems to me that many of the films that have been based on his material and that have failed failed because the filmmakers have neglected those finer details——oftentimes, incremental details. First thing is, they yank out the subplots. They yank out the texture. They yank out the supplemental characters and whatnot. What you wind up with then is purely the baldest kind of plot. You're left with the fur and the fangs, and you lose the Steve King, is what I'm trying to say. So, those subplots, frankly, are what make the storytelling so compelling to me. I couldn't imagine leaving them out, which is why *Shawshank* was a two-hour-and-twenty-two minute movie, and why *Green Mile* was a three-hour movie. Had I thinned out the narrative texture of those pieces by just pulling stuff out, and some people wouldn't be as vital, I don't think they would be the same movie, and I don't think they would be nearly as effective. As it is, they feel like very faithful adaptations of King's work, which is important to me. I want to speak in the tone of the author. I want to speak in his voice. Otherwise, why am I telling the story? Why go through the exercise and the trouble of telling the same story if you don't?

There is a mythic sort of feel to both of those films, but I think I really have to credit Steve King, because that mythic feel was in the source material that I was adapting. That stuff is all there. Both of those stories played to me; read to me, like, as mythic, iconic, tall tales. So, for me to capture that tone, really, was not so much a function of being a clever filmmaker and doing a lot of research as to the reality of prison life. It was really being a clever film-maker and just paying attention to my author and trying to tell the story as well as he did. That sense of myth really does spring from King.

On Choosing Cast and Crew

For me the casting process is usually a fairly straightforward one. I have actors in and read the pages, and for every actor that I give a job to, there is at least a dozen wonderful actors who came into the room and gave a great audition that you know would give a wonderful performance. But there's usually one who matches whatever picture you have in your head for that role. There's always the one who feels right for the part. I find casting to be somewhat emotionally difficult because so many wonderful actors walk through the door. And you want to give them all a job. You want to give them all work. But you can only say yes to one person for each role, and that's tough because I know how tough it is for them to walk in the room.

What I expect any actor to bring to a project—aside from their talent, which can be a considerable blessing—is a belief in the material. I would hope that most of the actors who come to the table are really excited about doing this film and not just because a paycheck is attached to it. They need to come to a film for the same reason I come to a film. It's never because there's a paycheck.

I've been very lucky with my actors in that regard, because the people I worked with have always had this belief in the script. I've never really had to fight any actor on the material. They come because they want to be there. The same holds true for the crew, too. I want the one guy who's excited to be there, who figures that we might be onto something. That we might be making something special that they're gonna be proud of. They take pride in their jobs. I've been very lucky in that regard, too. I've been able to work with some extraordinary crew people, and it makes a difference. I know some people don't necessarily think so, but it does. If you have a dolly grip working your hothead crane, who is really looking forward to seeing the movie, then this guy's out there really busting his ass to do a great job. It does make a difference across the board, no matter what function anybody performs in the film. And I'm happy to be there then, because enthusiasm and optimism, and not cynicism, surround me. "Oh, gee, I'm only doing this 'cause I have to send my kid through college" is not why I want anybody to be there. I still come from a place of loving the movies and wanting to make films that will last if I'm lucky. When you can gather those people around you, and you're all working toward the same goal, you're the same army trying to take the same hill, because you believe the hill has to damn well be taken, that's a wonderful work experience. I witnessed the other side of that quite a bit when I was crewing. Everybody shows up thinking, well, we're making a piece of whatever. It's like it's terrible to be there, shooting a movie where the people involved don't really care one way or the other. I like the other method better.

I would love to just comment on my actors a bit more. I mentioned this before, but I feel so blessed with the actors that I've been given the pleasure of working with. Not just the obvious big names like Tom Hanks or Jim Carrey, but everybody. The people who populate the film are the ones that bring the whole texture of the film to life. Guys like David Morse, Michael Jeter, Doug Hutchison, Sammy Rockwell, Jim Whitmore, and Jeff DeMunn. These supporting-cast members are really the unsung heroes of many films. They bring so much integrity and so much talent to the proceedings, and they wind up being so vital just being part of the texture, and they're all such pros. They're all such gentlemen and gentlewomen as well. And there is Patty Clarkson, Bonnie Hunt, and Laurie Holden. Those people I owe a great deal to because they're as vital to the process of telling the story as the story itself. They are the conduits through which the story flows. I mean, when you have actors of that caliber, half your job is done. When you get a guy like David Morse, all you have to do is point the camera at him. He's got the inner life of that character already figured out, and it enhances everything that you, as the director, do. So, I'm in love with my actors. And I'm incredibly grateful to all of them for what they've brought to what I've done.

The Majestic was an homage to Frank Capra, and it read like that and felt like that and we shot it with that kind of feeling.

Martin Landau—Actor

The Magestic (2001)

Jim Carrey; Martin Landau; Laurie Holden; Allen Garfield; Bruce Campbell; Amanda Detmer; Daniel von Bargen; Jeffrey DeMunn; Kris Anderson; Bob Balaban; Hal Holbrook; David Ogden Stiers; James Whitmore; Ron Rifkin.

I've always said that if somebody came to me with a script that I thought was terrific, I wouldn't be compelled to write one myself in order to direct. I'd be happy to direct somebody else's script as well, which was the case with *The Majestic*. Michael Sloane and I worked on the script, honing the material together. But, ultimately, that's his screenplay. What drew me to it was something really very simple. I thought it had a great heart. I thought it had a great sweetness to it and optimism to it that I really responded to. More than anything, it had this Frank Capra feel to it that I found irresistible, having been a Frank Capra nut all my life. I always thought, if I had the opportunity to direct something that might be deemed a Capra, if Capra is a genre, like a western, I'd love to do a Capra someday. He was an enormous influence on me as a filmmaker. Ask me my favorite movie, and I'll tell you *It's a Wonderful Life*. Does that make me a sap? Fine, I'm a sap.

So, I read the script, and I thought, my gosh, this is the Capra film that I've always wanted to do. I also thought that it would give me the opportunity to lighten up for a change as a filmmaker, because doing the prison films like *Shawshank* and *Green Mile* were both somewhat emotionally difficult places to go. You wind up living with these themes and these characters in your head. I guess it's like an actor getting into character. Directors do the same thing. You live with the reality of the movie that you're trying to make for so long. I thought, hey, with this one I get to lighten up. I get to be outside for a change. I get to do sort of a sweet romance. The guy gets to kiss the girl. That was really what drew me to the material.

Jim Carrey came to the film when Mike Sloane and I first were scratching our heads, thinking, who do we want to play what would have been Jimmy Stewart role fifty years ago? Who's out there? Who's like that? We had a very, very short list, and Jim Carrey was on that list. He was on the top of that list, actually. He's been sort of corralled by the nature of his success into a certain kind of filmmaking. So people really don't think of him in these terms. But I always saw a little bit of Jimmy Stewart in the guy. I always saw a little bit of that sort of easy, sweet, romantic, leading man in him. People look at me like I'm nuts when I say that because most people think of him as the wacky guy with the green face or he's talking out his butt. In the quieter moments of Jim's films, I've seen that little bit of Jimmy Stewart quality.

It was actually a fairly simple matter of sending him the script and hoping that Jim was at a point in his life where he was ready to cast aside the bag of tricks and come from a completely honest and organic place as an actor. Happily, I caught him at the exact perfect moment in his life where he was not just ready to do that, but very anxious to do that. He really wanted to take this kind of challenge on. As much as it unnerved him—terrified him, actually, to strip away everything that he knows and everything that is instinctive as a performer and everything that's made him successful—he was willing to put aside performing and really just embrace being. I thought he did an absolutely marvelous job.

Let me tell you something. There's a reason the movie business settled in L.A. I can say it in two words—consistent weather—and when you leave L.A., you're just begging for trouble. We were dogged on *Shawshank Redemption*. We were dogged on *Green Mile*. Boy, when you go outside and you're depending on the clouds or the sky to stay the same, forget it. Northern California was the worst of it. We shot *Majestic* in the beautiful town of Ferndale up in northern California, near Eureka. It was gorgeous. I mean it was perfect for our needs, though it was lacking the movie theater, a diner, and a town hall. These were things that we could build and have the perfect town. Ferndale is a town that's really been untouched. There's not a KFC and a McDonald's on every corner. If you go to any small town anywhere, you'd be surprised to find how few of them look like they used to look. Ferndale had this microclimate where it would change on a dime. It's the only place in the world I've seen where it can be sunny, rainy, cloudy, all at the same time. It was weird. We had precious few sunny days. I had to make the most of those sunny days because, after all, this was a Capraesque film and not *Shawshank,* where we had gray skies all the time.

I remember at one point I had eight scenes in play that I was juggling. Those were scenes that I had begun shooting and couldn't finish because the weather changed, and so I'd go on to something else. I'm like the guy on the *Ed Sullivan Show,* spinning the plates and trying to keep them all from falling. The weather would dictate what we could do. Luckily, the town was very small, so it accommodated movement okay. We'd go two blocks in any direction at most. Or we'd go down to the fairgrounds, where we had converted this building into a small soundstage, and we actually had cover sets built there. A lot of the time it was really pissing down rain. But the upshot of it was we had to think on our feet a lot. That's where you have the blessing of great actors or great crew, because they could adapt quickly. They can think on their feet right along with you. I said, "Okay. We have to go do that now." Boom. They're on it. They're scrambling to get it done.

The best example would be Martin Landau, a man who is one of the many joys of my life working with actors. Martin had this scene scheduled where he shows Jim Carrey the cemetery for the first time, and he talks about this kid and what they did in high school and who has since died during the war. It's a scene where he pulls out the medal of honor, and it's basically a three-page monologue. The first week we were there, this hole opened up in the sky only over Ferndale. The sun shined down on the town. I said, "This might be the only sunny day we get while we're here. We have to shoot that scene." Well, that scene wasn't scheduled for three weeks yet. Martin looked at me and said, "Well, we were scheduled for three weeks from now on this, so I'm not sure how prepared I am. But I'm certainly game to give it a try." I said, "Great. Let's block it out and while we're setting up the cameras you go off and prepare for the scene." And he did. He delivered this heartbreaking, gorgeous performance in that scene. But it was all on the fly. It was all on the spur of the moment. That's what happens when you have great actors and when you have a great crew. They can handle those problems that are thrown at them, and all you can do is accept the blessing.

I like to say that our schedule on *The Majestic* was like a thing of beauty. It was like this gorgeous classical symphonic composition. But by the end of the first week we were playing jazz. The arrangements for the symphony were thrown out the window, and we were improvising notes as we were going along. Everyone was just coming in and jamming on because we had no choice. The weather mandated that. I think it made us a little crazy sometimes. Considering how much trouble we had with the weather, we only went a week over schedule, and that's a testament to how talented all my colleagues were in adapting, thinking on their feet, and going for it. We never once stopped shooting.

That scene for *Sandpipers of the Sahara* that appears in *The Majestic* was the most fun I've ever had on the set as a director. It was wonderful fun. And, in fact, the entire five-minute sequence that we shot is going to be on the DVD as a supplemental piece. So many people have asked about it. It was fun because I was able to kind of lighten up. I was able to toss aside any concern of subtlety and texture in a performance and all those things that always wind up feeling like brain surgery to me. I was able to just go for it and kind of get back to my roots a little bit as a kid watching these wacky and not-very-well-executed films that had way more verve and enthusiasm than budget. I watched these things on TV growing up. We drew inspiration from not just the swashbucklers, but also stuff like *The Mummy's Hand*. It was great fun for me because it wasn't brain surgery, it was three takes and okay, let's move on. It was great.

If the dolly bumped something during a shot, I said, fine. My camera team who worked with me on *Green Mile* looked at me like I'd been kidnapped and replaced by an imposter. But the thing bumped! And I said, "Yeah. It would have bumped back then too. And they wouldn't have cared, so let's keep going." We all had such a blast. It was so much fun—and fun to work with actors who were in the spirit of it. Guys like Bruce Campbell, who is the apotheosis of the B-movie mentality as an actor, because he's done so many of them. Cliff Curtis, a very, very classy and very talented actor, asked to play this villain with this silly accent. I said, "For God's sakes, he's a genius with dialect. Don't give me a real accent. Give me the most stupid, fake, bullshit accent you can possibly come up with." It took him a moment, but, once he got it, man, he was on it.

We borrowed a lot of props for that scene. We had a statue from *The Ten Commandments* that had been sitting in the studio storehouse for years. I don't know how many movies it's been in. We borrowed stuff from my buddy Chuck Russell, who was directing *The Scorpion King* at the time. I called him up and said, "Chuck, you got to lend me some of your set dressing. I promise I'll get it back to you next Tuesday." We had all these wonderful Nubian statues lining this hallway, all courtesy of Chuck. We went over there, loaded up a couple of trucks, and brought them over to the studio and tossed them on the set. It was all this wonderful cardboard silly stuff. I just loved it. Maybe there's a part of me that just wants to be this real cheeseball, B-movie filmmaker. Maybe I should do something like that one day, just to get it out of my system.

Just an Old-Fashioned Guy

I've always thought of myself as a very old-fashioned kind of filmmaker. For me narrative is everything. A lot of films today seem to dispense with that. There's not actually that much that's sexy in my movies in terms of flash, not a lot of explosions. There's not a lot of dizzying cutting or extreme camera work. And then all of this stuff that kind of passes for hip today. Some of that stuff actually gives me a bit of a headache. I'm a real traditionalist, an old-fashioned guy. I grew up watching John Ford movies and David Lean movies and Frank Capra movies and Billy Wilder movies. Their films always focused so much on the story and on the characters, you never really saw the director's hand in it, necessarily. You never saw the director doing what a lot of directors seem to do nowadays, which is jump in front of the lens and say, "Hey, I'm the star here, not the story, not the actors." It seems like a lot of people want to prove something about their directorial style.

My directorial style is I want to have as invisible a style as possible. I want to stay behind the camera and be the man behind the curtain and let the story lead the way. So in that sense, yeah, I think I'm painfully old-fashioned. Whether that works in my favor or not in the long run, who's to say? I don't know. It's for other people to decide. I'm glad that there are enough people out there who want to see a movie like that and who are willing to put aside the MTV attention span and really absorb a film. I'm glad that there are enough people out there to warrant my making films. But boy, there are times when I really feel out of step. I feel like I'm a throwback. Am I a dinosaur? Is there room for my kind of filmmaking anymore? Luckily, there has been. At least there still is, because I don't know what else I'd do for a living. Maybe go back to the day job and write screenplays for other people. Who knows?

As for nudity in my films, well, the mouse was completely nude in *Green Mile.* In *Shawshank,* there was the guys in the shower. They were naked. But I think that's the extent of it. Not that I'm a prude. There's nothing I like better than nakedness when it's appropriate. But it has never quite seemed to lend itself to the kind of movies that I've been trying to make. So who knows?

Parting Words

How would I like my work to be remembered? Gosh, that's a really good question. If I had my fondest wish, I think I'd like to be remembered as a guy who really cared about the craft. I really care about telling a good story. I don't approach it lightly. I want to do something that people can embrace. I like timeless stories. So, hopefully, a hundred years from now, people will still watch these movies and still care about them. That'd be great. But, yeah, as a guy who tried to tell good stories that had some humanism in them, some humanity, some kind of optimism about people. "Movies were not cynical." I'm not a particularly cynical guy. I think it kind of shows up in the work. So, if I'm remembered fondly, and hopefully I won't be dying anytime soon, but when I'm gone, if I'm remembered fondly for those things, I'd be delighted. Of course I'll be dead, so I'm not sure I'll be delighted or I'm not sure I'll be feeling anything. But that would be great. That's a good legacy. That would be a worthy thing to leave behind.

Frank Darabont Filmography

The Woman in the Room (1983)
Buried Alive (TV, 1990)
The Shawshank Redemption (1994)
The Green Mile (1999)
The Majestic (2001)

Awards and Nominations

Academy Awards, USA
The Green Mile, Best Picture (nomination shared with David Valdes), 2000
The Green Mile, Best Writing, Screenplay Based on Material from Another Medium (nominated), 2000

The Shawshank Redemption, Best Writing, Screenplay Based on Material from Another Medium (nominated), 1995

Academy of Science Fiction, Horror and Fantasy Films
The Green Mile, Best Director, Saturn Award (nominated), 2000

Bram Stoker Awards
The Green Mile, Best Screenplay (nominated), 2000

Broadcast Film Critics Association Awards
The Green Mile, Best Screenplay, 2000

Directors Guild of America
The Green Mile, Outstanding Directorial Achievement in Motion Pictures (nominated), 2000
The Shawshank Redemption, Outstanding Directorial Achievement in Motion Pictures (nominated), 1995

Golden Globe Awards
The Shawshank Redemption, Studio Crystal Heart Award, 1995

Humanitas Prizes
The Shawshank Redemption, Best Feature Film, 1995

Online Film Critics Society Awards
The Green Mile, Best Adapted Screenplay (nominated), 2000

Science Fiction and Fantasy Writers of America
The Green Mile, Nebula Award, Best Script (nominated), 2001

USC Scripter Award
The Green Mile (nomination shared with Stephen King), 2000
The Shawshank Redemption (shared with Stephen King), 1994

Writers Guild of America
The Shawshank Redemption, Best Screenplay Based on Material Previously Produced or Published (nominated), 1995

About the Author

Robert Emery (right) with director Adrian Lyne.

President and CEO of Media Entertainment, Inc., ROBERT J. EMERY has been a writer-producer-director for thirty-six years. He has written and produced a wide variety of screenplays and television shows, has taught film production, and has been the recipient of more than eighty industry awards for his work. He wrote, produced, and directed the 2001 feature film *Swimming Upstream*. The movie received the Best Dramatic Feature award at the 2001 Angel Citi Film Festival in Los Angeles. His four-part documentary on the history of genocide, *The Genocide Factor*, aired on PBS stations nationwide in April of 2002. The project was awarded the Remi Special Jury Award for TV Series–Documentary from the Worldfest-Houston International Film Festival. Mr. Emery is a member of the Directors Guild of America.

Index

Books from Allworth Press

The Directors: Take One
by Robert J. Emery (paperback, 6 × 9, 416 pages, $19.95)

The Directors: Take Two
by Robert J. Emery (paperback, 6 × 9, 384 pages, $19.95)

The Directors: Take Three
by Robert Emery (paperback, 6 × 9, 240 pages, $21.95)

Get the Picture? The Movie Lover's Guide to Watching Films
by Jim Piper (paperback, 6 × 9, 240 pages, $18.95)

Shoot Me: Independent Filmmaking from Creative Concept to Rousing Release
by Roy Frumkes and Rocco Simonelli (paperback, 6 × 9, 240 pages, $19.95)

Documentary Filmmakers Speak
by Liz Stubbs (paperback, 6 × 9, 240 pages, $19.95)

Producing for Hollywood: A Guide for Independent Producers
by Paul Mason and Don Gold (paperback, 6 × 9, 272 pages, $19.95)

Hollywood Dealmaking: Negotiating Talent Agreements
by Dina Appleton and Daniel Yankelevits (paperback, 6 × 9, 256 pages, $19.95)

The Health & Safety Guide for Film, TV & Theater
by Monona Rossol (paperback, 6 × 9, 256 pages, $19.95)

Directing for Film and Television, Revised Edition
by Christopher Lukas (paperback, 6 × 9, 256 pages, $19.95)

Making Independent Films: Advice from the Film Makers
by Liz Stubbs and Richard Rodriguez (paperback, 6 × 9, 224 pages, $16.95)

Making Your Film for Less Outside the U.S.
by Mark DeWayne (paperback, 6 × 9, 272 pages, $19.95)

Surviving Hollywood: Your Ticket to Success
by Jerry Rannow (paperback, 6 × 9, 208 pages, $16.95)

The Filmmaker's Guide to Production Design
by Vincent LoBrutto (paperback, 6 × 9, 216 pages, $19.95)

Creative Careers in Hollywood
by Laurie Scheer (paperback, 6 × 9, 240 pages, $19.95)

Technical Film and TV for Nontechnical People
by Drew Campbell (paperback, 6 × 9, 256 pages, $19.95)

Please write to request our free catalog. To order by credit card, call 1-800-491-2808 or send a check or money order to Allworth Press, 10 East 23rd Street, Suite 510, New York, NY 10010. Include $5 for shipping and handling for the first book ordered and $1 for each additional book. Ten dollars plus $1 for each additional book if ordering from Canada. New York State residents must add sales tax.

To see our complete catalog on the World Wide Web, or to order online, you can find us at *www.allworth.com.*